Mark Colvin joined the ABC as a cadet in 1974. He was the first presenter of *The World Today* and worked for *Four Corners* for five years. After five years as London correspondent for the ABC, interrupted by six months in hospital with a life threatening disease, he returned to Australia as presenter of PM in 1997, a job he has continued to do despite three years on dialysis and a successful kidney transplant.

MARK COLVIN

LIGHT AND SHADOW

MEMOIRS OF A SPY'S SON

MELBOURNE UNIVERSITY PRESS
An imprint of Melbourne University Publishing Limited
Level 1, 715 Swanston Street, Carlton, Victoria 3053, Australia
mup-info@unimelb.edu.au
www.mup.com.au

First published 2016
Reprinted three times 2016
Reprinted twice 2017

Cover design by Josh Durham, Design by Committee
Typeset by Cannon Typesetting
Printed in Australia by Ligare

National Library of Australia Cataloguing-in-Publication entry

Colvin, Mark, author.

Light and shadow/Mark Colvin.

9780522870893 (paperback)
9780522870909 (ebook)

Includes index.

Colvin, Mark.
Broadcasters—Australia—Biography.
Journalists—Australia—Biography.
Transplantation of organs, tissues, etc.—Australia.

384.54092

For Nicolas and William

Life is a jest; and all things show it, I thought so once; but now I know it.

Epitaph on the tomb of John Gay, Westminster Abbey

Contents

Preface

I'VE BEEN A journalist for more than four decades. Yet I had no long-standing vocation to be a reporter before I became one. Even halfway through 1974, my first year as a trainee, I had real doubts about whether I would stick with the trade. I was one of those people who, at twenty-one, did not really know who they were, let alone who and what they wanted to be.

I did know I had a tendency to drift, and that some of the things I'd have liked to drift into—writing novels, making films—required more discipline about time and hard work than I thought I possessed. I wasn't totally indolent—I'd achieved a perfectly respectable 'good second' BA (Hons) in English at Oxford—but above all I didn't know what I was fitted for. I'd worked for nine months in a photographic darkroom at the Australian National University in Canberra, and for a while as a photographer at a local newspaper in the west of England. But, although competent, I thought I didn't have the 'eye' to be as good as my photographic heroes, and that I was better at writing the captions than taking the pictures.

As a 20-year-old, I took a walk in the Suffolk countryside with a friend of my father's, a man who'd made a lot of money in the Mad Men era in New York working for the advertising agency Ogilvy & Mather. He asked me what I wanted to do. 'Write, I think.' 'What do you want to write about?' 'I'm not sure. I've just spent three years studying the greats, and that's intimidating. And on top of that, I don't feel I've done enough or seen enough to write a real novel.' 'Well,' he said, 'people who can write but don't have a subject are generally advised to go into advertising or journalism.' And he confided that before he made a fortune writing ad copy with Don Draper types in the Big Apple, he'd once edited an English dog-owners magazine called *The Tailwagger*.

In part, though, this is also the story of growing up, unknowingly, as the son of a spy. My father joined MI6 officially in 1951 but was in fact recruited two years earlier. He was not at my mother's bedside when I was born because he was working in espionage: he climbed the ranks to seniority as an intelligence officer over nearly four decades, retiring just before I became a foreign correspondent. Until I reached adulthood, I knew nothing of the truth of his profession: even when I was told the truth, it was only a snippet of the whole story. Even now, I'm finding that some of the things he told me after his 'cover' was officially lifted were half-truths, and I'm having to accept that some were heavily embroidered, at best.

As such, an element of psychodrama enters in: the possibility that I stepped unconsciously into a field of work that I thought was the opposite of what my father did, but may have only been so in the way that the reverse sides of a coin are opposite to each other. Running in a great circle, only to realise you're almost back to what you were running from.

I grew up knowing that my father would never say much about what his work involved, and could be evasive or contradictory when he talked about it at all. But I thought that was normal among diplomats, especially on the 'political' side of the Foreign Office. He did not, as you will discover, formally reveal to me that he was a spy until I was twenty-five, though I'd pretty much reached that conclusion a year or two before. During my teenage and university years, we had disagreed vociferously about a lot, notably the domino theory of the Vietnam War and the relative merits of 'authoritarian' and 'totalitarian' regimes: he believed right-wing dictatorships were temporary by nature, whereas communist ones would never yield (like most of the intelligence community, he did not see 1989 coming). And so a substantial part of this book is an attempt to reconstruct, where I can, some of the parts of his life that I never really knew: the life of an active intelligence officer in MI6, which prefers to call itself the Secret Intelligence Service.

And there's this: a spy and a journalist, if they're doing their jobs properly, are both trying to find out the truth behind the lies and propaganda, even if they use radically different tools (or at least they did until the London tabloids started tapping people's phones and hacking into their emails). But there will always be this great difference: the journalist is trying to reach the largest number of people with their exclusive information, while the spy's audience is of necessity always tiny.

So in some way, by trying to be as unlike my father as I could, I was perhaps not so different at all: for both of us, information gathering was our trade, and constant doubt and questioning the knives we wielded.

This is a paradox I might have anticipated before I started to write this book. The history of modern journalism can actually be traced back to 'newsletters' commissioned by wealthy merchants in Florence and Amsterdam in the Renaissance. Information was worth money in the finance world, then as now. The people who wrote those newsletters were not called 'journalists' but 'intelligencers'. Perhaps intelligence is just reporting with a restricted audience: certainly my father once claimed that real intelligence 'product' was never more than a few per cent better or more comprehensive than what could be legitimately gleaned from a really careful combing and analysis of public sources.

The research I've done on my father for this book has yielded some surprises, and raised nearly as many questions as answers. As Adam Sisman's recent biography of John le Carré demonstrates, even the 'truth-tellers' who abandoned MI6, like le Carré himself and Graham Greene, leave a trail of ambiguous and contradictory stories. The ones who stayed in for life, like my father, became even more habituated to deception, silence and ambiguity, habits encouraged by their employer, which keeps up its walls of silence for many decades longer than any other branch of government. So I have had to accept that I may have got some things wrong, fallen for 'disinformation' in some cases, or misunderstood some episodes. This is my memoir, not a definitive history, and I will have to live with that.

Aside from all that, this is also, I've realised in writing it, the story of a whole world, a way of living and a way of thinking, that has become quite remarkably foreign. It's not only that I remember at first hand the early days of jet travel, and lived at a time when most intercontinental travel was still taken by sea. I didn't see a television until I was eight; our family didn't own one until I was ten or eleven. I remember when a radio small enough to put in your pocket was not just a novelty but a teenage life-changer. Memory, like looking through the wrong end of a telescope, can make these things smaller than they really were: some days I have to ask myself, as young journalists occasionally ask me, 'How *did* we do journalism before the internet?' So if a lot of this book is about my childhood, it's because I'm increasingly aware that the period itself is becoming history, and maybe I owe my own children a duty to document it.

But back to early 1974. Over the course of a month or two, I'd been laid off from a series of temporary jobs as a builder's labourer (I kept getting heat stroke in the December Canberra sun, among many other failings). So when I 'signed on' for the dole, I suppose the idea of journalism was somewhere in my mind, but I certainly wasn't set on it. That was such a different era: there was no Centrelink, but there was the Commonwealth Employment Service, the CES, a lino-floored, musty office with rows of uncomfortable metal chairs where you waited for hours to be interviewed by someone behind a thick glass window. Having filled in my forms and waited, I got to the front of the queue. The clerk riffled through my papers, looked up and said, 'You shouldn't be here. You have a degree.' 'What do you mean?' I asked. 'You should be upstairs,' he said, 'at the PES.' 'The what?' 'The Professional Employment Service.'

Somewhat bewildered, I walked up a flight of stairs into a different world: a suite of blue-carpeted offices with no barriers between staff and clients but comfortable armchairs around coffee tables strewn with careers brochures. A helpful man sat down for an earnest talk about what I wanted to do, at the end of which he asked me to come back in three days, when he'd have some ideas for me. I did, and he produced a folder full of employment ads.

Some were for jobs in the Public Service, none of which held much attraction: I suppose one thing I did know was that I wanted to do something in some way creative, and form-filling in the Department of Urban and Regional Development didn't fit the bill. Full employment was not just a phrase in Australia then, made credible only by massaging the statistics. It was a reality, or at least it was for me.

The remaining three ads were for cadetships (traineeships) in journalism. I applied for each of them and within days, all had asked me to come in for an interview. The first people I saw, Channel 7 Canberra, accepted me on the spot. I thanked them and asked for a couple of days to think about it: it was a good offer to have in the back pocket, but it was local journalism and I still had the possibility of a job in a bigger organisation and a bigger city.

As I wrote in a speech I gave in 2012, I was

> a half-English dilettante with an arts degree and a Pommy accent. I remember going for an interview at the *Herald*. First mistake—I went to the Hunter Street [Sydney] office, which was just their corporate headquarters, not the actual newspaper. Then I asked someone the way, but apparently the way I said 'Herald' was unintelligible, because I ended up at Harold Park. I did make it to Broadway on time despite all that, but the *Herald* found my minimal charm and talent easy to resist.
>
> Somehow, Aunty, where the BBC voice was still pretty prevalent in those days, saw something in me and, stylish in a denim jacket with patch pockets and a pair of flared trousers, I turned up on February the eleventh 1974 at 164 William Street, headquarters of ABC News.

I was now, at least in name, a journalist, but I still didn't feel like one. There were no journalism schools in Australia then. I had no complete sense of what the job might mean, or what it might lead me to.

The stories of my career in this book are, I hope, interesting in and of themselves, both because some record moments of high or low drama and sometimes historical significance, and because they all helped shape me as a *person* and as a *journalist*. Is there a difference, after four decades, or are the man and the trade inextricably entwined? I find it hard to tell, because so much of what I have absorbed as a reporter has become part of my personality. I react to much of what I encounter with an observer's scepticism, and I sometimes have to rein in a tendency to be too detached. The journalist's classic questions—What makes you tick? Where's the money? Who really runs this town? Cui bono? (Who benefits?) What lies behind what you're telling me? How will this actually work in practice? Why are you lying to me? Who are you loyal to and who would you betray, and for what?—have become second nature, to the extent that the greatest temptation and danger is cynicism. They also, again, almost uncannily, mimic the mindset of the spy.

But I was also told at the very beginning of my career that the greatest virtue of a good journalist is simple curiosity, and a broad interest in history, art, literature, psychology and philosophy has, I like to hope, kept the worst excesses of cynicism at bay. In other words, when I'm not working, I tend to read, and read, and read. And because I'm easily bored, my reading has always been wide and eclectic. It all feeds into who I am and what I am. Is there a difference between the who and the what? Who can say?

* * *

In the summer holidays of 1964, when I was twelve, I discovered the world of Sherlock Holmes, and over the course of a few weeks devoured it all. I've often thought that aspects of a reporter's extended career can acquire a Sherlockian tinge—bouts of frenzied activity followed by torpid meditation—but more recently I've been intrigued by the relationship between Sherlock and his older brother Mycroft. Sherlock is driven to experience the world for himself. He is a pair of eyes, sometimes aided by a magnifying glass or a microscope, but one who uses his capacious learning and fierce intellect to interpret what he sees. Mycroft, who rarely leaves the Diogenes Club, however, is almost like a disembodied mind, a brain that uses the eyes of others to see the world, then processes it.

Always a Sherlock by temperament (though not of course by genius), I found that from the mid-1990s, illness and disability gradually forced me to accept that going out and finding the story, seeing it through my own pair of eyes, was becoming increasingly difficult and would eventually be impossible. Presenting the *PM* program was the Mycroft alternative. I have tried whenever possible to use the program as a vicarious pair of eyes upon the world. I've encouraged all my colleagues, from young trainees to seasoned foreign correspondents, to bring me, and through me the program's listeners, a picture of the world through their eyes. If I sometimes push them harder than they expect for that first-hand view, it's partly because I miss being on the road so much, and partly because I know from experience that the view on the ground is never exactly what the predigested words of the news agencies or edited pictures off the satellite suggest. It is this that makes real journalism so important: the plethora of different pairs of eyes on a subject, each trying to view it as dispassionately as possible, but each bringing a different perspective. And it is that pluralism—not a pluralism of opinion but of observation—that is most at risk in this era of declining news budgets and shrinking foreign bureaux.

Some of this book is a record of a time when there was still a large and amorphous entity called, loosely, 'the foreign press corps': when there were budgets and time to dig into stories at home and overseas. They were sometimes extravagant days, but they were also days when Australian journalism was a way to see the nation and the world and bring it to an *Australian* audience, from an *Australian* perspective. Too often now, the financial stringencies of cash-strapped news organisations mean we get the view as edited in New York or London, seen through British or American eyes.

I understand all the pressures, economic and otherwise, that have worked on the news business, but I still believe in the need for more well-supported Australian eyes on the ground. There has been some fine citizen journalism, and I know young freelancers who have done great work self-financing or crowdsourcing their reporting of the world, but I worry for their future. Journalism on a shoestring won't support a reporter forever, and what's needed more than ever in an increasingly sophisticated world is the depth of experience that underpins complex analysis in reporting.

If I have a journalistic credo, it's this: don't make up your mind before you've gathered the facts. Never start with a conclusion. Test your theories against the evidence. If the facts contradict you, change your thesis: don't try and crush the reality into your pre-planned script.

Be one pair of eyes. Gather your facts, listen to others' opinions, cast your net wide. Then—and only then—draw your conclusions.

More than four decades at the ABC have given me the freedom to learn these lessons. I've not often been told what to write, and when I have, my counterarguments have usually been listened to. I know that there are many in journalism who have had far worse experiences with their bosses, and I feel no complacency about that. I'm aware, in other words, that what integrity I have has seldom been challenged. I'd like to hope that I'd have stood up to an overbearing editor with a one-sided political view who wanted me to change a story, or to a proprietor with vested commercial interests, but I've seldom been tested, so I have no intention of being self-righteous. Professionally, compared to so many others, I've mostly had a dream run.

So, like the legendary lost dog on the poster—'Three legs, blind in one eye, missing right ear, tail broken, recently castrated … answers to the name of "Lucky"'—I feel that despite near-death experiences and chronic illness I have had what AB Facey famously called A Fortunate Life.

This is a record of some of it.

Chapter 1

A Long Shadow

THE FIRST TIME I set off to cross a national border as a foreign correspondent, I forgot my passport. It was January 1980, and at twenty-seven years old I had just arrived as the greenest of green recruits at the ABC's London bureau. It was cold and dark when the bureau's veteran cameraman, Les Seymour, picked me up at 6 a.m. to drive to Dover.

It was hardly going to be an earth-shattering piece by any standard, let alone Seymour's. He'd covered massive stories, from the 1973 Yom Kippur War between Israel and the Arab states onwards. A constant fund of heavily embellished but usually hilarious anecdotes from his years on the road, Les would have regarded this story as run-of-the-mill, almost filler. It was in fact quite literally a 'boring' story we were off to film: a piece on the hoary proposal to bore a tunnel under La Manche, as the French call it—the English Channel.

Since the election of Margaret Thatcher seven months before, the idea of the 'Chunnel' had been revived. But as it had first been mooted by Napoleon in 1802, the digging begun in the 1880s had been short-lived, and sporadic attempts to revive it throughout the twentieth century had all fizzled out, the prospect of the great project ever becoming reality still seemed speculative at best. There had always seemed to be too much at stake in the idea of joining two nations with such a history of mutual hostility and misunderstanding, whatever the benefits to trade and tourism.

Nonetheless, there we were, with a couple of interviews under our belts and plenty of Victorian architectural plans, even the abandoned nineteenth-century borehole entrances on film, but nothing actually moving. TV stories need colour and movement and people, so the obvious thing to do was film the things the tunnel—if it were ever dug—would disrupt: the Channel ferries.

We'd arranged to film on the trip from Dover to Boulogne, and we had an appointment with the 9 a.m. ferry. Nothing could possibly go wrong. Until it did.

About half an hour from home, Les asked me casually: 'Got everything?'

'Of course,' I said. 'Tape recorder, notebook, mostly written piece to camera. All fine.'

'Got your passport?'

It took a moment to sink in. Somehow I'd thought that since we were just going to get on a boat and sail to Boulogne and back, without setting foot on French soil, I wouldn't need travel documents. It hadn't occurred to me that we'd have to go through Immigration to get on the ferry.

There was just one thing in my mind at that moment. I. Am. An. Idiot.

For the next three years in London, Les seldom let me forget that moment, the sotto voce 'Got your passport?' becoming a running joke, even on a short walk to the pub.

The story worked out fine, by the way: we turned back and I got the passport, then rang the ferry company to tell them we were going to be late. They obligingly put us on a crossing an hour or two later than the one originally planned. But over the next seventeen years or so as a travelling journalist, I scarcely ever left home without my passport. Some lessons you have to learn the hard way, and it's best you learn them as early as possible, with as little damage done.

* * *

I was appointed London correspondent in mid-November 1979. At the time I was working on a TV current affairs program called *Nationwide*, set up just that year by a brilliant journalist and producer named

John Penlington, who'd been a reporter in the early years of Australia's first real current affairs program, *Four Corners*, which began in 1961. At *Nationwide* I had felt incredibly lucky to work alongside far more experienced figures in TV journalism. I'd also had a brief stint at *Four Corners*, where people like Caroline Jones had mentored me with kindness and patience. I thought I'd kept my head above water—just—in exalted company, but I was still surprised, when I applied to fill the London vacancy created by the return of Richard Palfreyman, to be given the job. I'd be arriving in London on New Year's Day 1980, to work under Bureau Chief Ken Begg and alongside Tim Clark, both of whom I'd known as a cadet reporter in Canberra, and with the charismatic ex-*This Day Tonight* journalist Tony Joyce.

It was a daunting prospect, but I'd visited the bureau on a previous trip to London and I knew the lie of the land: there was a fair amount of grunt work, turning around and rewriting the day's international stories using BBC audio we had the rights to, handling the many freelancers who filed for *AM* and sent their pieces via the London office, and covering British politics, which in those early days of the Thatcher government was still making big news in itself. So I felt that I'd be able to do something useful day to day while putting down roots and trying to develop a feel for the bigger international stories. I was especially keen to try to get to Tehran, where the fall of the Shah and the return of Ayatollah Khomeini had precipitated a continuing revolution featured on TV screens almost every night, and where students had just taken over the US embassy and were holding fifty-two Americans hostage.

Then, just over a month before I was due to leave Sydney, came the bombshell—the news that Tony Joyce, the man I'd most looked forward to working with, and next to whom I was going to be sitting for the next couple of years, had been shot.

Tony was best friends with Paul Murphy, who worked at the desk next to mine at *Nationwide*. The two had a lot in common: penetrating journalistic insight, lacerating wit, and a near-heroic capacity for tackling that now almost-forgotten journalistic institution, the Long Lunch, while still being able (mostly) to function as broadcasters afterwards. Both were brilliant raconteurs and mimics, Paul in particular. He would recount, word for word, conversations he'd had with Gough Whitlam or Billy McMahon years before, in voices so convincing you'd swear they were in the room—he would later do all the voices on the satirical animation *Rubbery Figures*. He'd been my principal mentor and protector for the last couple of years, and I'd grown deeply fond of him. I arrived at *Nationwide* that morning to find the place in shock, with Paul at the epicentre.

The only thing we knew for sure was that Tony Joyce was in Zambia with a bullet in his head. He and cameraman Derek McKendry had flown there in a hurry: in one of the very last gasps of Rhodesia's attempt to maintain itself as a white-ruled enclave, a British-supplied Rhodesian Hawker Hunter jet had bombed a bridge and border post between that country (soon to become Zimbabwe) and Zambia. Zambia was at the time the main host for the training camps and bases of the anti-Rhodesian forces led by Joshua Nkomo and Robert Mugabe respectively.

Already, the Zambians had started to cover up the story of how Tony came to be shot. Paul, although in shock, was working the phones, trying to talk to Tony's wife Monica and taking other calls. One was from a senior ABC executive who told Paul that his 'intelligence connections' had told him that Tony had been unaccredited and in an unauthorised zone. This, as I and others would find out later, was a lie. Tony and Derek had checked in at the Information Ministry, told them they were going to the border to film the bomb damage, been given the all-clear and been told to return the next day to complete their 'formal' accreditation.

Derek McKendry is dead now—he had a heart attack in 1999 in his native New Zealand—but he was a fine man and a deeply experienced newsgatherer, having for instance been in the first Australian TV team to enter China after the Cultural Revolution, covering the arrival of Australia's first ambassador to the People's Republic of China, Dr Stephen Fitzgerald. I worked with Derek frequently in the years 1980–83, and over time, piece by piece, he told me the real story of what had happened in Zambia.

Tony and Derek took a taxi to the border post, filmed the bomb damage, talked to some locals, and recorded a piece to camera with the wrecked bridge in the background. On the way, they'd passed through a number of military checkpoints without incident, their papers in order. On their return, though, there was another stop, and here there was a problem.

In Derek's telling, this time there were not only soldiers but an angry, shirtless man with a pistol, apparently in charge, who shouted at them that they were spies, Rhodesian mercenaries, and who refused to be convinced by their press papers or Australian and New Zealand passports. His eyes were bloodshot, and Derek believed he was both drunk and had been smoking weed. He seems to have identified himself at one point as a local 'cadre', or official of the ruling party of Zambia's president, Kenneth Kaunda.

At any rate, although the soldiers appeared willing to listen, this man's rage did not abate. He insisted Derek and Tony get themselves and their film gear out of the taxi and into a police car. It was after my colleagues had complied that this armed 'civilian' fired his handgun into the police vehicle. Derek thought the shot was random, it could even have been the result of a reflex grip of the trigger finger, but he remembered clearly the sensation of the bullet whistling past his face and into the right side of Tony's head. Inside the skull, specialists back in London would eventually conclude, the bullet continued to ricochet, carving a path through Tony Joyce's brain.

For Derek and Tony, though, at that roadside stop in Zambia, the nightmare was only beginning. Evidently panicked by what had happened, their captors arrested them. Derek remembered Tony being apparently semi-conscious for at least part of the journey back to Lusaka, where his injured colleague was transferred to a poorly equipped hospital. McKendry was thrown into a fetid, cramped, sweltering jail cell, still under suspicion of being a Rhodesian mercenary, but, he would believe for the rest of his life, *actually* under pressure to lie about what had happened and help the Zambians cover up what amounted to a war crime.

Tony Joyce may have been doomed from the moment the bullet entered his head, but we'll never know. His skull was grotesquely swollen, the cranial cavity inflamed and full of fluid, and the only hope of survival would have been to get him specialist care immediately and medevac him back to London within hours. An English missionary doctor at a hospital in Lusaka did her best under difficult circumstances to keep Tony alive, but he needed much more.

While Tony and Derek endured the harshest possible conditions, a series of negotiations took place between Canberra, Sydney, London and

Lusaka, with the manager of the ABC's London office, Stuart Revill, and Ken Begg forced to fly to Zambia on the earliest possible plane, with Tony's wife Monica. As the Lusaka authorities were still making spurious allegations that Tony and Derek were Rhodesian spies, the negotiations were appallingly slow, the authorities obstructive at every turn, even to the point of refusing for some time to let Monica see her husband. In fact, despite a direct plea from Australian Prime Minister Malcolm Fraser to President Kaunda, new obstacles kept arising, with different officials countermanding each others' orders.

One of Britain's top neurosurgeons flew in to help, and eventually there was agreement that Tony Joyce could be put on a plane back to London, and the comparative safety of St Bartholomew's Hospital. But even as Tony's comatose body was wheeled out of the hospital on a gurney for transfer, with Monica Joyce at his side, they were surrounded by armed Zambian soldiers who shouted that he was a mercenary and tried to prevent him from leaving.

I remember Stuart Revill and Ken Begg both telling me months later of the intensity of fear and hysteria in those hours, and the sense that nothing would be settled until they were finally on the plane and in the air.

Meanwhile, Derek McKendry was still in a dirty, crowded cell, and under pressure to change his story. Zambia wanted him to agree to their version, which was that Tony had been in the taxi, not the police car, and had been hit by a stray bullet in a war zone. They even drove him back to the scene of the crime in an effort to persuade him, but he stood his ground. He was released after five days, and then only after intense, high-level diplomatic pressure involving the Australian and New Zealand governments.

When I arrived in London, Tony Joyce was still alive but had been in a deep coma for five weeks. His hospital room was one of my first destinations, and I will never forget it. He lay there with tubes and wires and an oxygen mask, and Monica sat beside him, talking cheerfully to him, playing Rolling Stones tracks. She told me how he would sometimes twitch or seem to squeeze her hand. 'You've lost a few pounds, Tony,' she told him, and turned to me with a smile to explain that he'd been worrying about putting on weight recently. She was there for him constantly, then and the next month. But the damage had been done: the bullet had not only driven through the brain tissue, but the days of largely untreated inflammation had ensured that none of the essence of Tony, the vibrant, courageous, irreverent man who had baited politicians and never flinched from war zones, would ever be back. His inevitable death finally came on a wet, dark London February day, and it left a family—and a bureau of his colleagues—grief-stricken.

And so it was that my life as a foreign correspondent began under a long shadow. The ABC's office at 54 Portland Place, just a couple of blocks from the BBC's great steamship-like edifice, Broadcasting House, was a mournful place at the beginning of 1980, one where the prevailing depression was such that it was difficult for many of us to do much more than go through the motions. Tony had been a ball of energy in the office, and I found that everyone had a fund of stories about him, from Les Seymour, who'd filmed with him, to soundman Paul Adams and production assistant Gill Kimsey. We all spent quite a lot of time at one of his favourite lunch haunts, the Cleveland Kebab House, where the owner, a young Cypriot named Sav, operated an informal lock-in system that allowed us to keep drinking during the afternoon. The self-medication of grief.

An inquest backed by a Scotland Yard investigation was given zero cooperation by Zambia. But it still managed, using convincing forensic evidence about the path and speed of the bullet, to totally discredit the theory that Tony Joyce had been shot in crossfire, backing Derek McKendry's account of how it had happened. It wasn't going to bring him back, though, and the gloomy finality of the memorial service, for which Paul Murphy had flown over to give the eulogy, and where Tony's six-year-old son Daniel held his mother's hand and stood straight and grave in a dark suit, left us all wrung out.

We were all still there, supposedly, as foreign correspondents, and the one thing all who'd known Tony agreed on was that he would never have wanted us to stop reporting from the field. I hadn't come to London just to do what Ken Begg used to call 'techno-hackery', or what *The Guardian*'s Nick Davies, decades later, would call 'churnalism': rewriting wire copy and recycling BBC actuality. That was an inescapable part of the job, but the point was to get out of the office, out of town, out of the country. But no-one—in Sydney or in London—particularly wanted to be the first to take the decision to send a reporter to another potential flashpoint.

And so it was Channel Tunnel stories and the like, and a trip to Rome for an EU summit, where I tried to cover a press conference by the UK foreign secretary, Lord Carrington, only to be rebuffed by a vote of the travelling British press, who didn't want any upstart colonials in there with them. *The Sydney Morning Herald*'s Ian Frykberg and I sat outside drumming our heels for forty-five minutes, wondering if we'd come on a wild goose chase, until it was over. Then I went up to Carrington and introduced myself as being from the ABC. 'Oh the Aussies?' he drawled. 'The dinky-dis? I've always got time for the dinks.' Carrington was a classic English political aristocrat, one of whose ancestors had been governor of NSW and who had himself been British high commissioner in Canberra in the 1950s, so his affection for Australia was real enough, but the language reflected a patronising post-colonial attitude that was a lot more prevalent in Britain then. Still, Carrington was quite forthcoming in the interview I recorded, and I filed a piece for *AM*, before going for a walk, buying some nice silk ties, then having a fairly uproarious dinner with the hard-drinking Frykberg and flying back to London the next morning. It beat sitting in the office, but it still wasn't what I'd become a correspondent for.

Chapter 2

An Innocent Abroad

IN EARLY NOVEMBER 1979, not long before the death of Tony Joyce in Zambia, Iranian revolutionary students besieged and then overran the US embassy in Tehran. They were enraged by Washington's decision to allow its long-term client, the now-exiled Shah of Iran, to enter the USA to be treated for what was by then terminal cancer. For President Jimmy Carter, it may have seemed a humanitarian gesture towards a man who had effectively been a US puppet dictator for more than three decades. For many in Iran, however, it was a decision that played to their own deeply held fears and resentments.

The CIA had run the 1953 coup that brought down the democratically elected Iranian Prime Minister Mohammad Mossadeq. It did so hand-in-glove with the British Secret Intelligence Service (the SIS), at the request of the British Government, because Mossadeq was proposing to nationalise Iran's oil industry. That was a resource the British, in the form of the Anglo-Iranian Oil Company, later to become British Petroleum and now known as BP, had controlled since before World War I. They were determined not to let go of it, and democracy was the price Iran had to pay.

The Shah had painted himself throughout his reign as a moderniser and a seculariser, but he was certainly not a democrat. Starting in the early

1960s, the Shah had introduced what he called the 'White Revolution': he distributed some government-owned land to the poor, and brought in voting and education rights for women. And in a country where most were then still peasants, he introduced a 'Literacy Corps' aimed at getting education out into the countryside, rather than confining it to the major cities.

For this, he was much celebrated in the Western press, culminating in a near orgy of media coverage in 1971 when Shah Reza Pahlavi, in reality the son of an army private who had used thuggery to gain the throne, threw himself a gigantic party at the ancient city of Persepolis, attended by scores of crowned heads, presidents and prime ministers, all housed in a fabulously luxurious tent city, and culminating in a five-and-a-half-hour banquet beginning with quails' eggs stuffed with the finest Iranian caviar and washed down with vintage pink champagne.

This celebration of the 2500th anniversary of the founding of the Persian Empire was intended to give to the world a sense of immense continuity—a royal family with antecedents stretching back two and a half millennia—and to Iranians themselves a sense of pride that the world was recognising the significance of their place in it. For many in the West, it was indeed an indication of a prosperous nation whose visionary leader had lifted it out of the Third World, liberated its women, and created a modern society fit for the twentieth century. But most ordinary Iranians could see the flip side: not only the vast extravagance of a $150 million party but the everyday expense of being governed by a dictator, albeit one on a Peacock Throne. They knew about the billions of dollars spent on US fighter jets and other sophisticated armaments, the corruption (and resistance to criticism) of the Shah's own court, and—the darkest underside—the activities of the Shah's secret service, SAVAK.

Even to those who knew little about Iran, SAVAK, with its practices of disappearing people, torturing and murdering political opposition, and sending even the clergy into exile, was notorious. It was often mentioned in the same breath as apartheid South Africa's brutal intelligence service BOSS, and was believed to share training and techniques with it, as well as the CIA. For Iranians, particularly those with an interest in freedom of expression or political opposition, SAVAK meant the fear of the 3 a.m. door-knock, the family member taken away and either never seen again alive or eventually returned broken.

So as well as a newly prosperous but small middle class, there was also in Iran a rising generation of well-educated young people who wanted if not revolution, then at least a transition to democracy. The Shah, however, cocooned in wealth and privilege, and in the certain knowledge that the USA saw him as a strong bulwark against the Soviet Union, saw no reason to give it to them.

And as for the things the West saw as progress, there was a powerful group that saw them as exactly the opposite. They were the fundamentalist Shi'a Muslims—by far the majority religion in Iran—who eventually coalesced around Ayatollah Khomeini, whom the Shah had exiled to Paris.

Khomeini saw the Literacy Corps not as progress but a threat to the virtual monopoly on education through madrasas that the mullahs had established in the countryside: a threat, in other words, to the system of education based on memorising the Koran. And, the Ayatollah thought, women's suffrage was not a liberation at all but a way 'to corrupt our chaste women'. As for the schools and universities where photos of the day show smiling young women bareheaded and wearing Western skirts and dresses, they too were anathema to the Ayatollah and his followers. He excoriated them in sermons which were taped in Paris, smuggled back into Iran, and, in those pre-internet days, dubbed onto hundreds of cassettes and distributed among the people.

Promising a government based 'on the will of the people as expressed by universal suffrage', Khomeini flew back to Tehran in January 1979. With threats being transmitted from the ground that the Iranian Air Force would shoot the plane down, and after years of exile, the Ayatollah was asked what he felt. 'Nothing,' he replied.

The year that followed was tumultuous, and left in tatters the hopes of secular democrats that the new government would fulfil their hopes.

Some of this I knew when, in late March 1980, not long after my twenty-eighth birthday, I went to the Iranian embassy in London to apply for visas. Back in Sydney, the ABC's federal news editor, a rumpled and kindly man named Bert Christie, who was in charge of foreign assignments, had finally let himself be persuaded that the time was right to allow someone from the London bureau to travel to a major story again: although with deep misgivings. The hostage story was simply too big to treat by recycling agency TV footage and freelancers' radio contributions. It was now five months since waves of young revolutionaries had smashed into the huge US embassy compound in Tehran, overwhelming the Marines while the local Iranian police melted away. It was five months, too, since the relatively moderate provisional government of Mehdi Bazargan had collapsed, leaving the way free for Khomeini to appoint his own hand-picked Islamic followers into all the positions of state power. (Much good would it do them: in this atmosphere of revolutionary fervour, most of them would themselves be exiled, executed or assassinated within a decade.)

For some months, the Iranians had closely restricted the number of visas they issued. The world had seen footage of gallons of alcohol flowing down the gutters as mullahs smashed bottles in the streets, and of women forced to wear the veil. Perhaps now the Iranians believed things were stabilising a little, and they could afford to let more journalists in.

* * *

The Iranian embassy in London was a tall, imposing, white stucco building in Princes Gate, overlooking Hyde Park. Its stately façade was soon to become world-famous as pictures flashed around the world showing members of Britain's SAS abseiling off the roof, the climax of an operation to free hostages held inside by a half-dozen gunmen, but that was weeks into the future. Besides, journalists entered through the far less gracious back entrance, into a dingy and windowless space where they were issued lengthy documents clearly only crudely modified from those issued by the Shah's regime.

While sitting in this airless waiting room, having filled in all the forms in triplicate, I got talking to a journalist named Jon Snow, of ITN News, then the UK's only commercial TV news service—nowadays Jon is the long-serving host of Britain's Channel 4 News. An imposingly tall figure, he was, at thirty-three, also extremely clever and very experienced, and he was kind enough to tell me a bit about his visits to Iran since the revolution. The more he spoke, the more I became aware of the size of the task ahead. I had travelled abroad a lot in my life, including through China during the Cultural Revolution, but never as a journalist, only as a diplomat's son. I'd seen my share of death and destruction covering train disasters and bushfires, but always in Australia. I'd never had a gun pointed at me or seen a shot fired in anger, let alone tried to make sense of what was then still an unresolved revolution with aspects of a civil war.

It became clear to me that this job was going to be very different from anything I'd ever done. It wasn't just the language barrier, or the difficulties of long-distance communication in that pre-internet era. It was also the reality of working in an environment where half the population automatically assumed that any journalist, particularly any Western-looking journalist, was a spy or an agent of the Great Satan (America) or the Little Satan (Britain). And there was the problem of censorship: every piece of film flown out of Iran had to be processed in a Revolutionary Government laboratory and checked by a government censor. Every minute of videotape also had to go via the government satellite station, where vigilant censors hovered over every frame and every word.

Jon kindly gave me a lift back to the ABC, only three blocks from his own ITN office, and I went back to my desk far less complacent about the challenge ahead. Looking back now, though, I still have the sense of how unprepared I was for the maelstrom of the next few weeks.

Eventually the visas came through, and I went shopping for some warm-weather clothes now that I'd be getting out of chilly London. I stopped short of following in the footsteps of Evelyn Waugh's William Boot and buying cleft sticks and a collapsible canoe. But, acutely aware that I was still the man who had forgotten his passport on his first assignment just nine weeks before, I could not shake the sense that I was an innocent abroad. And I could not forget the memory of Tony Joyce, comatose in the hospital.

As I walked down the stairs to leave 54 Portland Place for the airport, Ken Begg, the bureau chief, was standing on the landing with tears running down his face. I'd known Ken since 1974, when I was a cadet. 'Take care mate, for Christ's sake,' he said. 'Don't worry, Ken. I'll look after myself,' I replied. It was only two years later, while reading a lengthy *Sydney Morning Herald* article by Peter Bowers, that I learned that Ken had had an almost identical conversation with Tony Joyce the day he left for Zambia.

I tend to look back on myself now and see a young idiot. Why was I not terrified on my first real assignment? Why was I not more aware of the situation I was flying into? My younger self answers back: 'What more should I do? I've talked to colleagues who've been there. I've talked extensively to that Iran expert, Professor Fred Halliday, whose book I've also read. There is no internet, and there are no mobiles or satellite phones, you supercilious twenty-first-century geriatric. The only way really to find out is to go there.'

And so Les Seymour and I boarded a 747 at Heathrow, with the usual vast number of cases loaded with film gear and enough tape to last us a month or more, and many hours later landed in Revolutionary Iran.

Chapter 3

Drunk as Lords

WE LANDED IN Tehran early on a Friday morning. We were met as prearranged by a driver with a van—let's call him Hadi—who would be our transport and in a limited sense our translator over the coming weeks: his English was good enough to understand directions but not for interpreting interviews. Hadi's main subject of conversation was money, first expressed within minutes of the airport when we got stuck in a traffic jam and an ancient, toothless and clearly starving beggar knocked on the window. 'Keep window shut, give him nothing,' said Hadi. 'Why not?' Les asked. 'Is good money,' came the reply. 'He is fine, no problem, does not need. Begging ... is good money.'

I'd been counselled, if possible, always to hit the ground running on a foreign assignment. So I asked Hadi what was happening that morning and whether there was anything we could film on the way to the hotel. I thought he told me that Ayatollah Khomeini was preaching at Friday prayers, so I insisted we go there. This would be quite something: I believed that it had been some months since Khomeini had preached in public, and there was sure to be a large crowd. We got to the outdoor venue, and there were indeed some 50,000 people, but I had misheard: the Ayatollah preaching that day was Ali Khamenei. I felt somewhat deflated, but the pictures were good, and the crowd big and enthusiastic enough to report something, at least, about the state of the Islamic Revolution. I did a piece to camera and we filmed Khamenei, ramrod-straight in a long robe, holding his sermon in one hand and an AK-47 in the other, preaching hellfire and damnation to the enemies of Iran. The crowd chanted 'Marg bar Am'rika': Death to America.

Some in the crowd were hostile, though they tended to back away reassured when we said 'Australia'. It was a strange atmosphere, one that would be repeated again and again in the days ahead: a noisy public demonstration of hatred and anger, followed by attempts to speak English and ask if it was easy to emigrate to Australia, questions about kangaroos and koalas. But there was no ambiguity about Khamenei himself. His face, like that of his leader, Khomeini, was hard and unyielding, his air of utter rectitude unshakeable, his simultaneous embrace of the gun and the Holy Book the clearest possible symbol of the marriage of religion and state power. Dark-haired and granite-faced, he looked nothing like the smiling, white-bearded figure who appears in the modern iconography of Revolutionary Iran—and at the time we certainly had no idea that this was the man who would inherit from Khomeini the position of Supreme Leader, in which he continues implacably to this day.

We got back into the van reasonably pleased. Now we just had to check into the hotel and work out how to file the story, which I recently saw for the first time in thirty-five years:

> *Piece to camera in front of massive crowd.*
> The Islamic Revolution in Iran depends for its momentum on regular expressions of unity—occasions like this one when thousands of people get together to reaffirm their religious and political commitment.
>
> *Shot of Khamenei, tilting down to his AK-47.*
> The independence of the new Islamic Republic is a key theme. The Ayatollahs attack the United States and President Carter. But their message is that Iran must also arm against other potential aggressors, such as the Soviet Union.
>
> *Crowd chants 'Allah o Akbar, Allah o Akbar'.*
> The apparently united reaction to these pep-talks, however, conceals the real complexity of the situation.

Shots of people distributing propaganda leaflets in the crowd.
Also jostling for power and influence in Iran today are other less visible groups: the Tudeh, or Moscow-oriented communists, and the militant Mujahideen and Fedayeen.

Shots of bookstalls selling revolutionary literature.
Both these groups embrace a kind of Islamic Marxism, and the conservative Ayatollahs have accused some Mujahideen of being in league with the Soviet Union.

Shots of stall selling freshly squeezed orange juice.
A worsening of Iran's economy can only strengthen the claims of these groups that the revolution under the present leadership is not working.

Shots of worshippers bowing, praying; pull out to wide shot of huge crowd.
As the sanctions bite harder, and the prospect of long-term shortages becomes a reality, the government has to fight harder for its own stability.

Piece to camera in front of shouting, jostling crowd.
These meetings aren't only held to restore the faithful. They also strengthen the religious, Islamic content of what's essentially a political revolution. And in the present climate, the alternative to that could be a shift in power towards more Marxist-oriented groups. In Tehran this is Mark Colvin for ABC National News.

* * *

My home for the next few weeks, the Intercontinental Hotel, was a tall concrete building on what had been Pahlavi Avenue when the Pahlavis had occupied the throne, but which had since been renamed Dr H Fatemi Avenue, after the brilliant young foreign minister the Shah had ordered executed by firing squad in the coup against Mossadeq of 1953. It stood out from the Tehran skyline for height rather than beauty: its chief design feature was the way it stuck out at the roofline in a twin diamond shape. Otherwise, inside and out, it was a fairly standard piece of 1960s architectural Brutalism: but it wasn't for architectural merit that journalists stayed there.

There were a few foreign freelancers living in flats and houses around Tehran at the time, among them the ABC's own stringer Roger Cooper, but for the fly-in-fly-out reporters the Intercon was where you stayed. Journalism was constrained by a lot of difficulties in those days, but the chief of them was communication. Before mobile phones or even faxes, you needed, above all, access to a telephone switchboard which would take messages for you and connect you to the international exchange. You also needed to be able to send messages by teleprinter—the telex. And at that time in Tehran, you needed to be somewhere where, as a foreigner speaking no Farsi, you would be afforded some degree of protection.

Even at the Intercon, these things were hardly guaranteed. The previous year, the hotel had been attacked by left-wing militias, the siege only relieved after three days by Revolutionary Guards under Ayatollah Khomeini's control. Ownership of the hotel itself was also the subject of a protracted legal dispute, with its American owners trying to hold on in face of a concerted attempt by the Revolutionary Government to nationalise the place. Supporters of the Ayatollah would eventually succeed in ousting the German general manager and all other foreign employees, but when we were there they were still battling on against increasingly heavy odds. The result was that the hotel had been largely cut off from its US parent group, financially and personally. Rumour had it that, no longer able to obtain supplies from the rest of the Intercontinental chain, they were increasingly feeding guests on the remaining contents of the freezers. For whatever reason, many of us complained of various minor stomach ailments: I certainly didn't feel physically well for weeks.

There's a Garry Trudeau *Doonesbury* cartoon from the time in which a regular character, the Reverend Sloan, is on the phone in what to me is quite obviously the Intercon: 'Hello? Operator? I'm trying to get room service.' 'Sorry, sir. Everyone's out fighting the Leftists today.' In a subsequent strip, Trudeau's ludicrously self-important TV journalist Roland Burton Hedley III is doing a long-distance Q&A with the Rev:

> Hedley: This is Roland Hedley … only one man has been invited to see the hostages. He's Reverend Scot Sloan, and I talked with him today. Reverend Sloan, what's the condition of the hostages now?

Sloan: I have no idea. I've spent the last week waiting in my hotel room.

Hedley: Oh ... Well, what are conditions like in your hotel room?

Sloan: A little cramped, but I'm not being mistreated.

That's pretty much how you started to feel after a few days in the Intercon. It wasn't just the long hours spent writing or hunched over a tape recorder editing radio stories, then dismantling the phone and using alligator clips to transmit your audio down the phone line. It was also the waiting.

In the era of mobile phones, satellite phones, Skype, Twitter, Facebook and the rest, it's probably useful to describe how we did international journalism back then. The indispensable tool of my trade was the Nagra Mark 4 tape recorder. A marvel of Swiss engineering, it weighed about 8 kilograms with batteries, and you carried it over your shoulder. Colleagues from the time often grumble that the Nagra has kept more physiotherapists and back surgeons in business than any other piece of equipment outside the mining and construction industries.

The Nagra was as tough as it was heavy: years later, I saw one run over by President Mikhail Gorbachev's armoured limousine on the road outside the Soviet embassy in Paris. An outraged French TV sound recordist turned on the machine only to find it still working: bent out of shape, yes, but still working.

The reason you used the Nagra was that it really did work. Its technology ensured that, unlike some other reel-to-reel recorders, the tape always moved through the mechanism at the same speed. That meant no 'wow' or 'flutter' when the machine was being used in a moving vehicle or at walking speed (there was no real question of running with that much weight on your shoulder), or when the batteries ran down. So you could reliably use a clapperboard to synch your Nagra with a film camera—an Arriflex with its equally consistent speed of 24 frames per second. Ultimately, sound and vision could be remarried on the plates of a Steenbeck editing machine. In fact, the rushes *had* to be synched, shot by shot, before editing could even begin.

For radio, the Nagra also had an editing block, on which you used a razor blade and quarter-inch sticky tape to cut your story together. Again, you knew that whatever the state of the batteries (a row of no fewer than twelve big D-cells), the tape would flow past the magnetic play heads at the right speed.

Equally, the era of the laptop computer was still a few years away. Everything I wrote in Tehran, I wrote on a typewriter, two-fingered (I'd never learned to touch-type), but usually extremely fast. Corrections you made by hand or with Tipp-Ex, unless you decided you'd got the whole thing in the wrong order, in which case you often just had to type it all again. Cut-and-paste back then was not a word-processing metaphor—you used real scissors and real paste.

But once you finished your radio story, you still had to file it, and that meant getting a phone line good enough to send it down with sufficient audio quality to put it to air. That was when the waiting started. There was no direct international dialling in 1980: you had to go through international exchanges. But first, you had to go through the hotel exchange.

Ben Affleck's film *Argo* is set just a month before my arrival in Tehran, and it contains some good stuff—most of it in the first half—but much of the rest has elements of the ridiculous for anyone who was there at the time. And of those elements, none is more ridiculous than the plot point, as the closing crescendo builds, in which an Iranian agent tries to verify a piece of evidence by dialling direct from an ordinary office telephone at Tehran's airport to a film producer's office in Los Angeles. There simply was no way of doing that back then. You had to go through several operators—in my case, a hotel operator, then a Tehran international exchange operator, then an operator at the Sydney International Exchange.

Looking back now, I'm fairly sure that every experienced journalist in that hotel was regularly bribing the Intercon's operators to get them faster access to international calls. I was such a greenhorn that I had no idea. I would regularly wait six to eight hours, being told that my name had moved up the list and the call would come through 'soon, soon', to get put through to my colleagues on the desk in London, let alone Radio News or Current Affairs in Sydney.

In the pre-mobile, pre-pager era, that meant you were trapped, staring at the ceiling, thinking how now you finally understood why rock stars trashed hotel rooms and threw items of furniture out of windows. Once I made a virtue out of this imprisonment by writing a piece for *Correspondents Report* about what I could see out of my hotel window:

a family of desperately poor people who lived in a makeshift shelter on the roof of the building opposite; Tehran's always appalling traffic; the smog. And a bleakly hilarious incident in which a small car with a sunroof cut off a large Jaguar in the street directly below. I saw the Jaguar driver jump out at the next traffic light, walk up to the Fiat Bambino driver who had so insulted him, reach through the open roof, grab the driver by the throat, haul him up and punch him in the face. I resolved to be very careful to avoid inducing Iranian road rage.

There were also unwelcome incidents in-house, although they at least alleviated the boredom while you waited for that all-important call to come through.

A few months before I arrived, the morals police had raided the Intercon and seized all the hotel's alcohol—beer, wine and spirits—without exception. The mullahs had then destroyed it all, smashing bottles, opening cans, and letting it all pour down into the drains. 'Hard-bitten journalists wept,' one who'd been there told me with a lopsided grin. But the mullahs weren't finished. Almost every day I spent in that dreary hotel room, each time at a different hour, there was a knock on the door. I'd open it and there would be a brown-gowned mullah, stony-faced, flanked by a couple of Revolutionary Guards brandishing Kalashnikovs, ready to shoulder past you and start the search. They were brutish, thorough and wordless, and they didn't stop at a cursory look inside the fridge. They turned the mattress upside down, they looked behind the curtains, and they went through the bathroom cupboards, all in search of the demon drink.

Before my trip, I'd heard all the stories about the Revolutionary Government's hatred of the bottle, and had been quite resigned to being a teetotaller for a few weeks. But some kind of innate, sheer bloody-mindedness demanded a response to these repeated and ill-mannered invasions. I bought a couple of six-packs of beer on the black market, unscrewed the air-conditioning grille directly above the room entrance, and made my stash in there. They never once even looked: a small victory but a satisfying one.

Another regular visitor was far more welcome: the black-market caviar salesman. He knocked on my door about three days after I got to the Intercon, keen to sell me a large tin of the best Oscietra—high-quality Iranian caviar from the southern Caspian Sea—for a mere five pounds sterling. I was dubious. I'd never remotely been able to afford caviar, had never even tasted the stuff. Would I like it? Was it worth the price? I tried it and was hooked ... like a Caspian sturgeon. From then on I stopped ordering anything from room service except blinis, sour cream and lemons. There was more than one day in that hotel when I ate caviar for breakfast, lunch and dinner. On departure, I took a giant tub of the stuff—possibly a whole fifteen pounds' worth—back to London with me. I gathered that I probably could have sold it in the UK to the right buyer for about a thousand quid, but I liked it too much not to eat it myself and share it with my friends. Caviar is the cocaine of seafood. And I've never been able to afford it since.

As in the USA in the 1920s, Iranian alcohol prohibition, while theoretically absolute, was never without its loopholes. In this case, the loophole consisted of a Korean restaurateur called Mr Kim, whose well-appointed teppanyaki restaurant, Les and I soon discovered, was where half the foreign press corps went in the evenings. You sat on high stools around a flat, horseshoe-shaped cooking surface heated to a sizzling temperature. Inside the horseshoe, a chef, juggling large knives and cleavers as though they were clubs in a cabaret act, sliced beef and fish very thin and cooked it very rare in front of you. It was wonderful, and at the current rates of exchange ludicrously affordable. There were noodle soups and perfectly cooked vegetables, and always on the side the pungent spicy kimchi to flavour everything.

And there was beer, and whisky. Somehow Mr Kim, who appeared to speak only about twenty words of English and almost no Farsi, had done a deal with the local Revolutionary Committee whereby they would turn a blind eye to the alcohol—as long as he admitted no Iranians. That was fine with Mr Kim, who knew that thanks to the journalism crowd he could do a roaring trade every night without a single local entering his portals.

It was there, I think, that I first met the local BBC stringer Alex Brodie, a tough, tenacious, energetic journalist who'd made his name covering the revolution, mainly for the World Service. His name will recur in this narrative, but for now I'll just mention the night he and Les and I were the last people to leave Mr Kim's, none of us remotely describable as sober, and for some reason we couldn't get a taxi. After waiting an hour or more, during which we inhaled even more booze, we were starting to get a bit desperate, when Mr Kim himself offered to drive us home. We got in his extremely large and luxurious Mercedes, and he smilingly drove me and Les back to the Intercon before taking Alex back to his house-cum-office.

Drunk as lords in Revolutionary Tehran.

In the business of supplying foreigners with alcohol, prohibition or no prohibition, profits were clearly there to be had.

Chapter 4

We Are Corpses

If there were aspects of life at the Intercontinental Hotel that made you feel somewhat imprisoned, the reality was that there were plenty of opportunities to get out and see what was going on.

Employees of the giant American network NBC had much of the floor above us, converted into offices and editing suites, and the BBC TV correspondents would meet them every morning to plan the day's coverage. As a client of NBC and a longstanding international partner of the BBC, we were able to participate. This was fortunate, since there was so much going on in Tehran that one Australian correspondent accompanied by one cameraman could never have achieved much on their own. As it was, we were happy to contribute our eyes to a broader coverage, in exchange for the knowledge that we could use others' material as freely as they used ours.

The Americans, especially, were far better resourced than anyone else. For them, the continuing imprisonment of the hostages was a huge story, leading the bulletins every night, with the news anchors beginning or ending each broadcast by announcing 'Day X of the hostage crisis'. There was at least one producer for every on-screen reporter, and they had the money to employ a fleet of drivers and a large number of interpreters.

The story was of course much bigger than the US embassy where the hostages had now been held incommunicado for about five months.

The invasion of the embassy was a rogue act: it had been run by student revolutionaries, apparently without direction from the government, although possibly with encouragement from the most radical among the Ayatollahs, who had no patience for anything but absolute power over the civil government. But after an initial period of uncertainty, Supreme Leader Ayatollah Khomeini, in breach of every diplomatic convention and treaty, gave his blessing to what was essentially an act of terrorism—the takeover of a foreign embassy, by convention to be treated as foreign soil, and the brutal imprisonment of its employees. As such, the events of the last few months signalled a power struggle—a serious fracture in the Revolutionary Government and possible instability in the revolution itself.

There were mass rallies, liable at any time to turn into riots. There were bombings. Les and I went down to one of the town's central squares one day to film the immediate aftermath of a car bomb that had gone off minutes before. There was blood and twisted metal everywhere: the worst thing I'd seen since I'd arrived at the Sydney Hilton on a night in 1976 after a bomb blew up a garbage truck, killing three people and injuring eleven. On another day, a couple of pedestrians were blown up by a homemade device—nowadays we'd call it an IED—concealed in an innocent-looking wash bag.

The economy was also a mess. I remember getting up at 2 a.m. one morning to go and film bread being made at a bakery. The government had fixed the price of bread, but inflation on the raw ingredients was so high that bakers were desperate. They were going to go out of business unless the price went up in the shops. And if that happened, it could mean bread riots. The elements of the government that wore suits wanted to do something practical to deal with the situation. The elements that wore robes and turbans, shall we say, wanted the revolution to be more pure, and had no truck at all with economic and other pragmatic solutions. It was they who now decided to flex their muscles, by cracking down on the opposition.

In late April 1980, I reported for *AM* on student riots that left hundreds injured and one person dead. Iran's ruling Revolutionary Council had ordered the closure of groups and clubs across all universities, a move I assessed as deliberately setting up a head-on clash with the country's left-wing groups. The groups in question were the Mujahideen and the Fedayeen, Islamic organisations which claimed a significant role in the success of the previous year's revolution, but which the clergy accused of communist sympathies. And I noted that the clergy themselves commanded a formidable force called the Hezbollahi, a group of mostly illiterate youths with shaven heads who employed violence in the service of what they called the Party of God. But for the average Iranian, beneath the political infighting was a harsher reality, which I acknowledged in my report:

> Meanwhile, this new political row is diverting attention from Iran's drastically worsening economic situation. The country's President, Mr Bani-Sadr, produced the simplest summing-up, predicting 100 per cent inflation unless something was done urgently. Mr Bani-Sadr said, 'Economically speaking, we are corpses.'

'Corpses.' Even in the strongest political rhetoric, it doesn't come much starker than that.

Bani-Sadr had been Ayatollah Khomeini's pick for the presidency, but as well as being an Islamic revolutionary and having shared the Ayatollah's Paris exile, the president was to some degree a pragmatist, one who had studied finance and economics at a high level, and actually written a textbook on Islamic economics. Bani-Sadr knew that the economy was plummeting, with predictable consequences. Every foreign journalist could have told you from personal observation what those consequences meant. With international sanctions starting to bite, and with the exchange rate of the rial fixed, prices were starting to rocket to such a degree that Weimar-style inflation could not be far away. Any Iranian with the sense and the wherewithal was trying to get money out of the country—or get their hands on foreign currency.

As it was, some journalists were pulling outrageous scams by changing most of their expense, accommodation and telecommunications money on the black market at prices many times the official rate, but charging their employers at the official rate. I heard about one Visnews producer who actually hired a crane just to get one top-shot of a massive demonstration, purely because he'd be able to make such a profit on the exchange-rate differential.

There were also canny old hands who'd brought wads of their own dollars or pounds so as to work the Iran Air scam. That was the system by which you went into the airline's Tehran office with rials you'd bought on the black market for a fraction of their official value, and asked for two round-the-world first-class tickets. Iran Air was still trying hard to comply with the rules of the international airline organisation IATA, so when you got back to your office in London or New York and said you'd no longer be needing the tickets, they had no choice but to refund you the full value at the official exchange rate. Some people made illicit fortunes that way.

People who've had a revolution want more than the fall of the previous regime: they want their lives under the new government to be better, and the lives of Iranians were getting materially worse. Many of those who'd initially welcomed Khomeini and supported the fall of the Shah, particularly those who had hoped for a secular revolution, were now chafing.

There were also highly organised, quasi-military political organisations which regarded themselves as having played key roles in the revolt, but now felt keenly the Ayatollahs' determination to crush them. Les and I went to Tehran University to try to meet some of them. As I said in the report I subsequently filed for *AM* on 22 April, 'On camera, we got silence: granted the anonymity of the tape recorder, people were more than willing to speak.'

> Student: They had a cover-up here. They said that we want to do a Cultural Revolution in our universities. This is an internal matter OK, not for other nations, it's not anybody's goddamn business. And, and pre-judgement, false judgement, does not help us.
>
> Me: But this is not …
>
> Student: This is nothing, this is none of your business, this is an internal Iranian matter.
>
> Me: Well don't you think that the rest of the world has a right to be interested in what goes on here though?
>
> Student: No! Are you interested in people, in human rights? Go to southern Lebanon.
>
> At this point, we were told that if we left our camera in the car we could obtain an interview with one of the major political groups involved. We were led through a line of revolutionaries who were forming a barrier with arms linked. Then another line, then a third, to the front of the group's headquarters. There, several hundred men and women were sitting quietly with their legs crossed. There were no

> signs of impending violence. We were led into what turned out to be the inner sanctum of a group associated with the Fedayeen, a Marxist-Leninist group who played a considerable part in the revolution against the Shah, but who the present government regards with deep suspicion. We had scarcely begun our interview with their spokesman when we heard the riot.

At this point on the tape, there's a confused sound of shouting and chanting. I remember this as an extremely tense moment when we realised that we were in a locked room with high windows, too high to see through: we were trapped. It would be a few minutes before our shouts and banging on the doors were heard, and we could see what was going on.

> The noise signalled the arrival of the Hezbollahi. No-one knows whether this group actually contains any students. It certainly includes teenagers and old men in its raiding parties. But what's not in any doubt is its capacity for violent action against the left. And apparently the Hezbollahi were not only outside the gates. A small group of them had also infiltrated the headquarters beforehand. Within minutes, people were reeling into the office where we sat, bleeding heavily from the head. One man was carried through on a stretcher with a saline drip in his arm. Our hosts raided their store of bayonets for the defence effort. The weapons used included clubs, knives, rocks, crowbars and sticks, but no guns were fired at this stage.

Here I recorded a piece on the scene: 'I can see this man being dragged through the crowd, he's being beaten about the head, people using metal bars, a woman being dragged off. [Confused shouting] Incredible scenes.' It took more than half an hour before the coast was clear. It was all part of a bigger battle that would end that evening when Islamic fundamentalists—Ayatollah loyalists—claimed control of the university.

Les and I emerged shaken from that situation. The besieging forces had come very close indeed before being beaten back, and the fact that our hosts had been so frightened for our safety, more than our own immediate awareness of the danger, struck home. It was clear, among other things, that they themselves felt they'd lost face by putting us in peril, and they made sure to get in touch to let us obtain the interview that the siege had so rudely interrupted.

So the next day we were back on the (theoretically closed) campus, looking for the Mujahideen and the Fedayeen. The *AM* tape tells the story:

> At a secretly arranged rendezvous, the anonymous [Fedayeen] spokesman claimed that his group and the Mujahideen now had sufficient military power to take over. However, he admitted that their political base was inadequate to the task. He said both groups had made the mistake under the Shah of concentrating too much on guerrilla warfare and too little on 'political education'. As a consequence, he said, the revolution had been hijacked by the clergy. And his certainty of eventual victory was matched only by his contempt for the political ability of the Mullahs:
>
> Spokesman: They proved to be unable to solve the economic problems. The prices are going higher and higher with every day that passes. They haven't even food material and they haven't the money to buy it. And as I told you this situation is deteriorating with every day that passes.
>
> Me: But there will be a second revolution?
>
> Spokesman: Sure, sure.
>
> Me: Is there anything that could stop it?
>
> Spokesman: It's inevitable and nothing can stop it. It's inevitable because no such problems as housing, as inflation, as unemployment … have been solved.
>
> Me: How long before the second revolution will come?'
>
> Spokesman: One cannot say, but I think … less than one year. Because I told you, military speaking we are in a position now to stand against them.
>
> Me: When the revolution comes will it be a very quick one, or will it be very bloody and long-drawn-out?
>
> Spokesman: I think it will be bloody and long.

In retrospect, it's too easy to think of the Fedayeen spokesman's bravado as mere wishful thinking, with its Marxist assumption of the 'inevitability' of history. Historical inevitabilism has a nasty habit of being tripped up by unforeseen events. But to be fair, at the time, the revolution was genuinely under threat. The situation was extremely fragile. The foreign minister, Sadeq Qotbzadeh, was making frequent visits to our hotel to try to persuade the foreign press that things were not as bad as they seemed, but things were spiralling downwards.

They might have continued to do so, but that Wednesday no-one foresaw that the next day something would happen that would change everything: it would make the melting away of opposition to the Revolutionary Government inevitable, and cement in place the implacable hostility between the USA and Iran that had begun with the invasion of the embassy and the hostage taking—hostility that would continue for three and a half decades.

President Carter sent in an invasion force.

Chapter 5

Eagle Claw

'EAGLE CLAW', WE now know, was the codename for the secret operation mounted by President Carter, who was panicked by the mounting media pressure as the US embassy crisis dragged on, and under constant attack from the increasingly popular Republican presidential candidate, Ronald Reagan. The only thing that really worked about it, though, was the secrecy. There was no indication among any of our Tehran contacts, or those of any colleagues that I met then or afterwards, that the hostage rescue attempt was coming. Iran, though churning with revolutionary upheaval, was not braced for this.

The Americans mounted their attack on a Thursday, 24 April. From aircraft carriers in the Persian Gulf, they sent a helicopter force, backed by C-130 refuelling planes and more planes flying in with highly trained Delta Force commandos, to Desert One, a remote site in the Dasht-e Kavir desert. The plan was to fly onwards, on the Friday, to a site about 50 kilometres out of Tehran, then drive in trucks to the embassy, break in, free the hostages, and 'exfiltrate' them to the waiting helicopters that would fly them back out.

Even on paper, and without the benefit of hindsight, the operation looks ambitious, not to say crazy. As it was, it never got beyond Desert One, and probably never would have: the planners hadn't even calculated that the landing site was on a bus route, let alone that a bus would come along in the middle of their landings and they'd be faced with a coachload of eyewitnesses. Nor had they noted that April is dust storm season in the Dasht-e Kavir: some of the helicopters had even had the dust-protection removed from their engines to lighten their load and give greater range.

For the American military, it was an utter catastrophe. For President Carter, it was effectively the end of his hopes of a second term in the White House. It was the moment, we can see now, that ushered in the Reagan era, for better or worse.

There was indeed a dust storm, a bad one, which reduced visibility so much that one of the helicopters crash-landed and another was too badly damaged to continue. The commander cancelled the mission, but before the remaining helicopters could take off, there was a collision, in the swirling curtain of sand, between one of them and one of the C-130s. Both caught fire, leaving a tangle of twisted metal, rotors and rivulets of molten aluminium on the ground. The rescue force took off in the remaining transport plane, in such a hurry that they failed to blow up all the helicopters, leaving them, their arms, ammunition and comms equipment as an unwitting donation to the Iranian Revolutionary Air Force.

That was on the Thursday afternoon and evening, and even later that night, such was the remoteness of the site, the news did not break. All unknowing, Les and I loaded our equipment into a van at 6 a.m. the next morning. We were heading out to film a story we never did manage to complete: a platoon of young revolutionary women being trained at a firing range in the use of automatic rifles. We were going to talk to these veiled zealots, watch them drill and fire their guns, and hear—I suspected—the usual lines about the importance of combatting the Great Satan.

At 6.30 a.m., we arrived at the apartment of our stringer, translator and guide, Roger Cooper. A quietly spoken, scholarly Englishman who lived in a delightful old Tehran apartment full of carpets and Iranian artworks, Roger would later become world-famous as an alleged spy. He was to serve five years in appalling conditions in Tehran's notorious Evin Prison after a show trial in which he was denied a lawyer, and the judge, a mullah, told him before the proceedings even started that he would be found guilty. Roger was a man of great sangfroid—when he was finally released and returned to Britain, he told the waiting press: 'Anyone like me who has been educated at an English public school and then served in the ranks of the British Army is quite at home in a Third World prison.'

But that Friday morning, the stiff upper lip was not in evidence. Roger was waiting for us in some panic: 'What are you doing here? Haven't you heard the news?' No, I said, I hadn't had time to tune my short-wave radio in to the BBC World Service before we left. 'You probably shouldn't have come,' he said. 'It may not be safe to look even remotely American on the streets of Tehran today. The Americans have sent in a rescue force. It's been on the BBC and Iranian radio. It failed disastrously, but there's absolutely no telling how the crowds will react. Don't forget, it's just coming up to Friday prayers. You should get back to the hotel. Even there, there's no guarantee you'll be safe.'

Roger had lived in Iran, on and off, since 1958. I knew, from talking to him often on the phone while taking his freelance radio pieces, that he was a level-headed and extremely experienced observer, not in the least given to hysteria in these matters. Our shoot with the women revolutionaries was definitely off for the day. More to the point, would we survive till the next day?

Les and I got back to the Intercontinental to find the place in turmoil, with milling journalists swapping rumours and trying to assess the situation. The consensus was that no-one was going anywhere till the end of Friday prayers: as we'd driven back to the hotel, sitting low in our seats so as not to draw attention, we'd seen vast crowds moving through the streets to hear the Ayatollahs' sermons. The question was how the clerics would react. Would they whip the crowd up into an anti-American frenzy, recalling the fervour of the year before in the immediate wake of Khomeini's return? Or would they take a more moderate stance?

The NBC guys had some of their Iranian staff out on the street, and by the end of the morning we were fairly sure that it was the latter: the sermons had all been along the lines of 'Our glorious Revolution has survived, Allah has seen to it that the American Satan has been repelled once again. Allah o Akbar. Go back to your homes and rejoice.' But while this was a relief, the hotel—and the city—were still pullulating with rumours, chief among them that the Americans were now going to attempt a second mission. Such was the atmosphere of fear that this idea had really taken hold, and a number of old Iran hands told me that, should it happen, the Intercontinental would certainly be besieged again.

It was at this point—and I've never told this story before—that I was sufficiently panicked to do something I regard in retrospect as insane. I rang my father. That sounds normal enough, until you factor in my father's job. He was then head of station for the SIS at the British embassy in Washington. This was—is—Britain's chief on-the-ground connection with the CIA.

As a matter of personal principle as a journalist, I had never before asked my father to use his position as a senior intelligence officer to help me with anything, and never did again. It still leaves me with an obscure sense of guilt. But I was really scared. Really, really scared. So I put a call through to his home number, and we had a chat.

It started innocuously enough: 'Hullo, Polo' (his nickname for me). 'Are you all right?' I had some naive idea that if we just had a longish chat, maybe whoever else was listening would think it was only a father–son catch-up. So I told him quite a lot about the stories I'd been covering and the things I'd seen. Being an old-line Cold Warrior, he was particularly interested in the Moscow-backed Tudeh Party, and was quite surprised when I told him it now seemed irrelevant, having been superseded by more-Islam-oriented Marxist groups. Then we talked a bit—obviously—about the failed raid, which was massive world news by now, and I mentioned that there was an increasing conviction that another raid was in preparation. I can't remember how I phrased it, but since his job was officially 'counsellor' (political) I asked carefully if any of his 'political connections' might know the truth of the matter. I do remember emphasising that I was very frightened indeed. Amazingly, considering what must have been his certain knowledge that the phones were tapped, he rang me back about two hours later and told me basically to relax: there was not going to be a second raid.

He once told me it was the maddest thing (in professional terms) he'd ever done. But mulling it over since, I've sometimes wondered whether, just perhaps, he may have been using the connection to pass a message to the Iranians: it was certainly the sort of oblique way he worked, so it's not impossible. All I can tell you is that it gave me a sense of extreme relief, and the ability to tell Les that we could probably, in the next day or so, get back out in the streets.

* * *

I think it was two days after the aborted hostage rescue that someone from the BBC gave us the word that some reporters were about to be let into the US embassy. It seemed unlikely, more like a rumour than a genuine tip. No journalist had been inside since the hostages had been imprisoned there five months before. Still, we did as we were told. Along with a dozen other journalists, we waited by a side gate in the high walls of the sprawling diplomatic enclosure. More press trickled in over the next hour, as we speculated among ourselves about how long we'd all wait before deciding it was a hoax and going back to base. But eventually the gate did open, and we were ushered into the giant embassy compound.

We were led to a wide quadrangle, bounded by more high walls and the imposing central embassy building. Looking up, we could see Revolutionary Guards prowling the parapets, staring down at us with their automatic rifles at the ready. In the middle of the square, someone had put out about forty chairs in front of a dais set with several more chairs and a microphone.

It was cloudy but oppressively hot: probably well over 30 degrees Celsius, with Tehran's customary pall of smog. We'd been waiting outside for a long time already; now we had to wait some more. Our questions—Were the hostages still in the embassy? Or had they been moved after the siege?—were brusquely rebuffed. We could be silent, they said, or talk among ourselves, but there would be no information until Ayatollah Khalkhali arrived.

Described in his 2003 London *Daily Telegraph* obituary as 'a small, rotund man with a pointed beard, kindly smile, and a high-pitched giggle', Khalkhali was better known to Iranians at the time as the 'Hanging Judge' for his enthusiastic embrace of the death penalty. Appointed by Khomeini to head the new Revolutionary Courts, he set about his task with relish. In Kurdistan, for instance, he was known for having tried, sentenced and executed up to sixty people a day. He made this task easier for himself by inventing a concept called 'obvious guilt'. As the phrase implies, this meant that you could be 'presumed guilty' if the judge decided before your trial that you'd done whatever you were accused of.

Khalkhali's was also a name I'd heard before, mainly because one of the NBC producers had told me he was nicknamed 'The Cat Strangler'. The reason was that, allegedly, in footage never aired for reasons of taste, he had replied to the interview question 'What would you do if the Shah came into this room right now?' by picking up the cat on his lap and breaking its neck.

And we were soon to discover—to paraphrase a joke made by the late Christopher Hitchens—Ayatollah Khalkhali was 'not as nice as he sounds'.

About an hour ticked by in the broiling heat. Every reporter there knew that we had, at the very least, one story: we were the first journalists allowed into the US embassy since the start of the siege. But in those pre-mobile phone, pre-laptop days, we couldn't file it. We were thirsty, hot, headachy with the heat and increasingly impatient. On the other hand, with all those guns pointing at us, there was nowhere to go and nothing to do but wait.

Eventually Khalkhali swept across the gravel, dark-robed, turbanned and accompanied by a phalanx of Revolutionary Guards, apparently his permanent protection corps. He took the microphone and began a lengthy rant in Farsi. Various translators started trying to interpret as he declaimed, but the armed minders quickly went around silencing them. So we were in the surreal situation of having to listen to a half-hour speech in a language most of us didn't understand before we could get even a summary of what was being said. For the first ten minutes or so, this was just frustrating. But then the lack of translation became, if anything, an intensifier of the drama.

Behind the dais was a mysteriously shaped object, or collection of objects, covered in tarpaulin. Pausing in his speech, Khalkhali ordered his bodyguard to remove the tarpaulin, revealing a number of wooden packing crates piled on top of each other. He then directed the men to start opening them.

The first thing that hit you when the wood started splintering and the nails came out was the smell. It was hard not to retch. As the guards started pulling out unidentifiable blackened objects, and Khalkhali's rant continued, our nostrils filled with the scent of rotting, cooked human flesh.

It took a little time to sink in. What we were seeing was the desecration of corpses, the flaunting for the cameras of the hideously charred bodies of the US servicemen who had died in the conflagration in the Dasht-e Kavir. I still couldn't quite believe what was happening until Khalkhali brandished one blackened stick-like object, about half a metre long.

One of his guards gave him what was either a bayonet or a large hunting knife and he started hacking at the charcoal surface. As he scraped away, he revealed what was recognisably an aviator watch. This was a man's arm he was holding, a man who had been alive a couple of days before.

It was certainly the worst thing I'd seen to that point in my life, and to this day, along with that unforgettable stench, it remains in my memory, as indelible as a brand.

Chapter 6

An Actual War

THE SPIRIT IN Tehran now was not just angry, or defiant of the USA, it was overweening. Intensifying international sanctions meant that the problems with the economy would not go away. By September that year, in fact, Iran would reach such a parlous state that Saddam Hussein was emboldened to invade, starting a hideous trench and artillery war between Iran and Iraq that would last until 1988. But the stories we had been pursuing, about dissent from and opposition to the revolution, now had been clearly rendered obsolete. There's nothing like a renewed foreign threat, like the American desert raid, to bring the populace behind a populist government. The opposition groups we'd been speaking to lay low or melted away.

To exploit and intensify this new unity, a few days after the failed American hostage rescue, the Ayatollahs decided to mount a mass demonstration in celebration of their victory. We went to film it. I estimated—as did others—that there were at least half a million people there. My TV piece began like this:

Chanting crowd—pan across to piece to camera.
One of the most remarkable things about the Iranian Revolution is its incredible capacity for mass mobilisation. The revolution itself was

> marked by several demonstrations of a million or more, and it's still possible to get hundreds and hundreds of thousands of people pouring into the centre of Tehran in buses, in cars and taxis, and on foot.

After a while, we had a fair bit in the can, and all had been well. Any potential anti-Americanism from the crowd towards us was usually diffused by the fact that we'd drawn a large kangaroo on the side of our camera, with the word 'AUSTRALIA' in English and Farsi. But everything we'd shot was at ground level, so there was no real sense of the actual magnitude of the crowd. There was a big Iranian television outside-broadcast truck, and its crew told Les he was welcome to stand on top of it to film a panoramic shot that would capture the scope of what's probably the biggest demonstration I've ever covered.

My piece went on:

> *High shot from truck roof panning across vast crowd …*
> It's this ability to demonstrate support by sheer weight of numbers that's one of the keys to power in the country today. These huge demonstrations, however, also add considerably to the uncertainty and danger of life in post-revolutionary Iran.
>
> *Pick-up truck drives through crowd carrying young men, some armed with machine guns.*
> A mass of people this size may look united and purposeful at a distance, but on the ground it's a shifting and volatile coalition of different and sometimes conflicting groups.
>
> *Marchers carrying Khomeini posters.*
> In this gathering there were liberal supporters of President Bani-Sadr, devout Muslims faithfully following the Mullahs' line, groups of the derelict and unemployed seeking violence, and a sizeable element of the simply curious.

It was being visible on top of the truck that did it. Just as we decided we'd filmed enough and were trying to make our way out of the crowd, with me carrying the Nagra and Les the Arriflex, the attack began from behind. I felt a couple of punches to my shoulders and back, and saw teenagers running past after they'd hit me, but far more blows rained down on Les.

My script doesn't fully capture the intense fear we felt at that moment, completely surrounded, separated from our driver, and a long, long way from the edge of the crowd.

> Emotions run high. Anti-Americanism is often the strongest emotion of all, and when that happens there's no discrimination exercised. A group of youths, some as young as eleven or twelve, punched ABC cameraman Les Seymour several times in the back a few moments after he took these pictures. We were told they'd refused to believe we were not American. Only the arrival of armed Revolutionary Guards prevented further violence. Moments before, the crowd had been friendly and helpful.

The fact is that we may well have owed our lives to those Revolutionary Guards. We heard them first as a klaxon behind us, then looked back to see their big American pick-up truck ploughing towards us through the crowd, its front doors wide open and with an armed man balanced on each sill—it was like a bulldozer, scattering demonstrators as it came. Les and I both thought the guards were going to arrest us and lock us up, at best, but instead they scooped us into the truck and drove us to our van, well away from the mass of the crowd. They were friendly and business-like, and not for the first time I reflected on the duality of Iran: how you could meet deep hostility at one moment yet find it replaced by the greatest hospitality.

Les was feeling really sore. He went to the hospital, where a doctor told him he might have a broken pelvis and insisted he have an X-ray. He waited in a room full of women in chadors, before, as he told me later, the doctor put the pictures straight up on the light box to show him, in front of everyone. The trouble was, as I could see when he showed me the pictures, that there was inadequate shielding in the X-ray machine, so the pelvic images showed rather more than bone. Under the chadors, Les claimed, eyes were swivelling. The fact that he could laugh about it was in itself an indication that there was no fracture, but he was in pain, and for the next few days I concentrated on radio so he could get some rest.

Then, on 30 April, the focus decisively went off Tehran and onto another massive Iran story elsewhere—the takeover by an Iranian Arab separatist group of the country's embassy in London. After what had happened to us, and with the London office covering events at the embassy in Princes Gate, Bert Christie, to whom I answered in Sydney, wanted to make a decision on whether to keep us in Iran or pull us out.

I already had a counterproposition. 'Let's go and cover an actual war' was basically how BBC correspondent Alex Brodie had pitched it to me. 'Let's go to this place up in the north-west that's trying to make itself independent of Ayatollah Khomeini's regime.'

* * *

The self-declared Republic of Iranian Kurdistan was a place that did not exist in the eyes of the country's central government, or those of the United Nations, or in the consciousness of most of the world. But it was a place that had been fighting for its life since the spring of the previous year—a place whose capital had been besieged and sacked by the Iranian Army, with its American equipment inherited from the Shah, but then retaken by ill-equipped Kurdish Peshmerga.

Alex's friend and interpreter, Bahram Dehqani-Tafti, an Anglo-Iranian poet and teacher not long out of Oxford University, said he'd come with us and translate. We took a plane to Tabriz and drove towards Kurdistan with absolutely no idea what was going to happen next. Eventually we reached a ramshackle sort of border post, an oddity given that officially there was no border: how could there be, to a place that didn't exist? The sergeant told us to go and see his major, and detailed a young recruit to sit in the car as we drove there. This kid sat between me and Bahram, with his rifle between his knees, idly picking his teeth with the sight at the end of the barrel. 'Don't look,' said Bahram, 'but he's got the safety catch off.' The next five minutes on a bumpy track were spent praying this hayseed wouldn't blow his head off, because if he did we'd undoubtedly get the blame.

When we reached the major, Bahram somehow persuaded him to let us continue. Before dusk we were in Mahabad, the Kurdistan capital, a neatly laid-out town that bore few traces of the mighty battle to recapture it only a few months before. What I remember, after the near-anarchy of Tehran, was an aura of civil peace and military discipline: well-organised, neatly dressed Kurdish soldiers who knew how to handle their weapons.

'A Kurd kills with one shot,' one of them told me. 'We have always been short of ammunition.'

In the days spent in Mahabad, we met the Kurds' spiritual leader, Sheikh Ezzedine Husseini, a man who had always argued for a secular republic and insisted that clergy like himself had no business running a country. We also met their political leader, Dr Qassemlou, a grave, Sorbonne-educated democrat who spoke eight languages and had espoused Kurdish nationalism all his life.

Then we drove south, because that's where the Iranian Army counter-attack was coming from. We thought they were a long way off, south of Sanandaj, but halfway to Saqqez, a helicopter gunship rose over a bluff about 100 metres away, its heavy machine gun pointed straight at us. It hovered for what seemed like an hour but was probably a minute, then peeled away. Not long after, I was congratulating myself on my own coolness when we stopped, I got out of the car, and my knees literally gave way. I lay on the ground in a heap. Your body tells the truth about fear, even when you try to lie.

We got to Saqqez and debated whether to go on. There was a convoy leaving for Sanandaj straight away, and maybe not another till the next day. We'd had a conversation before leaving Tehran about safety and agreed that in the event of debate, any one of us would have a veto. In this case, Alex and Bahram thought the convoy would be a good idea, I wasn't sure, and Les, the veteran, said no. We took Les' advice and decided to wait, sitting talking to local Kurdish leaders, drinking small cups of thick sweet coffee and smoking. We all still wondered if we'd made the wrong decision, if we should have just gone on in the convoy. Then a man, white-faced and shaking, came in and started talking to the chief. Translation: the remnants of the convoy we almost joined were on their way back.

We came out of the house as the convoy limped in. We filmed the damaged trucks that had survived, the survivors and the charred bodies of the dead. An air-to-ground rocket attack is an ugly thing.

I've seldom felt so remote from the rest of the world. The feeling didn't dissipate when we got lost, in the dead of night, on the way back to Mahabad. We pulled into a hamlet and asked the way to the provincial capital. 'I've heard of it,' came the unhelpful reply. We found it the next morning.

In Mahabad, the Kurds were deeply concerned about the safety of our film, which I knew was enough for a 10–15-minute *Weekend Magazine* feature. They were sure—and everything we had seen confirmed this—that we would not be able to get it past the censors, or to smuggle it out of the country. The Iranians at that time were insisting on seizing all unexposed film and processing it, just in case, because others had used the 'unexposed film trick' before. But film is bulky, and we had about eight flat, round cans of it, each the size of a discus. How to get it out?

The Kurds had a solution: 'One of our people will smuggle it across the mountains into Turkey.' Alex and Bahram agreed that we'd be unable to get the film out any other way, but we were all concerned for the safety of the smuggler: we didn't want a man to put his life on the line for our film. Yet the Kurds persuaded us that, within two weeks, the film would be delivered to the Qantas office in Istanbul. We gave them the cans and then headed back to Tabriz en route to the Iranian capital.

* * *

Late on the evening of 5 May, I was in a Tehran café with Alex and Bahram, the latter shaking slightly and clearly in a state of shock, with his girlfriend Elisabeth at his side. He had been in his top-floor flat when he'd heard a rattling at the door from the roof. Fortunately the door was chained and bolted, and it appeared the intruder went away. But he couldn't be sure, and he'd rung Alex and arranged to meet.

Bahram had more reason to be fearful than most people. Although himself not notably religious, he was the son of the Anglican bishop in Iran, Hassan Dehqani-Tafti. The bishop had welcomed the revolution but had been rebuffed by Khomeini, and worse: clergy he was responsible for were arrested, the authorities confiscated the properties and equipment of the church's charitable work, and his house was looted. Then, in late 1979, in Esfahan, two gunmen climbed over the wall surrounding the Dehqani-Tafti house and broke in. They got into the bedroom and started firing. The bishop's wife, Margaret, tried to shield him, taking a bullet in the hand, but by some fortunate chance the rest of the shots missed. The couple kept the pillowcase they'd used that day, with its evidence of four bullet holes, when they went into exile in London.

The mullahs of Esfahan were not finished with the Dehqani-Taftis yet, though. They mounted a campaign, free of evidence, to accuse the bishop of stealing from and defrauding his parishioners. One lever they had was that Bahram was still in the country and unable to get an exit visa. So when Bahram said he thought someone was out to get him, we took it seriously.

We were telling Bahram to spend the next few nights away from his flat, and not to go to work at his day job teaching English, and he was being stoical and saying he would probably turn up for work, when all our eyes were drawn to the café's television screen. It showed something extraordinary happening, live from London. Some black balaclava-clad figures were abseiling down from the Iranian embassy's roof while others were clambering across its balconies. A bomb thrown through a window was detonated, men rushed in, and eleven minutes later, the six-day siege was over. The SAS is famous now, as famous as the US Delta Force or Navy SEALs, but that moment, beamed live around the world, was the first time most people, even in the UK, had ever heard of the ultra-secretive Hereford-based force.

It was an extraordinary event, but in the circumstances only a momentary diversion from the real human problem in our midst. I told Bahram he was welcome to stay in my room at the Intercon if he needed to, but he said he'd go to Alex's house. I still had the audiotapes from Kurdistan: the Iranian censors never bothered with those, for some reason, so we knew that there was going to be no problem getting them out of the country. We agreed that the hotel was a safe-enough place, and made an appointment for Bahram to meet me there the following afternoon to do word-for-word translations, to supplement the running interpretation he'd done on the spot.

The next day, when Bahram was a couple of hours late, I started to worry. I called Alex, but he'd heard nothing. I went up to the NBC offices, where Bahram sometimes translated, and where they liked him, to ask if they'd heard anything. They hadn't, but they sent a couple of drivers out to look. It was a few hours later, at dusk, that one of the drivers came back to say that Bahram's corpse had been found slumped against an outer wall of Evin Prison. He had gone to his teaching job that morning after all. On his way to my hotel, thugs had forced him off the road, transferred him to their vehicle, and taken him to a piece of waste ground to die.

Bahram was a remarkable and exceptionally intelligent young man. He'd arrived at Oxford to study politics, philosophy and economics the year I graduated, and we had a lot in common. We had all bonded under fire in Kurdistan, too: friendships form very quickly under those circumstances. His death left me in utter turmoil, especially coming so soon after that of Tony Joyce.

I wrote a story about him which became a tribute and an obituary. I pictured his death—correctly, I still believe—as a symbol of what had happened to the revolution as a whole: the betrayal of the young, secular and idealistic at the hands of the fanatical and ruthless. I still do not know if the ABC used it: if so, it's lost. However, I was an ABC News appointee, and ABC Radio News and Current Affairs were almost at war in those days, so I occasionally found my best stuff capriciously dropped.

Somebody read it, though, and it was raw enough to ring alarm bells in Sydney. Bert Christie rang to say it was time to pull out, and Les and I now needed no persuading. As our plane left Iranian airspace, we each ordered a fuck-you gin and tonic, even though it was only just past breakfast time.

* * *

If I've devoted a lot of space to this first part of my life as a correspondent, it's not only because of the deep personal effect it had on my life, the impressions it made, the scars it left behind, but also because it was, on a broader stage, an extraordinary and perhaps pivotal moment. If the students had not taken the hostages, and the Supreme Leader allowed them to continue, or if the desert raid, by some miracle, had succeeded, so much might have been different, in Iran and in the rest of the world.

In Iran, I still believe there was considerable fragility in the Ayatollahs' regime. There was an outside chance of a second revolutionary upheaval. There was, indisputably, conflict between clerical hardliners and civilian pragmatists: a genuine power struggle which did not have to end with the triumph of the Velayat-e Faqih—Khomeini's doctrine that the state must be governed by a Supreme Leader from the highest ranks of the clergy; that is, himself. Jimmy Carter's failed raid shifted the balance definitively to the fundamentalists, and soon many on the pragmatic wing, including the president and foreign minister, would be in exile or dead. The idea of a 'separation of powers' between mosque and state was dead, for a generation at least.

In the USA, most historians agree, the hostage crisis was a pivotal factor in ending Carter's presidency, and thus helping usher in the Reagan era. Economically, free-marketeers definitively defeated Keynesians, not only in America but throughout the Free World. Strategically, Reagan's obduracy also forced the events that led to the end of the Soviet Union, so this was also a key turning point in the Cold War.

* * *

A few days after returning to London, I travelled to Hampshire for the wedding of my cousin Belinda. A splendid affair, it was held in Winchester Cathedral, with a lavish reception afterwards. There were men in morning suits and pearl-grey ties, and girls in beautiful dresses, and rivers of champagne. Belinda's husband Tim sang with his band, the wonderfully named Dicky Hart and the Pacemakers. The English spring weather, which can be treacherous, was instead warm and clement. It should have been a delight, but in some sense most of me wasn't there. I was back in Tehran.

When people asked me what I'd been doing, I'd start to tell them, and watch their eyes glaze over. You couldn't blame them: why ruin a good party with tales of upheaval and bloodshed? And at the back of my mind was something else: a growing fear about the film we'd tried to smuggle out of Kurdistan. The courier had not yet arrived at the promised drop-off. I rang regularly to check, but weeks went by, then months, and it never turned up. Eventually I had to come to terms with the probability that a man had died in a vain attempt to get the truth about his largely forgotten people across the border, in order that I could tell his story. It weighed on me, and still does.

A new correspondent, Peter George, arrived in London, keen to cover a part of the world I had subconsciously come to want to avoid. I still had Africa, and parts of Europe when the Brussels correspondent was on leave or had his hands full. But I couldn't face the Middle East again. It would be a decade before I would go back.

Chapter 7

The View from the Back Seat

YOU COULD DESCRIBE my birth as an accident of Empire. My mother grew up in western Victoria, my father in the English county of Hampshire. The cause of their meeting, albeit indirect, was that my paternal grandfather, an admiral in the Royal Navy, was posted to Australia in the years leading up to World War II to command and rebuild the RAN, which had been much depleted of both ships and officers during the Depression. I don't believe my maternal and paternal grandparents ever met during this posting, and my father, John Colvin, was still in England at the Royal Naval College, Dartmouth. But his sister Prudence was at school with my mother, Anne Manifold, and that connection was what would ultimately bring the two families together. When, after the war, my mother escaped what she had begun to find the stifling and parochial atmosphere of 1940s Melbourne and sailed for Britain, that tenuous link would eventually lead her to meet and fall in love with my father.

They married on 18 December 1948, my father distinguished in naval uniform complete with sword, my mother elegant, slim and beautiful in pleated white satin. They honeymooned in Paris, a blissful short break from the rigours of postwar British rationing: staying at the Royal Hotel in the Avenue de Friedland; eating a Christmas dinner at the Brasserie

Perigourdine Rouziers Freres, which styled itself 'The Temple of Gourmets': oysters, foie gras, turkey and a buche de Noel—Yule log cake.

I was born just over three years later, by which time the deep chill of the Cold War had really settled in. And it was the Cold War that dictated our movements as a family and defined the first half of my life, because my father was a warrior in its front line.

My earliest memory is of looking through the back window of my parents' car at a white chalet against a background of green forest. It is early 1954, less than a decade after the end of World War II, and I am two years old. The visual memory is now a little indistinct, but the emotion remains strong: we are leaving our family home—the first I can remember—in Krumpendorf, just west of Klagenfurt in the melodiously named region of Carinthia in south-eastern Austria.

The Gasthof Jerolitsch, where we lived, was a popular summer resort for Austrians and Germans: it still is, though the hotel and its chalets are now slightly overshadowed by a large motorway overpass. The picturesque lake called the Woerthersee was nearby, beautiful in summer and winter and the inspiration for a thousand postcards. Our view was of the Karawanken mountains, beyond which lay Yugoslavia.

The retreating back-seat image in my mind is tinged with sadness because, my memory tells me, I have been happy here: photographs show me tobogganing in winter with my mother, or sitting in my pram with our dachshund cross Otto. My mother has since often told me how affectionately the people in Krumpendorf treated the small, ash-blond English toddler whose father had some unspecified diplomatic role 'on attachment to the British Army'.

I have thought about this single flash of memory so often over time. I think it has remained with me because it was my first conscious realisation that things change, that the ground can shift, after which life will never be the same. There's a lovely Portuguese word that describes the feeling of the constant traveller: *saudade*, which the *Oxford Dictionary* defines as 'a feeling of longing, melancholy or nostalgia'. A ridiculously large concept for a tiny child, but something of that sense of melancholy and nostalgia has permeated my consciousness, and perhaps infuses the consciousness of all those who are forced by circumstance to move in childhood—army brats, diplomatic brats, refugees—and who spend half their lives trying to work out what 'home' really means. Along with that picture in my head of the white house growing smaller in the window, somehow, there is the clear knowledge that my parents and I are not ever going to come back here. A part of my existence has ended.

It wasn't the first life upheaval I had gone through: we had moved from Norway when I was one. But it was the first I was old enough to remember. Now, my parents told me, we were on our way to Vienna, where as it turned out I would also be perfectly happy, but it's hard to convince a child of that. Somewhere in my little head was the inchoate idea that we were heading out of Paradise and into the Unknown.

* * *

My father's identification card for 1949 reads: 'Marina Mercante Nacional, Republica de Panama'. John Colvin: National Merchant Marine, Republic of Panama. It gives his age as twenty-seven, his hair as *castaño* (chestnut), his colour as *blanco* (white) and his status as *casado* (married). The photograph shows a lean, good-looking young man with large ears and a slightly receding hairline, in a dark suit and spotted tie. He's looking up and off camera, with a slightly sardonic expression.

Most oddly, in a handwritten addition, this yellowing card describes my father—who studied at the Royal Naval College, Dartmouth from the age of thirteen, joined the navy as a midshipman six years later at the outbreak of World War II, and rose to the rank of lieutenant-commander before leaving the service—as an 'official trainee'. What is this experienced naval officer doing, four years after the war, as an apprentice on a tramp steamer sailing under the Panamanian flag?

Now we enter the realm of detective work, pieced together from scraps, first- and second-hand, including the testimony of my mother (usually careful and reliable); the anecdotes (often unreliable, sometimes positively misleading) that my father sparingly doled out; the official silence of his employer, the SIS, better known as MI6: the difficult job of making sense of a life that was lived on two levels, the public and the secret.

For much of the first half of my life, I believed that Dad had left the navy a few years after the war to join the Foreign Office in Whitehall. His story was that they'd sent him to London University on a language course to learn Serbo-Croat, then to work on a tramp steamer plying the

Yugoslav ports of the Dalmatian coast in the Adriatic, for six months, to get language experience. He claimed that he worked as a stoker on this steamship, shovelling coal into the boilers, and that the Srpski and Hrvatski language training he got was mostly curse-words from his below-decks colleagues. My uncle Colin, who retired from the navy as a commander in the 1960s, used to tease Dad, who was rather proud of his lieutenant-commander's braid, with the nickname 'Stoker John'. Looking back over a long time spent with them over Christmases and school holidays, I rather think Colin and my father's sister Prudence knew quite well what his real profession was, and that they often talked above the children's heads in a sort of teasing code.

Because of eye problems that developed during the war, Dad's naval career had been blocked: he could remain in the service, but only as a paymaster, or 'pusser'. He was the kind of person who loved books, not bookkeeping: for most of his life he was fairly irresponsible with money—a boy who had at one stage run away from Dartmouth to go on the stage, and been hauled back by his father, Admiral Sir Ragnar Colvin, then president of the Royal Naval College, Greenwich. He told me he'd never particularly wanted to be in the navy, but if he had to be, he wanted to be a proper sea officer.

Somewhat frustrated, by 1949 he was looking for a way out. But, my mother tells me, it was a period when, unless you were sacked, the only way out of the navy for an officer was to transfer to another government department. So when, staying with friends in the country, my recently married parents went to a hunt ball and Dad was approached by an SIS recruiter, he was keen.

If that sounds like the classic Old Boys' Club recruiting system that produced the Cambridge spy ring, I suspect there was an element of that, but it's certainly not the whole picture. It was, admittedly, a couple of years before Burgess and Maclean's defection and the suspicion which that threw onto Philby, but I've come to the conclusion that my father's recruitment was probably based more on his own service record than questions of class and contacts.

In the mid-1990s, after my father had been named in print as a retired senior intelligence officer (with a nod and a wink from his former bosses at SIS), it became possible to talk a little more freely about his life.

In the last year of the Pacific War, he'd been seconded to South East Area Command under Earl Louis Mountbatten, based in Colombo—the jumping-off point for a plan to retake South-East Asia from the Japanese. Dad told me that, several months before the war's end, he'd been dropped into Vietnam on a midget submarine, and once 'in-country' he ran a ring of resistance agents against the occupying Japanese. Indeed, one Sunday lunch, he told my eldest son Nicolas, then eleven, a (to Nicolas) satisfyingly grisly story about using cheese-wire to garrotte Japanese guards. At any rate, when the atomic bombs were dropped at Hiroshima and Nagasaki, and the Japanese in Vietnam surrendered, he was able to emerge from the shadows and, as the most senior British officer in the country, receive the ceremonial swords of the officers commanding the Japanese garrison in Saigon. He was twenty-three years old.

Incidentally, he nurtured to his grave a deep disappointment that somewhere between Saigon and Southampton, the Royal Navy managed to lose those swords, which again led to family teasing, there being apparently no other proof of this extraordinary story. But over four decades after the loss, a photograph surfaced of the very scene he'd always described, the young RN lieutenant flanked by resentful French majors and colonels (the British being the senior invading power, this was the protocol).

While writing this book, a dozen years after his death, I discovered another aspect of my father's wartime Special Operations work, clearly undertaken before he went to Saigon. The intelligence specialist Professor Richard Aldrich, of Warwick University, who knew my father and hosted him at seminars, wrote to me to confirm some of what I knew, and more, including that 'John Colvin ferried agents across to Yugoslavia in motor gunboats during World War Two'.

This must have been roughly in the same period Evelyn Waugh, Fitzroy Maclean and Randolph Churchill were working with Tito and his Yugoslav partisans against the Nazis and the Croatian Ustashi crypto-Nazis they backed. Waugh and Maclean in particular were deeply disillusioned with the way they were ruthlessly used to help bring in a communist dictatorship, and that bitterness suffuses the last volume of Waugh's *Sword of Honour* trilogy, one of my father's favourite books. But Dad never once told me of his own experience in that theatre of war.

I remained sceptical until I came across a passage in his memoir, *Twice around the World*, that I'd managed to skip over on previous readings, about the store in Hanoi called 'The State Department', as it was in 1967:

> The State Department was, in fact, the State Shop. It was always crammed with customers, sometimes fifty to a line, for the meagre stock of goods dispensed by one or, rarely, two young female assistants to each counter, *but it made a wartime British Woolworth's or the Balkans in 1945 seem like Asprey's* [my emphasis].

These, it seems to me, are clearly references to first-hand experiences, so it is certainly possible that Aldrich's account is correct. Yet another reminder of how little I knew about my father in his lifetime. And given the deep secretiveness of his employer, there is no doubt much more that I will never know, however hard I dig.

Given his record in Special Ops, the recruitment of Lieutenant-Commander John Horace Ragnar Colvin would have made some sense in the postwar world. He was if anything sentimentally patriotic about a dream of England that was already on the verge of disappearing, what Orwell described thus:

> When you come back to England from any foreign country, you have immediately the sensation of breathing a different air … the diversity of it, the chaos! The clatter of clogs in the Lancashire mill towns, the to-and-fro of the lorries on the Great North Road, the queues outside the Labour Exchanges, the rattle of pin-tables in the Soho pubs, the old maids biking to Holy Communion through the mists of the autumn morning—all these are not only fragments, but characteristic fragments, of the English scene.

One day in conversation about the 1930s, I quoted WH Auden's line about that 'low dishonest decade', to which my father took exception. He was vehement in his insistence that for him, the 1930s—his teens, in effect—had been dominated by a growing sense of the need to defend Britain against fascism. This came partly from his naval cadet schooling; partly from his own father, who as a high-ranking naval officer himself was firmly convinced of the need to re-arm; and partly from the influence of Winston Churchill's long campaign in the wilderness years against the appeasement of Hitler.

From Churchill, my father also learned to detest communism. This passage from his memoir is heartfelt and represents what was his consistent position for decades:

> Behind the communist order lay a horrible idea, the conviction that mankind, God's creatures, should be bent to a single, disproven economic theory, to whose requirements all nature, love, frivolity, laughter, decency, truth itself should be subdued, to which indeed the virtues as well as the defects of humanity were irrelevant, even hostile. To dedicate the spirit to a cause, even a wrongheaded cause, was one thing. To submerge the spirit to the exclusion of everything but the mechanics of the cause was another.

Dad was recruited when the Cambridge Five—Philby, Burgess, Maclean, Cairncross and Blunt—were still burrowing deep inside the system, but even in the far more paranoid years that followed, I doubt his loyalty would ever have been in question. From every conversation we ever had about politics, the one thing I'm sure my father could never have been was a double agent.

So was he actually a 'stoker' on that ship in the Adriatic in 1949, four years on from his apparent Special Operations work in the navy? I don't think so. As a new recruit in the SIS, was he just in training, or using that war experience from his navy years to recruit and run agents in Dalmatian ports, this time against communists instead of Nazis? Or was he genuinely just honing his language skills? Questions I may never answer.

There is now, however, a description available of the training he would have undergone between his recruitment in 1949 and the 'official' date of his joining the SIS, 1951. Adam Sisman, in his biography of John le Carré, who joined the SIS a few years later, describes the field operations centre in Hampshire, Fort Monkton. There, would-be officers practised the 'tradecraft' familiar to readers of spy fiction. They learned to use dead-letter boxes and safe houses; they were taught pistol shooting; they were put through their paces on the techniques of surveillance; they learned how to blow things up, how to code and decode enciphered communications and transmit them secretly by wireless. And, as my father used to mention in occasional mysterious asides, they learned how to fight and if necessary kill, using unarmed combat, or such lethal but silent weapons as lengths of cheesewire.

By 1953 (after his first posting in Oslo), in Klagenfurt, just north of the border with what was then Yugoslavia, my father was a fully trained intelligence officer, running agents against Tito's communist regime. Ljubljana, now the capital of Slovenia, was not far to the south; Zagreb, now the capital of Croatia, was a little further but still within striking distance. The purpose of my father's agent-running job in Klagenfurt was to find out as much as possible not only about the politics of Yugoslavia, but especially the state of military preparedness, equipment and plans in that country and whatever other Soviet satellite states he could penetrate. I don't know much about how he did it, but he did tell me that much.

He also once told me that he had an agent who discovered a fatal flaw in Eastern Bloc military security, literally through the rear. This weakness consisted of a paper shortage. It was so acute in the Yugoslav military, he said, that the monthly tactical plans and 'order of battle' showing the disposition of troops, tanks and artillery were being recycled when only a month or two old: the recycling consisted of cutting them up into small squares and hanging them on hooks in the soldiers' latrines, to be used as toilet paper. My father said his agent was able to get his hands on enough of these to provide intelligence gold.

As I understand it, this copious source, straight from the army's privies, was reliable enough that it became one of the factors that got my father noticed and promoted. And that was why, at the beginning of 1954, we were on our way from the SIS sub-station in Klagenfurt to the central one in Vienna.

Chapter 8

Maximum Ambiguity

GLIMPSES AND SNAPSHOTS, faces looming out of the haze. The feeling of love and warmth; the first moment of extreme pain when my finger gets accidentally slammed in a car door; Italian sun and sand and gelato after the greyness of a postwar Central European city; kicking out my legs in my mother's firm grasp in the warm Adriatic, or floating along in a blow-up ring. From my three-year-old self, I can't retrieve memories so much as a blurred series of little filmstrips, some of them burned at the edges by the projector bulb, too many of them melted and lost forever.

I remember leaving Klagenfurt, but not the rest of the journey to our new home in Vienna. My mother remembers it clearly, though, especially the moment of slight dread at a Russian checkpoint. When we lived in Austria, the country was still divided into four parts: the Russian, American, French and British zones. Only the central part of Vienna, the Inneren Stadt, was neutral. To get from Klagenfurt to Vienna, you had to drive through the Russian zone.

The Soviet Army had been the first into Austria at the end of World War II, and the whole country found itself for the next ten years in a strange state of limbo between East and West. Stalin was reluctant to leave: he wanted a 'string of pearls'—buffer states around the Soviet

Union that would stand between Mother Russia and another invasion. 'We' were the West, and our forces had not 'liberated' Austria (which had in any case fulsomely welcomed Hitler in the Anschluss): the Russians had. And 'we' were not welcome guests in the Russian zone.

My mother remembers the British Government Humber car stopping, and the hard faces of the Russian soldiers, and the examination of the diplomatic passports, and a sense that, whatever the rules laid out in international treaties, they just might still not apply *here*. She remembers too how, in shops in the Inneren Stadt, when a Russian walked in, the Viennese would walk out. And how, stopped at a traffic light, you would see a Russian Gazik, or jeep, pull up beside you, and the hostility in the soldiers' faces, and the way they held their Kalashnikovs or their pistols with no real care about who they might be pointing them at.

I myself remember none of that, nor anything of what my father was doing: that I can only reconstruct from the experiences of other SIS agents during that period.

Gordon Corera, in his book *MI6: Life and Death in the British Secret Service*, describes the SIS officer in Vienna, Anthony Cavendish:

> His task, like that of every MI6 officer, was the recruiting and running of agents. MI6 officers only occasionally spy themselves in terms of collecting secret information. More often than not, they gather intelligence by recruiting agents—people with access to secrets who are willing to risk their lives by passing it on.

Vienna was a place of maximum ambiguity, 'filled with its own tricksters, fraudsters and charlatans on the make', says Corera. 'Intelligence was a commodity for sale like everything else on the black market and often just as fake, with refugees running paper mills churning out fabricated documents to satisfy the demands of the spies.'

This was the Vienna Graham Greene depicted in *The Third Man*, a city full of touts and shysters, blackmailers and black marketeers, a city where, as Corera points out, Greene got his inspiration for the film's climactic tunnel chase scene from reality: 'The Russians controlled the sewers and refused to lock the entrances, which were disguised aboveground as kiosks. These allowed their agents to disappear from one part of the city and suddenly emerge ghost-like somewhere else.'

The Russians weren't the only ones using tunnels for espionage. Daphne Park was an SIS contemporary of my father's, and was in Vienna not long before him. In his biography of Park, *Queen of Spies*, Paddy Hayes describes how the Vienna station had

> figured out a way to build a tunnel under the streets of the city that could be used to tap into all telephone and telegraph communications between the Soviet High Commission in the Imperial Hotel and the Soviet Central Commandant in the Epstein Palace, and between those two locations and the Kremlin.

When my family was in Vienna, Hayes says, this system was in full operation: 'An underground control and recording centre, called "Old Smoky" because of its poisonous atmosphere, was established underneath a shop selling Scots tartan and Harris tweed. Here banks of recorders recorded all voice and signal traffic passing though the monitored cables.'

I am three. None of this means anything to me. My world is a warm kitchen, and a boxer puppy called Bamse—Norwegian for 'little bear'—who had replaced Otto and become my dearest childhood friend. The wonder of the ocean, never to be extinguished, enters my life during our first beach holiday, at Caorle, just north of Venice. That beach is still vivid to me, and not only because of the family albums. I'm walking up a little flight of steps off the sand into a hut on stilts where there is dark sacking instead of windows, keeping out the heat and light. A man hands me a cornetto of something cold and white: *gelato di limone*. Even today, it only takes one taste of lemon gelato to catapult me back into that moment: a tiny person holding his father's hand, standing in a dark mysterious space out of the hot sun.

I had words that would remain in my family's vocabulary for years: 'eckybock' for apricot, 'num-nums' for food of any sort, 'diggun' for drink. To the end of his life, my dad would say, 'It's news time, switch on the la-la', because in Vienna that was my word for the radio. And a little of my toddler talk was in German: I remember that for months after we left Austria, I habitually said *mittagessen* instead of 'lunch'.

Mittagessen was a good word. I definitely liked to eat. The classic family story, from those days of currency restrictions all over Europe, was of another Italian holiday when my father had brought enough

Italian currency from Vienna to pay for our board and lodging, on the basis that he would pay full price for him and my mother, and half-price for me. When the time came to settle up, he was shocked to see that he'd been charged full price for three people. Remonstrating with the hotelier, he was finally forced to concede and pay up when told, 'Signor, if your son had only eaten half as much as you and your wife, naturally I would have charged you half, but as it was, signor, he ate as much as either of you.' As a result, my parents spent a nail-biting few hours on the drive back, wondering if the fuel tank would last until the Austrian border, putting the car into neutral when going downhill in a desperate bid to save petrol. (They did make it back into the land of the Austrian Schilling: just.)

Despite these indications of a gargantuan appetite, photos from that time show a healthy toddler, certainly not thin, but not unhealthily fat. Nonetheless, a love of Italian food is one childhood addiction that has never left me.

My grandfather Ragnar Colvin had died in early 1954 while we were in Klagenfurt. The heart trouble that invalided him out of running the Royal Australian Navy in 1941 had not been severe enough to stop him serving for most of the rest of the war in a quieter job, as the naval adviser to the Australian High Commission. The doctors who treated him had advised that he should rest as much as possible, and on no account take vigorous exercise—advice which would horrify modern cardiologists, but then again, they have far more pharmacological weapons in the fight against heart disease.

I have no memory of him, but my grandmother Sibyl was a big presence in my childhood. She visited us in Vienna and would often tell me about how bad an influence my father, who habitually swore like a sailor, had been on me. In the back seat of our car one afternoon in those pre-seatbelt days, aged three, I had stood up, waved my fist at a passing truck, and shouted 'GO TO BUGGERY'. As anyone who works with me knows, variations of this sentiment are muttered to this day, loudly or under my breath, generally at obstreperous spin doctors or politicians. (I'm still blaming Dad.)

* * *

In my father's world, dark doings were afoot. They involved two of the most effective traitors in the history of espionage.

One, Kim Philby, became a household name when he was named in the British Parliament as The Third Man in a Soviet espionage ring, only to be cleared by Foreign Secretary Harold Macmillan, who told the House of Commons in 1955: 'I have no reason to conclude that Mr Philby has at any time betrayed the interests of his country, or to identify him as the so-called "Third Man", if indeed there was one.'

The other, George Blake, was not even under suspicion at this time, and would not be unmasked until 1961. He was a hero inside the SIS, having endured three years of imprisonment in North Korea. The service appears to have harboured no suspicion that Blake had in fact converted to Marxism during his imprisonment and volunteered to spy for the KGB. But for the next few years, he would indeed feed vast amounts of information from his jobs in London and Berlin straight back to Moscow: he would say later that he had betrayed so many agents that he'd stopped counting. We know from his confession that the numbers of agents 'blown' in East Germany alone ran into the hundreds.

More relevant to my father's work, George Blake's first job on return from North Korea was at Y Section in London's Carlton Gardens. This was, according to the *Encyclopaedia of Cold War Espionage*, 'an especially secret section of the SIS to exploit special technical information sources by using sophisticated listening devices'. The SIS' Vienna tunnel should have been one of the great intelligence coups of the century, but Blake's presence at Y Section, where his job was overseeing the translation and transcription of the tapes from Vienna, meant it was compromised from the start.

Rather as Winston Churchill had deliberately refrained at times from saving some lives by acting on decrypted Enigma machine information during the war, because doing so could alert the Nazis to the breaking of their codes, the KGB were very careful at first not to act on their knowledge of the tunnel. According to Daphne Park biographer Paddy Hayes, 'the KGB waited a full year before even alerting the Soviet military to the possibility that the conversations of their soldiers were being monitored by Western intelligence. Even then they were careful to avoid saying anything that could point to Blake's existence.'

In *Near and Distant Neighbours: A New History of Soviet Intelligence*, Jonathan Haslam says the Vienna tunnel let the British re-create the Soviet order of battle in the Balkans. 'Discovering the Soviet order of battle in the Balkans' happens to be the precise phrase my father used when I asked him what his job was when we lived in Klagenfurt. However, Haslam says, 'The Balkans was not the crucial theatre of battle, so the information obtained was not of the greatest value', thus explaining why the KGB felt able to hold back before acting on it: because when the Americans and British followed up the Vienna success with tunnels under Berlin, the Soviet forces started rolling up agent networks.

But Blake's total access to the Vienna intercepts raises the possibility that my father's own cover was blown as early as 1954–55, and that the KGB would have known that he was an intelligence officer, rather than, say, a mere third or second secretary in the embassy, throughout his career. It would help explain why he never had a posting in Moscow itself. And there's another reason to speculate on this: according to a number of sources, the Vienna head of station when we were there was Nicholas Elliott, who happened to be one of Kim Philby's closest friends.

When, in 1955, Philby was 'cleared' in the British Parliament of being a double agent, it was over the vociferous protests of MI5, the domestic counter-spying agency, up to and including its head, Dick White. They were convinced he was guilty as hell, and frustrated that his conviction was overruled. The old guard at SIS/MI6 had run a 'fair play' defence of Philby, on the grounds of innocence until proven guilty—grounds which are legitimate in a court of law but more dubious in the defence of a country. Philby's bland denials and the absence of anything but circumstantial evidence, no matter how strong, had meant that he could, however, be ejected from the service without being prosecuted—or ever quite disgraced. Kim Philby still had strong defenders in the service, and one of them was his old and close friend Elliott. Philby, to his backers, could not be guilty because he was 'One Of Us'.

You can get the flavour of this way of thinking from the transcript of a vetting session with Nicholas Elliott which has appeared in more than one intelligence history of the time:

Security Officer: Sit down, I'd like to have a frank talk with you.

Nicholas Elliott: As you wish, Colonel.

Officer: Does your wife know what you do?
Elliott: Yes.
Officer: How did that come about?
Elliott: She was my secretary for two years and I think the penny must have dropped.
Officer: Quite so. What about your mother?
Elliott: She thinks I'm in something called SIS, which she believes stands for the Secret Intelligence Service.
Officer: Good God! How did she come to know that?
Elliott: A member of the War Cabinet told her at a cocktail party.
Officer: Who was he?
Elliott: I'd prefer not to say.
Officer: Then what about your father?
Elliott: He thinks I'm a spy.
Officer: So why should he think you're a spy?
Elliott: Because the chief told him in the bar at White's [exclusive gentlemen's club in London's St James' Street].

The intelligence histories which cover Elliott's career, most recently and comprehensively Ben Macintyre's *A Spy among Friends*, do not suggest that Elliott himself was on any level a traitor. But they do paint a picture of someone who could easily be construed as thoroughly incompetent and in some areas naive, especially by intelligence community standards. Macintyre's book suggests that Elliott may have been one of the two interrogators whose kid-glove treatment and helpful suggestions of less damning answers to difficult questions finally led to the foreign secretary's 1955 parliamentary exoneration of the country's worst traitor.

Even after Philby's ejection from the service, Elliott's relationship with his old friend continued to be warm and strong: Elliott actually helped Philby reforge his relationship with the service, this time not as an intelligence officer (agent handler), but as an agent. MI6 used its close relationship with David Astor, owner of *The Observer*, to get Philby appointed as the paper's Middle East correspondent. There in Beirut, Philby also reactivated his KGB contacts. His guilt—as a double agent recruited in Vienna in the 1930s who rose to become MI6's man in Washington, apparently destined for the organisation's top job, 'C' (controller)—would not become irrefutable in MI6's eyes until 1963 when, after an apparently botched interrogation by—again—Nicholas Elliott, Philby disappeared into the night: he boarded a Russian ship and eventually resurfaced in Moscow.

As it turned out, Nicholas Elliott would not only be my father's head of station in Vienna. He would also be head of the London station when Dad returned to SIS headquarters in 1956.

Chapter 9

The Last Roar

IF LIFE CAN be hard for a spy's wife, it was very hard in the 1950s—I use the word 'wife' deliberately: there were no spies' husbands then, because although there were a few women in the service, they were forced to resign if they got married. A spy's wife had to maintain the fiction that her husband was a conventional diplomat, knowing that this was a lie, but never allowed to know much more than that.

During my father's first posting in Oslo, when I was a tiny baby, my mother remembers SIS colleagues arriving from London and going out all night with him, clad all in black from gloves to balaclavas, on what was clearly a mission of burglary. Of what? An embassy? A Russian diplomat's home? She didn't know, but she held a long vigil wondering if they would get home unscathed.

Fortunately, Elizabeth Anne Manifold was a strong, intelligent and resilient woman. Raised on a sheep station in Victoria during the Depression, a lover of horses who became an accomplished rider for practical reasons, rather than for show, and a voracious reader, she might in another era have pursued any number of careers. In the last years of World War II, she briefly attended the University of Melbourne, but seeing the tide of wounded soldiers coming home, she left to train as a nurse.

She was already finding Melbourne suffocating, however, and as soon as she turned twenty-one, at the end of 1946, she decided to get out. She and some friends, accompanied (or chaperoned) by an older friend of the family, Ines Thornthwaite, boarded a Blue Funnel Line steamer, the *Nestor*, en route for London via South Africa. The ship was crammed with passengers and cargo. Britain had won the war, but the peace had brought austerity and rationing. In the holds were goods from Commonwealth countries like Australia that were at a premium. And in the cabins, my mother and her friends were among the first of that wave of young Australians who wanted to see a bigger world than their own country in the 1940s had to offer.

The group landed at Durban, where the ship was to take on coal, and made their way across South Africa to rejoin the *Nestor* at Cape Town. My mother, who had been brought up in a family with a tradition of charity and philanthropy, remembers the shock, not only of the rules of racial segregation but of its realities. In Johannesburg, where at 1753 metres the nights are cold, poor black miners slept on the streets, many of them showing what she recognised as the signs of tuberculosis. And she remembers the misery evident in the black shantytowns, seen from the train to Cape Town.

The *Nestor*'s penultimate stop was the Canary Islands, where the deck cargo load became even heavier with produce such as bananas, which during the war had been a dreamed-of impossibility for the British, and even now were still a luxury. My mother's first sight of Old Blighty was of little white houses dotting green fields in northern Wales as the *Nestor* ploughed towards Liverpool. Then, on the starboard side as they sailed up the Mersey, with Liverpool to port, there appeared Cheshire's Wirral Peninsula—the place her great-grandfather had left more than a century before. Two years later, she was married, in London's Savoy Chapel, to a dashing young British naval officer she'd met in Hampshire, John Horace Ragnar Colvin. There was then no hint in either of their minds of the clandestine world that lay ahead.

* * *

By mid-1955, returning to London from Vienna with a three-year-old in tow to prepare for her second child, my mother was relatively used to the espionage life. There had been the long absences, during my father's 'language training' in the Adriatic and his 'tradecraft training' in centres in London and Hampshire; he had often been away when they lived in Klagenfurt and Vienna too. And when you're married to a spy, the question 'How was your day, darling?' is never going to get an informative answer.

There's also doubtless an element of not really wanting to know. Espionage is a form of licensed villainy: burglary, blackmail and bribery are tools of the trade, and with a few exceptions almost everybody is greedy for money.

My father told me one story of his time in Vienna, about an assignment on which he was a third-party observer of an exchange between a CIA agent and an Eastern Bloc informant, at an outdoor restaurant by a lake. The informant had brought a briefcase full of documents. The CIA man had brought a case full of greenbacks. My father was looking down from a table on a slightly higher terrace when, as the men opened their respective cases, a sudden, violent gust of wind blew up. Documents and dollars fluttered into the air, towards the lake. 'And you know what?' grinned my father. 'Both of them grabbed for the dollars.'

Dad stayed on in Vienna when we returned to Britain: these were the last months of Partition and the race was on to shore up Austrian democracy, and to identify Soviet sleepers and potential booby traps, literal or metaphoric, that Moscow might leave behind when it withdrew. That left my mother on her own in London with me, with the job of finding us somewhere to live. It wasn't easy, given the ingrained sexism of the era. A lawyer told her that, as a married woman, she could not purchase the house she'd decided to buy, even though she was using money she'd raised by selling her own life insurance policy: the only signature that would be valid was her husband's. It seemed almost as though nothing had changed since Jane Austen's time: when a woman married, her husband took charge of the finances. It was particularly ridiculous in this case, as my mother was always careful with money, whereas my father seldom was.

Somehow my mother overcame this apparently insuperable obstacle, despite Dad's absence, and we moved into a nineteenth-century terrace house near the World's End part of then very unfashionable Chelsea. She always had a good eye, and spent a lot of time in junk shops finding bargain antiques. Though heavily pregnant, she got the nursery ready for the new baby, furnished and decorated the rest of the house, and continued, with the help of a Swiss au pair called Erica, whom I loved with a passion, to look after me.

On 8 December 1955, my father came home, literally just in time for the birth of my sister Zoë. He only stayed a few days—maybe a week—before returning to Vienna to work. He had never attended a birthing class, because they didn't exist then: hospital rules would never have let him be in the room when Zoë was born, even if he'd asked to be; and I very much doubt that he ever changed our nappies. That was how things were.

My own memories of this time are longer and brighter and clearer than earlier ones, and involve what I think I can describe as conscious thought as well as sense impressions. I recall quite clearly being told Mummy was going to have a baby, and somehow convincing myself that it would emerge, aged the same as me, as another little boy with whom I could play football. I also remember my paternal grandmother Sybil, a terrifyingly bad driver, taking me to the hospital to meet my little sister for the first time, but braking so hard on the way that I hurtled into the windscreen and arrived at my mother's bedside with an egg-sized bump on my forehead.

At the end of our street was the terminus of the no. 31 bus route, with a café where the drivers would smoke, drink mugs of tea, and eat huge fried English breakfasts. Directly opposite was a little hole-in-the-wall greengrocer's owned by Ted, a tirelessly cheerful Cockney who flirted with all his women customers, called my mum 'Annie', and used to have a raw egg for a snack—I can still see him tilting his head back and cracking it into his mouth. Across the big road, the King's Road, was Cullens the grocers, smelling of coffee and spices, where you bought flour or rice scooped out of barrels into brown paper bags by men in buff-coloured work coats. There was Timothy White's the chemist, with strange liquids in blue and deep-red glass jars displayed in the windows. Next to that was a travel agent, through whose windows I gazed covetously at large scale-models of aeroplanes and ocean liners. Round the bend in the King's Road there was a stationers', where if you were lucky enough to have a farthing, with its reverse illustration of a wren, a halfpenny, one of those big worn pennies with Queen Victoria's head on them, or, joy of joys, a twelve-sided threepenny (pronounced 'thrup'ny') bit, you could buy paper and crayons and erasers. A little further and you reached MacFisheries, with its open front and big white slab displaying sole and plaice, haddock, cod and flounder, all so fresh you could sometimes imagine you smelled the North Sea.

Then it was on to the newsagents, a shop which I called the Smoking Man, because it was where my dad got his cigarettes. They were called Player's Navy Cut and they had a picture of a sailor in Royal Navy uniform on the front. My godfather John Villiers, who could make a penny disappear and then re-emerge behind your ear, also used to make a little hole in the sailor's mouth, roll up a little of the packet's paper lining into a tiny cigarette, insert it, and then blow smoke into the empty packet so it came out through the little tube. 'Look, Mark! The sailor's smoking!'

There was smoke inside the house and out. Some of the Great Smog of 1952, which had killed 4000 Londoners—fortunately that was the winter we were in Oslo—was still around: the Clean Air Act which eventually tamed it was not passed till 1956. I can remember one morning walking to kindergarten with the au pair, putting my arm out straight in front of me, and scarcely being able to see beyond my hand. There was an eeriness about the swish of tyres and the honk of horns from slow-travelling cars you could not even see.

On clear days, though, when you ventured further afield, there was the Thames, a source of endless fascination to a child, with tugs hauling dozens of roped-together barges against the tide, and smaller vessels plying their trade. There were houseboats at Chelsea too in those days, and what small boy has not wondered how it would be to live on a houseboat? You could cross Battersea Bridge and head into Battersea Park, a child's wonderland. Attractions built for the Festival of Britain in 1951 and still in operation included the Treetop Walk. You climbed a spiral staircase up a tree trunk, then went along a walkway through the branches of the trees that lined the Thames—as you progressed, just out of your reach, were fairyland creatures, and coloured lights at night. I loved the Crazy Golf and something called the Crazy Cottage, with its madly canted walls and floors. There was a paddling pool and a boating pond, and behind the big fence the glorious temptations of Battersea Park Fun Fair: forbidden for this four-year-old, but, I remember thinking, Dad might take me there one day, maybe when I'm five.

For now, though, there was the near-endless fascination of the Guinness Clock, an amazing array of wonderful mechanisms which performed a series of routines every quarter of an hour or so. A shiny golden sun would begin to rotate, and a large parasol would swivel to reveal a park keeper who rose up and rang a bell. Doors opened to reveal a pair of toucans (the Guinness mascot of the time) pecking at a tree. The Mad Hatter emerged from a tower with a fishing rod. He caught a small fish, which was pursued by a larger one, then a bigger one still, then a fourth, the biggest of the lot. And so on. In my memory, I must have sat cross-legged watching that clock a hundred times. These were the days when the company's main slogan was 'Guinness Is Good for You', and my mother had been advised by a doctor, just after I was born, to drink a small bottle of stout every night (she refused), but I'm still not sure what possessed them to create such a magnificent and elaborate advertisement-cum-attraction aimed specifically at children. I loved it. And I don't mind a drop of the black stuff either, as it happens.

* * *

Some time in early 1956, my father's Vienna posting was finally, officially, over. He returned to MI6 headquarters to serve, again, under Nicholas Elliott. In the public mind, these were the James Bond years. Ian Fleming's fourth book, *Diamonds Are Forever*, had just come out; *From Russia with Love* was in the pipeline. The Bond image of British intelligence—swashbuckling, daring, glamorous and above all successful—was magnetically attractive to a British public economically crippled by six years of war, whose cities were still pockmarked by bomb craters, and which had hardly begun to come to terms with the fact of its rapidly shrinking Empire. Britain needed its heroes, even if they were imaginary. And that year of all years, in intelligence at least, they certainly were.

Theoretically, my father worked at the Foreign Office, a grand edifice on Whitehall, just down from Number 10 Downing Street. In fact, his workplace until the mid-1960s, along with most London-based SIS officers, was in Broadway Buildings, a shabby maze of offices which could hardly have been less like the fantasy world James Bond inhabited. Situated next to St James' Park Tube station, Broadway Buildings was notoriously dingy and spartan: it had a creaking lift, lino floors, bare lightbulbs, ancient metal filing cabinets, and a sign outside claiming it was the headquarters of the Minimax Fire Extinguisher Company.

Years later, after his retirement, while walking around Westminster, Dad would point it out to me. He did so with some nostalgia, which I think he felt largely because Century House, the Brutalist tower block south of the Thames where SIS moved in 1966, was even worse. He also showed me the little building nearby in Queen Anne's Gate, joined to Broadway by some sort of secret passage, he said, where 'C' had his office and a flat for when he needed to stay overnight. Somewhere under there, he said, was also a sort of bar or club: a secret drinking den for secret people. He liked the general area around Broadway too: it was close to Westminster Abbey, an easy stroll to the National Gallery, and a pleasant walk across St James' Park and Green Park to his club on Piccadilly.

SIS was then still largely peopled by 'decent chaps', either recruited via clubs and the Old School Tie system, or because they'd had a 'good war'. Gordon Corera, in his SIS history *The Art of Betrayal*, writes:

> The service recruited incestuously from within small circles in the tight-knit British elite. Fathers recruited sons, officers married secretaries and they all socialised with each other, partly because it alleviated any security concerns and partly because of the sense of superiority it provided. MI6 was a gentlemen's club and a gentleman could always be trusted.

But all this had left MI6 profoundly vulnerable to its enemies, as the defections to Moscow of Guy Burgess and Donald Maclean and the sacking of Kim Philby had shown. And not only vulnerable but also still full of people who were blind to its own failings. Depending on your point of view, 1956 and 1957 can be seen either as MI6's nadir, or the start of its revival—the beginning of the end of the service's nightmare years. It certainly began with disaster, in the shape of the Buster Crabb affair, initiated and directed by Elliott, as London head of station. It was also destined to go catastrophically wrong.

Soviet leader Nikita Khrushchev had arrived in Britain for an official visit on board a new cruiser, the *Ordzhonikidze*. Elliott commissioned Commander Lionel 'Buster' Crabb, a diver with a distinguished war record, to swim under the ship while it was docked in Portsmouth

Harbour. But for all Crabb's wartime heroism, he was now a 47-year-old chain-smoking gambler with depression and a heavy drinking problem: he drank five double whiskies the night before the early morning dive. Crabb was never seen alive again. Years later, a Soviet ex-diver would claim that he had caught Crabb planting something on the ship's bottom, grappled with him underwater, and cut his throat, but other accounts suggest an encounter with a moving propeller or some other accident.

As Freedom of Information documents confirmed half a century later, a top-secret briefing paper was prepared instructing government spokesmen on how to lie to the media about the whole affair. The cover-up failed, as cover-ups often do: the story leaked, infuriating Prime Minister Anthony Eden, who was already close to concluding that SIS had a tendency to go out of control, and had decided to appoint MI5 head Dick White to replace MI6's 'C', John Sinclair. This in itself was a massive cultural challenge to the organisation my father had entered less than a decade before. For a start, MI6, full of upper-class former Special Operations daredevils, 'robber barons', and Empire-builders, looked down on MI5, which was seen as being staffed by ex-policemen and colonial bureaucrats. Even more substantially, the Philby question continued to divide the two services like a chasm.

MI5 had been rightly certain that Philby was a traitor, and was enraged when he was allowed to leave with a large payout, publicly exonerated by the prime minister. In MI6, however, he still had many defenders—admirers, even. As late as 1950, one SIS officer said to Gordon Corera, 'one new recruit was told that he should "model" himself on Philby, the "star of the service"'. Many of those who had had him on a pedestal in the 1940s could not bring themselves to see him as a pariah even now. I know that my father, certainly in later life, utterly loathed and despised Philby, but his boss at the time, Nicholas Elliott, was among those who could not shed their personal loyalty.

Worse was to come, for Britain and for the SIS, though this time the impetus to disaster was driven at least partly from 10 Downing Street itself. The Suez affair remains one of the key turning points in British postwar decline. And in this case, I know that my father was a minor player, close enough to observe key events at first hand.

In Egypt, Colonel Gamal Abdel Nasser had led the overthrow of the monarchy in 1952 and now, as president, had decided to nationalise the

Suez Canal. Oil was the key. More than two-thirds of Western Europe's oil supply had to pass through Suez at the time, and the cost, if the canal was cut off, of taking it around the Cape of Good Hope and up the west coast of Africa, looked alarming. British Prime Minister Anthony Eden, deeply shaped by his political experiences in the interwar years, saw Nasser as a Middle Eastern Mussolini. He took Nasser's decision not only as a challenge to Britain's interests, and by extension (because of the canal's key role in Eastern trade) the Empire, but also, it seems, as a personal affront: some reports suggest that he had felt slighted by Nasser's behaviour on the one occasion the two men met.

Most accounts portray Eden at this time as physically ill and increasingly mentally unstable. Gordon Corera says Eden made his wishes explicit: 'One of his ministers recalled Eden calling him up on an unsecure line and saying, "I want Nasser murdered, don't you understand?" This was the licence to kill.'

I know of my father's involvement in the Suez affair only because of a conversation we had in 2002, the year before he died. I told him I'd been remembering life in London when I was four, and that one of the things I recalled especially strongly was a postcard he'd sent me from America of a Pan American Boeing Stratocruiser, the luxury airliner of its time. It was a cutaway diagram of the plane, so you could see the pilots behind the great multi-paned dome of the cockpit window, the comfortable chairs in the 'stateroom', the 'berths' where passengers slept, and the spiral staircase that led up to a comfortable lounge and bar. The memory was reinforced by the fact that on his return, he'd brought me a jigsaw puzzle of the same picture, and I had treasured it.

'What were you doing on that Stratocruiser to America anyway?' I'd asked him. 'Ah,' he said. 'I was the junior member of a delegation that went to Washington to try to bring the CIA on board with SIS's plans for Suez.' This was certainly the meeting referred to by the University of Birmingham's Professor Scott Lucas in a BBC program on the Suez Crisis in 2006. Lucas' proof of the meeting was a CIA memorandum dated 1 April 1956, covering two days of meetings between CIA representatives and MI6 Deputy Director George Young. It read, in part:

> Following emerged as MI6 position. Nasser's aims are the total destruction of Israel, Egyptian domination of all Arab governments,

> and elimination of all western positions in the Arab area. In order to realise his ambitions Nasser has accepted full scale collaboration with the Soviets ... MI6 asserted that it is now British government view that western interests in the Middle East, particularly oil, must be preserved from Egyptian–Soviet threat at all costs.

Lucas said that to deal with this imminent threat, 'Young suggested regime change in not one but three Arab countries [Syria, Saudi Arabia and Egypt], and for the first time he mentioned the possibility of working with a new Middle Eastern partner: Israel.'

This is an extraordinarily aggressive proposal, going far beyond the eventual operation in which the Israelis would invade the Egyptian Sinai, and British and French forces would step in, in a phoney peacekeeping role, to 'protect' the canal. The Americans certainly regarded it as wildly over-ambitious, asking, among other things, how Nasser's toppling could be brought about if Saudi Arabia was in collapse at the time. 'Use the snip-cocks,' Young replied, using a vulgar and offensive term for the Israelis.

The Americans told the British delegation that they would consult at a higher level and get back to them, but they never did: the Eisenhower administration's opposition to the scheme, Professor Lucas told me directly, was conveyed to Prime Minister Eden via back-channels. My father, on his first visit to America, would have been agape. 'It was pretty much doomed from the beginning,' he told me.

Not being in favour of maintaining or increasing British and French interests in the Middle East, and unconvinced that the British plan was well enough conceived, diplomatically or militarily, the USA ultimately remained opposed to the invasion. The Suez Crisis ended in humiliating defeat, the withdrawal of the Anglo-French invasion force, and, within months, the fall of Anthony Eden as prime minister.

It also marked, for many historians, the dividing line in Britain's postwar pretensions as an Imperial power: the beginning of a belated realisation that the victory against Hitler had left the country too indebted, financially, diplomatically and geopolitically, to maintain its status as a real superpower. It was, as the CIA man in London at the time, Chester Cooper, would later title his book, *The Lion's Last Roar*.

Chapter 10

Worlds I'd Never Known

WHATEVER EARTH-SHATTERING EVENTS were going on in the adult world, for me the year I was four was life-changing in another way. It was the year I learned to read. This was the one thing in my entire childhood that seems in retrospect to have been almost completely effortless.

At home, I had a series of books called *Ant and Bee*, who lived with a Cat and a Dog, and had sequential adventures involving all the other letters of the alphabet. They were small-format books, just right for a child's hands, and wider than they were high. My parents had read to me at bedtime for as long as I could remember, but *Ant and Bee* somehow started to make the transition for me from hieroglyphics to letters. At kindergarten I started to take my reading textbooks home. After a few weeks, the teacher asked my mother to stop me because I was about ten books ahead of the rest of the class—it wasn't a plea to stop me reading, just a suggestion that I stop leapfrogging the class. Fortunately, both my parents were lifelong readers, and books were not just encouraged but showered on me.

The first 'real' book I read on my own, though, I found for myself on a bookshelf behind the living room sofa. It was sometime around my fifth birthday. With *The Secret Garden* by Francis Hodgson Burnett, suddenly, the days of Ant and Bee, John and Jane and their dog Spot, were over. The book itself was a thing of beauty, one of a number that my mother had been given as a child, illustrated with pre-Raphaelite-influenced pictures and re-cased in gold-tooled leather by her two spinster great-aunts who had taken up bookbinding after the Great War. It wasn't the cover or the illustrations that sucked me into the book's pages, though, but the power of story. There was something about the sullen, sallow child Mary, exiled to a great echoing house in Yorkshire by her parents in India; something about the eponymous secret garden, the growing friendship between her and the gardener's boy Dickon, and their gradual rehabilitation of her crippled cousin Colin; something about the way the book catapulted me in both time and space to a world and an era I'd never known.

At difficult times in my life since, I have often read for sheer escapism, but the attraction of books at the beginning was not escape in that sense: I was a happy little boy in a happy house. It was more about exploration. Reading, I could somehow see immediately, offered you freedom and adventure without the accompanying danger. You could travel to volcanoes and treasure islands, under the sea or into space, laughing or crying, all while sitting on the sofa or lying on the carpet with your chin propped in your hands.

And it wasn't only that I'd learned to read. I'd become a reader, one of those kids who has to be called repeatedly at mealtimes because a book has them so completely in its thrall, a boy who occasionally bumped into lampposts while walking along the street deep in a book. Or deep in a magazine—I remember getting my first subscription to *The Robin*, the junior member of the stable that included *The Eagle*, home of spaceman Dan Dare and his evil nemesis The Mekon.

I loved the printed word, but there were limits to my literacy. I thought the sign outside my grandmother Sybil's neighbour's house in Hampshire, which read 'The Bungalow', was a warning that the property contained a Buffalo, so I would sprint past it in terror, until I told Granny my secret fears and she explained. And when, asked by my mother what I wanted for my fifth birthday, I asked for an encyclopaedia, what I actually wanted was a tricycle. It's my first memory of having to hide disappointment, though I'm not sure I was very good at it. As it turned out, the illustrated children's encyclopaedia I was given, which I still own, was a treasure hoard, full of interesting stories about trains and planes and cars, dinosaurs and—for some reason this stuck—the then recently rediscovered coelacanth, a bizarre-looking fish long thought to be extinct.

My real fifth birthday treat, though, in 1957, was a trip to Heathrow Airport, or Heath Row as it was still called then. Flying was such an expensive rarity that a lot of 1950s families used to make the trip out to the viewing area, to watch the KLM Constellations and the Pan Am Stratocruisers come and go. It was the beginning of the commercial jet age, a time when aviation was a badge of national pride, and BOAC's De Havilland Comets had been the pioneers—until they started falling out of the sky with metal fatigue. The problem was eventually addressed, and soon the Comet 4B would become Britain's jet aviation workhorse, but the country's edge of being first was lost. Within a year the Boeing 707 would dominate the international skies, and would do so for decades. But on 13 March 1957, what I saw was a magnificent collection of turbo-prop airliners, taking off, manoeuvring on the tarmac, landing.

Back home that evening, my birthday dinner was roast chicken, a relatively expensive rarity in the 1950s. My Big Present was a little red pedal-car.

* * *

In my father's world, the SIS was coming to terms with the fact that not only had Suez been a disaster, it had helped draw the world's attention away from the Hungarian Revolution which had erupted at exactly the same time.

Joseph Stalin had died in 1953, increasingly paranoid and sclerotic, and at the beginning of 1956, Nikita Khrushchev made his 'Secret Speech' denouncing the great dictator. By the middle of the year, versions of the speech had been printed in a number of Western newspapers, and rumours of it had spread widely in the Eastern Bloc. Hungary, with its strong cultural and historical links to Western Europe, had never been an enthusiastic colonial vassal of the Soviet Union, and by the end of October 1956, the whole nation appeared to be in revolt. For a brief moment, it appeared that the liberation, or at least partial autonomy, of a Soviet buffer state from communism—a key aim of Western intelligence since 1945—was about to happen. The Kremlin seemed to hover on the brink.

The broadsheet *Pravda* published a statement that included the words: 'The Soviet Government is prepared to enter into the appropriate negotiations with the government of the Hungarian People's Republic and other members of the Warsaw Treaty on the question of the presence of Soviet troops on the territory of Hungary.' It was seen as an extraordinary concession, almost cause for celebration, in Budapest. But then, at the precise moment the French and British became mired in Suez, the Kremlin drastically reversed itself and sent in the tanks. Within a fortnight, the revolution had been utterly crushed. Thousands were dead. Two hundred thousand Hungarians, seeing no end to totalitarianism, fled across the borders, in many cases enriching the business, political and cultural lives of the countries like Australia where they ended up.

Both my parents, having lived so close to Hungary and understanding at first hand from their time in Austria exactly what Soviet occupation meant, and why people would flee it, were deeply affected by the turmoil. I remember years later finding a November 1956 copy of *Picture Post*, entirely devoted to Hungary, at the bottom of my father's sock drawer. He hadn't wanted me to see it because of the pictures of corpses (I was only ten or eleven), and he had tears in his eyes as he explained to me what the front page headline, 'CRY HUNGARY', and the whole story of betrayal and abandonment meant to him and to the democratic world.

It would be twelve years before another Eastern Bloc country, Czechoslovakia, tried again to defy Moscow, with the same result; another twelve years before the groundbreaking rise of Solidarity, a non-government labour union, in Poland; and a total of four and a half decades after World War II before the countries Stalin had annexed were able to become free. For many Western converts to communism, however fervent, Khrushchev's denunciation of Stalin, followed by the ruthless crushing of the Hungarian uprising, meant enough was enough.

Britain, meanwhile, was losing its own Empire piece by piece, in some cases without resisting. In August 1957, when I was five and my sister nearly two, what was then called Malaya became independent. We did not know it, but this event was about to play a major part in our lives.

* * *

In London, I had moved from kindergarten to the Chelsea Froebel School. It was 'progressive', and I remember it with great affection: mostly there was a lot of painting, storytelling, learning numbers with blocks and rods, and only desultory attempts to get us to learn our times tables. In summer, we put on grey Aertex shirts and went to Battersea Park for running races and to play rounders. I had my first crush, on a girl in my class called Beth. I would go red if I had to speak to her and not know what to say.

I have no visual memory of flying back from Vienna in 1955. The first aeroplane ride I remember was in 1957, my first visit to France. It was a twin-prop Bristol Freighter whose enormous nose was in fact a pair of doors. A ramp was placed in front of them to load two or three cars per trip. Behind the cars there was seating for twenty people. It was just a short Channel hop to Le Touquet—less than 70 kilometres—but even though Le Touquet was a traditional haven for the English, from HG Wells, Edward and Mrs Simpson and Noël Coward to Winston Churchill, even a child could tell that it was Foreign. You had croissants for breakfast, which you were positively encouraged to dip into hot chocolate, which came in a bowl, not a cup. The lavatory was called a WC, pronounced 'doo-bluh vay-say', and it was not a 'throne' but a hole in the floor with places for your feet. There were bolsters instead of pillows on the beds. I watched men playing boules in the park, and wished I was old enough to have a drive on the go-kart track. The grown-ups played golf and tennis; the food was good. It was, in its small way, the beginning of a long love affair with France.

That winter, as often through my childhood, I went to stay with my grandmother for a week or so. Granny Sibyl lived near Winchester, in a tiny white cottage on a very steep slope. She subsisted frugally on the naval pension, gluing china back together if it broke rather than buying new plates. She kept an immaculate garden on this sharply angled hill, and took her disagreeable poodle, Suki, for long walks across Twyford Down, meeting other elderly ladies with dogs along the way.

At the top of the hill near the cottage was a fence, beyond which the ground sloped steeply down into a railway cutting. I was allowed to sit at the top of the slope and wait for the steam trains to go by. Down in the cutting, the engines puffing along were almost small enough to imagine them as Thomas and Gordon and Henry on the island of Sodor. I waved to them and sometimes, thrillingly, the engine drivers waved back as they slowed to a stop at Shawford station. Down the hill from the cottage was the river Itchen, small and slow and reedy, one of England's most famous trout streams. Near the bridge that crossed the stream in Shawford village lived a man who had built a tiny, realistic town out of matchboxes in his garden. If you walked further downstream, there was also a little wooden bridge where you could be like Christopher Robin and play Poohsticks.

Granny's hallway had a glass case with all my grandfather's medals. There were an awful lot of them, up to and including Knight Commander of the British Empire and Commander of the Order of the Bath. I could never quite understand what this mysterious Bath was for. Could you wash in it? And how would you command it? Elsewhere in the house were a portrait of Nelson with his eyepatch and missing arm, a tableau of the victor of Trafalgar dying on the deck of the *Victory*, surrounded by Hardy and his comrades, and a framed replica of a letter from Nelson himself. You were never in doubt that you were part of a naval family. If you grazed your knee or banged your head, you were told to 'Remember Nelson'—translation: even if they lose an eye or an arm, boys don't cry.

Granny was a terrible cook: we ate frizzly overfried eggs and burnt bacon for breakfast, and greasy overdone chops for lunch, at a table with a lazy Susan in the middle: 'We bought it because your grandfather couldn't bear to speak or be spoken to at breakfast. Not even "Pass the marmalade."' The lazy Susan was also where she kept the half-melted silver ashtray that was one of the few things she'd salvaged from the 1923 earthquake in Tokyo, where my father was born while my grandfather was on posting as naval attaché to Japan. Granny told me how her own father, General Kays, had been so choleric that once, on seeing the housemaid carrying a decanter of port with insufficient care, he had shouted, 'That's right girl, give it a good shake,' and she, unfortunately, failed to pick up the sarcasm and did.

Granny was from another age. She talked about 'gels' instead of 'girls', used 'weskits' for waistcoats, 'forrids' for foreheads (I still do this), and often uttered phrases most people had stopped using in the 1920s. Years later, when I got my first job, she asked me, 'And do you get a good screw?' which apparently meant 'Are you well paid?' It was hard to keep a straight face.

She often told the story about how, when Queen Mary (grandmother of the present Queen) visited the Royal Naval College at Greenwich, they were warned to hide their valuables, because the old lady was notorious for 'admiring' people's knick-knacks in such a way that they were obliged to offer them to her as a gift. Luckily, the only things at Greenwich the royal personage who historians sometimes describe as a 'kleptomaniac' took a fancy to were all already the property of the state. My grandfather, at the time, had the job of president of the college, and my aunt, then a very small girl, used to ride her tricycle around the ground, telling the sailors on duty to 'Salute the president's daughter'.

Granny would prove indomitable throughout her long, lonely decades as a widow. She read, and in the case of Jane Austen re-read, constantly. She worked her way through the *Daily Telegraph* every day, and listened to the BBC. She kept in touch with friends from the old days and made herself busy around the village. When I stayed with her that winter, we bought fresh eggs from the chicken farm down near the Poohsticks bridge, and that Christmas we went to the village pantomime. I shouted with laughter at Widow Twanky and practically rolled in the aisles at all the terrible jokes. I loved it so much that she patiently took me again the next night.

But soon there would be no more stays in Granny's cottage, no more Chelsea Froebel School, not for a while. We were going to live overseas. West Africa was the original destination, but my father was strongly of the view that his interests and abilities were better suited to middle Europe or the Far East—he would later boast about how he finagled his way out of the Ghana job and into a posting in Kuala Lumpur.

The result was that in 1958, not long after my sixth birthday, we boarded a ship at Southampton, bound for the country that was still called Malaya but would soon become Malaysia.

* * *

The *Falstria* was a cargo and passenger ship, long, white and sleek, belonging to Denmark's East Asiatic Lines. 'No other means of overseas transportation,' said the brochure, 'offers such complete relaxation and pleasure as a sea voyage.' They might also have mentioned that it was a six-year-old boy's dream.

This was pre-containerisation, so there were the ship's cranes to watch as they loaded heavy netted bundles containing rice and grain sacks, barrels, wooden crates of different shapes and sizes, even sometimes motorcars, onto and off the ship. There were the Danish sailors, coiling hawsers and manning winches, usually kindly and ready to offer a word as long as you didn't get in their way. And there was the smell of heavy engine oil mixed with sea spray, as I went forward to visit my beloved dog Bamse in his kennel on the foredeck. There was also a children's room with toys and books where Danish child-minders looked after me and my sister Zoë.

We sailed out of foggy England, down to the Mediterranean, and docked in Marseilles, where we spent a day with our London neighbours, Freddie and Jean Shaughnessy, who were holidaying nearby. Heading for the southern Mediterranean, it got steadily hotter, and the ship's small, square seawater pool came into its own. With the help of an inflatable rubber ring I began to learn to swim.

The Suez Canal, which had been closed since the invasion of 1956, had now reopened, and I still have a vivid mental picture of the vast crowd of people in white robes clustered on the dock at Port Said, trying to sell us souvenirs, mostly leather goods—saddles, brightly coloured curly-toed sandals, toy camels—but also ornaments and knick-knacks and a type of red felt hat which I'd never seen before but my parents told me was called a fez. There was a dry intensity to the heat as we passed slowly through the canal, dunes on either side: I did not know it, but I would not truly feel cold again for about two years, though the heat I was soon to experience was different, dense with tropical humidity.

I've never taken a long sea voyage since: jet travel quickly superseded it as a way of getting from country to country. But even on island ferries during Aegean holidays, the smells and sounds and sensations of the deck of a ship at sea have always wafted me back to 1958 and those idyllic days as we skimmed across the Arabian Sea and the Bay of Bengal, heading for the Malaysian Peninsula.

I remember little more detail of the voyage, just sunny days and swimming and endless sea horizons, until we docked in Penang, our first landfall in our new country. I was startled to see small Malay boys, hardly older than my own age, shinning up trees to fetch coconuts in return for coins from tourists. In Kuala Lumpur we stayed in a hotel for a few days and I ate Chinese food for the first time: a taste explosion after 1950s London in the wake of rationing, and the excellent, but generally bland, Danish cuisine on the *Falstria*.

Soon we moved into our new home, 7 Lorong Kuda, right next to the Kuala Lumpur racecourse. A high hedge separated us from the track, but from our first-floor windows on race days you could see the tiny jockeys on their great horses come thundering round the bend as they gathered pace to enter the straight in front of the grandstand. We had a spacious garden, far bigger than our little backyard in London, and of course tropically greener. There were banana trees at the back, and a mangosteen tree in the middle, the trunk of which I would later use as the wicket in cricket games. It was in some ways my Garden of Eden. The front door had a portico, where you could get out of the car, a blue Ford Zephyr, without getting wet, even in a monsoonal downpour. Right in front of that were a big tree and a concrete fishpond.

Inside, there were big comfortable cane chairs downstairs, with a dining room which led down to the kitchen at the side. That was the domain of Ah Kwong, who cooked for us, and his wife Ah Kwai, who did the laundry and housework. Poor Ah Kwai: a hardworking middle-aged Chinese woman with a son of her own but with limited English, she was confronted with two children who wouldn't do what they were told—and wouldn't do it in pidgin English: 'No wantee, no likee.'

Even though, since independence the year before, Malaya was no longer a colony, we were typical little Anglo-Australian colonial children: most of our friends were English or Australian children too, and we lived a life semi-removed from the local culture. I was a bit frightened of the older Malay and Chinese boys who hung around the racecourse and walked through our garden (it was a public right-of-way) to get there. They played a game with a rattan ball that involved keeping it in the air as long as possible, and they used to shout at me, 'Hey, Johnny, come here Johnny.' Why 'Johnny'? That wasn't my name, I thought: what did they mean? They meant no harm, but I was still quite a timid child, and generally scuttled off as fast as I could.

Upstairs, there was a long room that stretched from the rear of the house to directly above the portico. Here there was a gramophone, though we had few records that were particularly attractive to children. I liked *The Man from Laramie*: 'The West will never see a man with so many notches on his gun.' For some reason, my sister and I listened again and again to the original soundtrack of *The Boy Friend*, a West End musical my parents had seen in 1953, and which I would recognise with hilarity, years later, in a Monty Python sketch which reimagined it as directed by Sam Peckinpah, with massively bloody consequences. And there was an EP of Pablo Casals playing the cello, chiefly memorable because my father would point out gleefully that in the quiet passage in the middle you could hear the great man fart.

There was no television in Malaysia then, and I don't recall hearing any radio. You played indoor games or read, or went outside and played in the garden. For my mother, who had been missing the presence of horses since she left the family sheep station in Victoria a decade or so before, living by the racecourse meant she could ride again regularly, and she made sure I took riding lessons, too, on a pony called Merah.

School in Kuala Lumpur started in the early morning and ended at lunchtime. In the afternoon we would go to the Royal Selangor Golf Club, not far away, where there was an Olympic pool. I was taught by a tall, rangy Australian called Miss Cairns to swim breaststroke, backstroke and freestyle, which was still called the Australian Crawl. Mum would sometimes take us shopping in the central markets, where there was the noise of shouting hawkers, and the mixed smells of South-East Asia: spices and herbs, coriander and chilli and fish, glorious arrays of tropical fruit, and the open-sewer smell of durian.

At weekends we'd go for walks around the reservoir above the city. There were caves, one of which was huge and contained a religious shrine and stank of the guano of millions of bats. At one place on the reservoir walk there was a small cave outlet through which, towards sunset, thousands of swifts would fly in great sky-darkening flocks.

Once, Dad took me with a friend of his who was a butterfly hunter on a trek through thick jungle. Another boy on the walk started screaming: he had a leech on his penis. The treatment—holding a lighted cigarette to the leech's tail so it would let go—seemed almost as terrifying as the leech itself. The butterflies were huge and exotic, some with gorgeous colours, others with long, trailing, almost tasselled wings. I never liked the idea of collecting them: they seemed too beautiful to kill.

More than once, we visited the kampongs, villages set among the rubber tree plantations. Village relocation and close political engagement with key local figures had been central to British tactics in the so-called Malayan Emergency, a guerrilla war against communist insurgents which had raged for most of the 1950s, but which was essentially almost over by the time we arrived. Independence in 1957 had deprived the communist MRLA forces of their strongest selling point in what they saw as a 'war of national liberation'. The gravitas and political savvy of the new prime minister, Tunku Abdul Rahman, had also helped neutralise the threat. As far as I can make out, one of my father's tasks was simply to consolidate the victory, ensuring that the jungle warfare of the past few years would not return.

I have a clear memory of him taking me on a drive into the jungle. I was six or seven, and we were in quite a remote part of the highlands. We walked into a clearing and there was a tribal longhouse, where we took off our shoes and sat on the floor to eat. My father was meeting a man called Colonel Dick Noone, and after lunch, he 'reviewed the troops'. They were hill tribesmen, who marched in soldierly fashion up and down the clearing, shouldering arms and demonstrating their skill in dismantling and reassembling their weapons. Small, wiry brown men, they looked disciplined and fierce.

Noone was a sinewy character in well-pressed khaki who could have stepped from the pages of an H Rider Haggard or John Buchan novel. He's a shadowy figure in the historical documents of the time, but my researches have revealed that Dick Noone had a long track record in guerrilla warfare. When Singapore fell to the Japanese, he made his way to Australia, where he served in the Z Special Unit, an Australian secret operations force which ran raids against the Japanese in occupied territories in Papua New Guinea and South-East Asia. According to Leon Comber's *Malaya's Secret Police 1945–60: The Role of the Special Branch in the Malayan Emergency*, Noone was instructed in 1956 to form and command a fighting force of Orang Asli (hill tribesmen). The British Army's 22 Special Air Service (SAS) Regiment was brought in to train them. Comber says Noone's job involved passing any intelligence he collected to the Special Branch. One of these troops of Orang Asli men must have been what I saw that day.

There is also what's on the record about what Noone did afterwards. From 1960–65 in Bangkok, he was the rural border security adviser with the Southeast Asia Treaty Organization. In that role, Comber says, Noone led 'an MI6 team of Malays, Bornean tribesmen and ethnically similar Montagnard tribesmen in operations against the Vietcong'. This was part of the little known British Advisory Mission to South Vietnam. So one of my father's jobs was clearly coordinating that kind of secret police and counterintelligence work.

Although independence had formally come to what was then the Federation of Malaya, there was more to be done. The federation consisted of the mainland peninsular states, but along with the British, Malaya had a larger plan: for a federation with North Borneo, Sarawak and Singapore, to be called Malaysia. This was prompted partly by arguments for strength in numbers and territory (though Singapore, which joined initially, would eventually decide to go it alone), but also by gradually rising alarm at the actions of Indonesia's founding president, Sukarno, who'd been getting increasing amounts of aid from Mao's China and the Soviet Union. For centuries, the Straits of Malacca, a classic strategic chokepoint for shipping, had been one of the fulcrums of world trade: now they were shaping as a potential Cold War flashpoint. The secret war in Borneo, when Sukarno decided to challenge the whole integrity of the Malaysian Federation, in what became known as Konfrontasi, would later, along with the fate of West Papua, become my father's central preoccupations. But for now, he was mostly working in peninsular Malaya itself.

In mid-August 1959, we went on a cruise on a motor yacht around Malaysia's southern islands. It wasn't technically a holiday: my father was officially acting as an election observer in the country's first post-independence national poll. I assumed for a long time that he'd swung the trip as a junket, but I now believe that he was intelligence-gathering too: with signs of Sukarno's incipient expansionism, it would have been useful to know what people in these outlying parts thought.

Many of these islands are now luxury tourist resorts, but then they were simple villages with houses on stilts and few resources except coconuts and the abundant fish on the reefs. I went snorkelling one afternoon while my father was working, and I still dream sometimes about the intensity of colour in the coral and the tropical fish. It was the last time for a while that I would feel so gloriously free.

* * *

I had an accident-prone streak in 1958 and 1959. It started on our first day in the new house, when I picked up a cat and tripped over, cracking open my head. Five stitches. Then my mother was in the changing room at the pool when a woman came in and said, 'The pool's full of blood, a boy's just cut his chin open.' Mum's intuition was instant and correct: yes, of course it was me. I'd been standing with my back to the water, about to try a backflip, when a schoolmate called Johnny Callaghan ran past and gave me a push in the chest. Instead of leaping, I went straight down, hitting the underside of my chin on the pool's edge. Straight to the doctor. Six stitches.

Another day, I was playing in the empty racecourse grandstand when I sprinted across what I thought was a shortcut, not noticing a thin band of metal at face level. Upper lip cut open, four stitches. My seventh birthday present was a bicycle. High-speed race down the Lorong Kuda hill with Roddy from next door, brakes on too hard, hurtle into ditch. Three stitches, left knee. I think it was that time that, when my mother rang the doctor, he answered wearily, 'Is it Mark? Does he need stitches?'

This was just normal boy stuff, though, even if slightly extreme. It was about to be eclipsed by a real disaster. It was just after we got back from the election-observer jaunt around the islands, and it happened on the racecourse.

I'd had enough time in the saddle to be a fairly confident rider. I could get Merah to walk, trot, canter and even gallop, and I'd had quite a lot of practice taking small jumps without falling off. She was only a small, fat pony, and adults trusted me enough to let me go around the racecourse on my own. We were in an inner ring of the course, quite close to my house, when I urged Merah into a canter. I was feeling the breeze on my face and enjoying the speed when disaster struck. A Malay boy had been flying a kite and its string had come down across the track, dangling at waist height. The pony saw it and jumped over it. I didn't see it and so was not braced for the jump. I was thrown, landing hard on my right arm. In the total shock that followed, only one thing was in my mind, the safety advice I'd always been given: if you fall off, get out of the horse's way, so you don't get kicked or trampled. I staggered towards the fence, to find that although I could crawl under it, there was a monsoon ditch between me and the next track. I stopped.

Merah, no danger to me or anyone else, was standing cropping the grass as though nothing had happened. I looked down at my arm. For the first time I noticed it was covered with blood. I could see something white sticking out of the elbow, and more of it sticking out at the wrist: bone and blood were about all that was visible from the elbow down. I started to scream. My mother came out—Dad was away that day, I think—and I was carried back to the house. I lay on the back seat of the car as I was driven to the hospital. In my confusion and pain, I couldn't remember the word for 'stretcher'. I asked my mother instead, 'Will they put me on a coffin?' which brought her to tears: 'No, darling, of course not.'

At Kuala Lumpur's British Army hospital I remember the nurses giving me the standard line that I was a 'very brave boy' as they wheeled me along a corridor, the pattern of ceiling tiles and lights flashing past my vision as they raced towards the operating theatre. Then an anaesthetist saying, 'I bet you can't count to a hundred before you go to sleep.' 'Bet I can. One, two, three, four, five …' Then nothing. I woke up in bed with my arm in plaster from fingers to shoulder. It had been a nasty accident, but in normal circumstances I should have been home within a week or two. Instead, that hospital room was to become my prison for the next six weeks.

Children's hospitals have changed a lot for the better since the 1950s. They needed to. Visiting hours, even for parents, were restricted to once a day for an hour or so. The idea of setting up camp beds so a parent could stay with a child overnight hadn't been thought of. There was no TV in the country, and being an army hospital, there were few other children I was allowed to play with. I think there were two others in my ward for the first week or so, but after that I was mostly alone, and I wasn't allowed to talk to children in several other wards because they had infectious diseases. So the compendiums of games I was given—Ludo, Snakes and Ladders, Draughts—weren't much use, because I had no-one to play them with. I was very, very lonely, and my arm would not heal. The Chinese woman who came to clean my room every day mocked me because I had a teddy bear: 'How old you? Seven? Too old for toy like that.' I had no comeback, except to guiltily hide Teddy every time she came around.

The heavy plaster itched horribly in the humidity. How long was this going to go on? I wasn't feeling well, either: sickly and occasionally feverish, I didn't seem to be getting better as expected. Then, when I'd had my arm in plaster for about three weeks, my mother and the doctor came to tell me I was going to have to have another operation, to re-break and reset the arm. The reason was something called osteomyelitis, an infection of the bone and bone marrow, more common in the tropics. It turns the bone soft and brittle. My arm was not healing at all as a consequence. As well as another general anaesthetic and weeks more in plaster, I was going to need a lot of penicillin, then still pretty much the only drug in the antibiotic arsenal.

I woke up again after the second operation, in the same room, feeling worse if anything. I missed home and school, and cricket in the garden, and the swimming pool, and my little sister. My only escape, as had been the case ever since the accident, was into the world of books. I'd already read the first few *Billabong* stories by the Australian Mary Grant Bruce, which my mother had had as a child: now I read my way through all fifteen. This was interspersed with the *Tintin* series, which in the late 1950s was gradually coming out in English translations; Arthur Ransome's *Swallows and Amazons* titles; most of the *Greyfriars* series featuring Billy Bunter; RL Stevenson's *Treasure Island* and *Kidnapped*; a whole series of Edwardian animal novels with titles like 'I'm Nick: A Yorkshire Terrier's Story', 'Jerry: The Story of an Exmoor Pony' and 'Bellman the Beagle'; and André Maurois' wonderful anti-war allegory of an underground world where the skinny take up arms against the obese, *Fattypuffs and Thinifers*.

I was still bored and lonely, though, and after six weeks in hospital, still not getting any better. I was pale and ill and losing weight. My mother asked the doctors to let me come home. They also decided that I seemed to have become immune to penicillin: she thought it was actively making me worse.

It was wonderful to be home, and my mother was right: I put on weight and started to look less deathly pale, though as it turned out my arm would still be in a sling for a long while. The plaster eventually came off, replaced with a splint, but the osteomyelitis had done its damage. The arm would never straighten again at the elbow, and the wrist end of the ulna was pretty much gone. It would become clear over the years that the radius continued to grow while the ulna remained foreshortened, so X-rays of my forearm show it as looking like a tensed longbow, with the ulna as the string.

I had just begun physiotherapy when the news came through from Australia: my beloved grandfather, Walford Manifold, had died suddenly while gardening at home in Victoria. He was sixty-seven, and there had been no warning. I had only known grandfather during a brief holiday he took with us in London, but I was devoted to him, and I remember crying for hours. So my poor mother, grief-stricken and in shock herself, also had to cope with a sobbing seven-year-old who would not be consoled. Soon we were on our way south to Australia, a country I half-belonged to in my mind but where I had never been.

Chapter 11

Not-So-Elysian Fields

MY IDEA OF Australia before my first trip there had been almost entirely shaped by old books: Mary Grant Bruce's early-twentieth-century outback adventures, CJ Dennis' *A Book for Kids*, *We of the Never Never*, *The Magic Pudding*, *Blinky Bill*, *Snugglepot and Cuddlepie* and more. My voice was that of a little English boy, but several of my friends and schoolmates were Australian, and, knowing I was half-Australian by birth and dreaming of a far-off literary Australian past, part of me wanted to be more like them.

I'd been bursting with anticipation of our first visit as we'd been planning a family Christmas, but the suddenness of my grandfather's death changed everything. My mother's youngest sister, Bindy (Belinda), had had coffee with him after lunch on the verandah of the family house, Mondilibi, that day, and told him she was just going to pop into the nearest town, Mortlake, to go shopping. She came back to find the place in shock, the men who worked on the farm embarrassed and not knowing how to tell her.

Grandfather had been working with Paul, the Yugoslav gardener, when he sat down with his back to a tree, said he didn't feel too good, and asked Paul to fetch some water. When Paul came back with a glass, Grandfather was dead. We would all wish for ourselves a sudden and painless death, when it comes, but few of us would wish the attendant shock and grief on our loved ones. I know that myself now, having lost my own father that way.

Mondilibi was a beautiful old homestead in the lee of a hill, with old trees and a large, well-tended garden designed by my grandmother, who had died in the year of my birth. By the time we arrived it was nearly November, warm and far drier than I was used to after Kuala Lumpur. It was very much outback Australia as I had imagined it reading books: horses and cattle and sheep, a big old shearing shed, a hot summer landscape. The paddocks stretched out across the Western District landscape, with only distant landmarks like Mount Elephant to orient you. It was my first taste of farm life, and I wanted to stay forever. Paul the gardener used to welcome me and my sister into his shed to eat buttered toast, drink from enamel mugs of hot sweet tea, and talk about Grandfather. Zoë remembers how Paul pulled his own tooth out when it got too painful, a lurid detail I can't work out how I'd forgotten.

My mother's other sister, Jill, had come up from Melbourne with her four children, Richard, Sarah, Margaret and David. And one day we went to meet older cousins nearby, who thrillingly had an 'old bomb'—a 1930s car that was too old to register on the road, but which still ran—and they were allowed to drive it around the property, with us on the back. Dad, who'd stayed in KL to work, flew down for Christmas: my present was a complete cowboy outfit: Stetson, waistcoat with sheriff's badge, chaps, and two chrome-plated plastic six-guns in their holsters.

But hanging over it all was a pervading sense of sadness and impending loss, which even at seven I could feel. This place I'd fallen in love with at first sight, my mother's childhood home, had to be sold. Grandfather had had a son, Derek, but he'd died of meningitis when he was fourteen and my mother was just eleven, leaving her and her parents grief-stricken. Now Mondilibi was left equally to his three remaining children, all daughters. There were state and Commonwealth death duties to pay, and no way to keep the place going, so their only option was to divide up the assets and sell the property. So the months we spent there were tinged with melancholy: not just the grief of bereavement after the death of a much-loved parent and grandparent, but the sense of an ending for my mother and my aunts. After we went back to Kuala Lumpur, there would be no coming back to Mondilibi.

And my broken arm was still not right. We had begun seeing a specialist in Melbourne, and eventually, several months after the original accident, I had some freedom. But the damage was done: the arm would never straighten and always look somewhat deformed. Because of its peculiar malformation I would never be able to play the piano or to bowl properly in cricket, a game my dad had already started to teach me. Because of the way the radius and ulna were aligned, I would also always have some pain or discomfort writing for any length of time. Eventually, thanks to boarding-school bullying, it would also leave me with a humiliating sense of physical inadequacy and a grating self-consciousness about baring my arms in public.

On the other hand, I could still swim, and, thanks to all those lessons in Kuala Lumpur, I did so confidently and strongly, especially once the arm began to regain some strength. We went to the beach at Anglesea, my first Australian beach experience: white glare off fine sand and Tarax lemonade and learning to bodysurf. To be able to harness the power of a wave, even a small one, to emerge with your head and shoulders clear as its power propels you towards the shore, even to crash out and get dumped, was liberating and intense. Later, those memories kept me going through a lot of cold English boarding-school winters.

Australia, when we flew back to Kuala Lumpur in early 1960, was now fixed in my mind as one of the places I'd call home, wherever I ended up in the meantime. I wouldn't actually be back in person till 1969, but some part of me always remained here.

* * *

Accidents and bereavements apart, my life to this point had been largely protected and idyllic. My father was away a lot, but when he was around we played cricket in the garden. My little sister 'fielded', which mostly meant sitting in her little wicker chair reading the *Beano Annual*. My parents took us on breaks and holidays: driving through the Cameron Highlands, visiting the Chinese old town in Malacca, going to the beach. But in September 1960 this was all set to change. I was to go back to England, to boarding school.

Again, my expectations were all derived from books, mainly the *Billy Bunter* and *Jennings* series. On the whole, I had an impression of fun, companionship and jolly japes. I had read Tom Brown's *Schooldays* but assumed, since it was a century old, that its portrayal of misery and uncontrolled bullying was as outdated as, say, that of Victorian animal cruelty in *Black Beauty*. I had no sense of foreboding.

My mother and Zoë and I flew to London, where we went to the (now-long-defunct) Gorringes department store with a long list of uniform items and equipment to buy, starting with a school trunk which would be emblazoned with my initials. It gradually filled as we marched around the shop, with a blazer, shorts and trousers, sports clothes, socks and underwear, and so on.

It seems insane now, but there was a machine where you stood and looked down through a viewer as it X-rayed your feet. It was called a 'shoe-fitting fluoroscope', manufactured by the British Pedoscope Company, and it showed your feet inside the new shoes in glowing detail. You had to wiggle your toes so the salesman or your parent could see whether there was 'growing room' or you should go up half a size. The only 'shielding' between you and the radioactive tube was a thin sheet of aluminium.

Once I was well irradiated and fully equipped, my mother took me and my trunk to Summer Fields, a prep school on the outskirts of Oxford, and hugged me goodbye. Here I would be 'educated' from the age of eight to thirteen. 'Mens Sana in Corpore Sano' was the school's Latin motto: 'A Healthy Mind in a Healthy Body'. Opened in 1864, it was still, almost a century later, imbued with its founder's values of 'muscular Christianity': sport and discipline, inculcated with copious doses of corporal punishment.

I was not in the least surprised when the son of the Prince of Wales' second wife, Camilla Parker Bowles, told the media a few years ago that an adult master at Summer Fields had shared communal showers with little boys when he was there in the early 1980s: that was a daily occurrence in the early 1960s. But although I believe some masters were (in practice highly repressed) paedophiles, the way most of them expressed it was not through sex but sheer violence. The system made that easy for them. If 'carrot and stick' was the guiding principle, the carrots were all collective, while the stick (and it was a stick) was all personal.

During my first year there were cold baths every morning, though after that they were abolished—luckily, because in the Big Freeze winter of 1962–63, the coldest of the century, they would have been intolerable. As it was, with the nearby Cherwell River so solid with ice that year that boys who had the right equipment skated on it daily, we were made to carry on playing rugby on fields still thick with snow.

The school was divided into four 'houses'—Congreve, Moseley, Maclaren and Case—though your house bore no relation to where you lived; each was just associated with a different colour. In any case, you were a number as much as a name: I still occasionally think of myself as 'MRM Colvin 138'. I was in Case, whose colour was red. If you did well, academically, in conduct or in sport, you added points to your house's total. If you did badly, you yourself were punished.

Summer Fields was a collection of nineteenth-century buildings around a large Victorian-Gothic Hall and a chapel in the same architectural style. Its dining hall was arranged like that of an Oxford college, with masters sitting at a table on a raised dais and boys at long refectory tables down the length of the hall. Wooden plaques lining the walls carried the names of old boys who had died in the world wars. The youngest boys slept in the main housing around the hall, the older ones in dormitories in houses dotted around the campus.

You had to learn the rules on day one, and there were a lot of them. Punishment could descend if you were seen running in the corridors, had your hands in your pockets, gave 'cheek' to one of the male masters (there were no women on the teaching staff except for a couple of classes for the very youngest boys), were late to class, had forgotten or lost a textbook, were found anywhere off the school premises, or for a host of other infringements. Breaking one of these rules meant a 'blue'. This could mean either an hour or more of copying out Vergil's *Aeneid* or Caesar's *Gallic Wars* during after-school free time, or a 'ten-minute discipline', which entailed running up and down a path during the whole of the brief morning break. Despite the tedium, I preferred the Latin 'lines': I suffered from what was then called 'chronic bronchitis' but which modern medicine now calls asthma, and even five minutes of running during the English winter could turn my lungs to sandpaper and make me double up with coughing.

But a ten-minute discipline, under the martinet history master HWH Hartley, was just the beginning. If you got two blues, or, worse, were found doing something more serious, like fighting, that added up to an entry in the Black Book. The Black Book meant the cane. And the cane meant lining up for a soul-eating half-hour or longer, in a line of other small boys, on a Wednesday or Saturday evening—sitting on hard chairs in their pyjamas and dressing-gowns outside the green baize outer door of the headmaster's study, waiting for a thrashing.

It first happened to me in the middle of my first week. Lost, frightened, and above all conscious that my family home was an impossible six and a half thousand miles away, I was crazy with loneliness and anger, and I reacted by striking out. I think that first time, in a red mist of rage, I threw a chair across a classroom, just as a master came in.

The canings took place in the office of the headmaster, Patrick Savage, but the man who did the beating during my first few terms was his deputy. His name was Pat Marston, but he was universally known—to his face, not just behind his back—as The Ogre. A heavy, thickset man with beetling brows, his quietest register seemed to be an angry shout. In a commemorative book commissioned by the school at the time, one Summer Fields old boy from years before suggested this was a mere front: 'His appearance was formidable. He growled and shook the room as he entered. But once I learnt that he didn't actually eat little boys, even on Black Fridays, the classes became amusing, exhilarating and even relaxing.' This genial portrait—in a rose-tinted book the school used extensively as a sales pitch—was completely misleading, certainly by the time I arrived. Any honest account would have described Pat Marston as a brutal sadist. 'Bend over the arm of that sofa and pull down your pyjama trousers, boy.' And then the beating would begin.

In theory, the barrack-room lawyers among the boys would whisper, there were supposed to be rules about the cane. Masters were not allowed by law to give you more than 'six of the best'. Masters were not allowed to take a run-up. Masters were not allowed to draw blood, and if they did they had to stop. But we all knew that was just rumour, and even if it had been true, who were we going to tell?

In the headmaster's study, Pat Marston would take a step or two back, so he could really get some force into his backswing. Lash! Down came the thin, whippy cane, then again ... Lash! It stung horribly on the stretched skin of the bare bottom, and it stung equally badly when Marston missed. Is his eyesight failing, you'd think, or is his aim deliberately bad? None of us knew, but the result was a web of welts and cuts that descended as far as the backs of your knees, or even lower, on to the backs of your calves.

This happened behind a heavy oak door, inside the green baize door. Sitting in your dressing-gown in the line outside, you could not hear the cane (known as The Swish) land on your predecessor, nor whether he was crying (known as 'blubbing'). It was a guarantee of actual silence, in a culture of psychological silence. Even if you blubbed, you'd have to wipe away the tears and make it look, as you walked out and down the line, as if you hadn't been.

One of the other key lessons I learned in my first week came in a class called 'Letter Writing'. 'Now, boys, time to write a letter home to your parents so they know that you're all right.' I wrote a note saying I hated it here and wanted to go home, put it in the envelope and wrote the address. The master in charge took it from me, read it and tore it up. 'Start again, and this time don't say anything bad about the school.' It left me with a lifelong loathing of censorship, and it added to the claustrophobia, the sense of being in a prison, which had closed in on me from the first day.

I believe it was in the third or fourth week that a boy a year older than me was paraded at High Table before the whole school at dinner. He had run away, said the headmaster, and been found at Oxford station trying to get home. Now he was going to get six of the best. Let this be a lesson … I had hardly even thought of running away. After Oxford station, where would I go? Heathrow? Stow away on a plane? It was inconceivable.

Telling tales on other boys was 'sneaking', and by the end of your first term you had internalised the idea of censorship and extended the concept of 'sneaking' to encompass the masters and the school itself, as well as your coevals. It was rare for a boy, even in the holidays, to tell his parents the truth about the school, which was, as the literary agent Toby Eady (another Summer Fields old boy) said in an interview with the *Independent* in 1994,

> completely based on fear. We were frightened children, living in suspicion and fear, fear of the masters, fear of the people who were meant to be giving us an education. And because they could punish you totally at will, and you had no one you could appeal to, you never trusted any of the teachers, and children should trust adults. To learn to trust again is very difficult when it is taken away from you so young.

I wonder, now, why no adults, not even the under-matrons, some of whom did seem to care about the boys, seem to have ever reported or protested against this abuse. Blood-stained pyjama legs should surely have been enough of a clue.

It diminished only in my third term at the school, the summer term. My mother was back in London and came to take me on a day out. For the first time, I was wearing shorts instead of grey flannel trousers. 'What are those cuts down the backs of your legs?' she asked. Some of them were old and scabbing over, others were fresh and new. I told her rather matter-of-factly, 'Oh, The Ogre beat me last night.' It was so normal to me by then. I'd inured myself to the beatings to such a degree that I would never give Marston the satisfaction of blubbing, even while he was thrashing me. I kept a stiff upper lip: the literal expression of what English private-school education had been intended to create in future Empire-builders.

My mother was furious, more furious than she let on to me that afternoon. Dropping me back at school, she went to see the headmaster and told him what was happening. It didn't stop the canings altogether, but from then on, every time I was braced for another encounter with The Ogre, it was Savage who beat me, not Marston: in fact, though there was never any formal announcement, The Ogre was never allowed to beat anyone again.

Savage's beatings were more accurate, it's true, but to me there always seemed something slightly odd about his manner: I see it in retrospect as bordering on the prurient. Savage's obituary in the London *Telegraph* called him 'a tall, spare, meticulous bachelor with beautiful handwriting … He anticipated personal tutors, taking boys for walks with his two King Charles spaniels, and introducing them to the pleasures of smoked salmon and James Bond.' If so, those boys were, shall we say, few and attractive.

Summer Fields was a school where those who excelled at sport, particularly, could lead golden lives. On my part, academically I was reasonably clever, but I was completely inept at games, and hampered by my deformed arm, which both drew down the bullies and made me the butt of the sports masters, because I couldn't do press-ups, climb a rope, bowl, or properly leap a jumping-horse. Given my disability, it still staggers me that my father insisted on having me enrolled in boxing classes.

Though I never heard that Savage did worse than play favourites with some pupils, the headmaster's reaction when he came into the dormitory one night when I was changing was bewildering. I had committed the 'crime' of taking off all my day clothes before putting on my pyjamas. Something about my brief nakedness triggered a red-faced explosion. I was to go straight to his room, where he caned me very hard indeed.

Sexual abuse of children is rightly at the forefront of people's minds now, but isn't it time people also recognised the profound trauma that sadomasochistic brutality, even without an overt sexual aspect, wreaks on small boys and girls? At Summer Fields it was routine, and not confined to the cane. One geography master who was also the cricket coach had an extraordinarily powerful and accurate throwing arm, and a boy looking out of the window was liable to be struck on the side of the head by a piece of chalk or even a wooden blackboard duster. The same master once managed to pull an eight-year-old's fine blond hair so hard that a small clump of scalp tore bloodily free.

Some masters were generally benevolent, but with a few of them there was a volcanic sense of lurking danger. Of all the beatings I took, one which remains with me happened on a very hot summer night in my first year. Three other boys were having a pillow fight. I was trying to sleep, but my sheets had got tangled, so I got up and started to remake my bed. A master came in and decreed that all those out of bed were for it: six of the best: 'Downstairs. Now.' I tried to explain but was told to be quiet. 'It's unfair, it's unfair, it's unfair, it's unfair' kept going through my head. By then I'd accepted that it could be 'fair' to be beaten for breaking written rules, internalised a system of values that said it was all right for adults to hit children regularly and sometimes mercilessly, as long as they had a reason. But that one night, I took my 'six of the best' with fury and resentment.

The prevailing sense of injustice, a system without any recourse or appeal, stays with you for the rest of your life. That and the physical bullying by other boys, which, again because of the 'no sneaking' ethos, you could do nothing about, even if the masters had been willing to listen. The British journalist Nick Davies, who uncovered the *News of the World* hacking scandal, told me recently that he thought his lifelong drive against injustice was fired by childhood physical abuse. I can't help seeing a similar pattern in my own career. I don't trust authority, because authority early on proved itself to me to be brutal and arbitrary.

On some emotional level, arguably, I have found it hard to trust anyone, certainly until they've given me reason to do so. This fits a pattern that comes up again and again in accounts of the many who have joined boarding school 'survivor groups' in Britain. The writer Alex Renton, himself a boarding school abuse victim, says there are now at least 150 private schools with serious current or recent allegations against them. It's a system that psychiatrists describe as 'attachment fracture', one which seems almost purpose-built to turn out dysfunctional individuals, and which perpetuates itself because so many of those individuals in turn find parenthood too difficult and send their own children away.

Renton, who was deluged with survivor stories after he wrote in *The Observer* in 2014 about his own experiences, says his correspondence is

> full of people apologising for not having a story of sexual predation to tell. 'It was only bullying', people write, 'not what you'd call abuse'. But emotional cruelty is what exacts the greatest toll on the developing mind ... what most reliably damages children is long-term emotional neglect, the absence of safety, the failure of justice, the loss of love.

* * *

The first friend I made at Summer Fields was another new boy that day, Caspar Fleming, son of Bond's creator Ian. Although neither of us knew it—Ian Fleming's own intelligence history was not then public—both of our parents were spies or former spies with a naval background. We walked around together until we found the school's World War II air-raid shelter, a long grassy mound with a padlocked iron door. We were both fascinated, but only he thought of picking the lock, and insisted he could get the tools to do so during the Christmas holidays. (It never happened.)

Caspar had the full collection of Bond books, of course, claimed to have given his dad the inspiration for one of the paperback covers, and would lend copies to anyone who asked. A storyteller himself, who would spin terrifying yarns about ghosts and banshees in the dormitory after lights out, Caspar was a strange, unhappy creature, pale with a shock of black hair. His parents were much older than mine, his mother in her late forties and his father in his fifties. Both of them were hard-drinking, heavy-smoking socialites with little time to spare for their son. He told extravagant stories about his famous father, but even then I had the sense that at least some of them were fantasies.

Caspar also claimed to own an enormous collection of guns, swords, crossbows and hunting knives, a claim which may have been true: he was taken to Juvenile Court a few years later when a number of pistols and a quantity of ammunition were found in his study at Eton.

I lost touch with Caspar at thirteen when we both left Summer Fields, but chanced upon him again at a Kensington antiques market five years later. He had a stall selling Nazi memorabilia. He remembered me and we talked briefly, but he avoided all eye contact, staring at the floor or at his shoes most of the time. He looked like the acid casualties I'd encountered, an increasingly common phenomenon in 1970. Whether because of drugs or not, he was, it transpired later, deeply depressive. I was saddened but not surprised in 1975 when I pulled an item off the Reuters wire reporting that, despite a series of hospital treatments including electro-convulsive therapy, he had killed himself. He was twenty-three.

In my last few years at Summer Fields, life eased a little. School was still a prison: even now I can instantly summon up dread and misery by humming the first line of the hymn 'The day thou gavest, Lord, has ended', which began Sunday Evensong after your parent or relative dropped you off at the end of one of the carefully rationed days out. But I had begun to conform to the system, or rather, I had worked out a method of locking my feelings of fear and entrapment and hatred away, creating a separate, socialised self. It worked in that the beatings, at least, grew fewer. And I continued to try to free my mind from its physical confines by reading constantly, beginning a lifelong addiction to PG Wodehouse and Charles Dickens, both discovered somewhere around my eleventh birthday. For a little while at least, you could be on the road with Mr Pickwick or with Lord Emsworth at Blandings Castle, and somehow no longer at school.

The other escape was through music. Transistor radios were forbidden, but they were tiny and easily smuggled, so most boys had one: mine was a birthday present in 1963, around the time of The Beatles' first LP. Especially at night, under the pillow, the transistor gave you the illusion of freedom: the illicit sounds of Fabulous 208, Radio Luxembourg, so different from the staid tones of the BBC Home Service and the Light Programme. On early Sunday evening, though, everyone listened to the BBC's *Pick of the Pops*, with the transplanted Australian disc jockey Alan Freeman counting down the top twenty. The charts in the early 1960s were a constant battle between the listening tastes of the young and the middle-aged, so our favourites kept being pushed out of the top spot by yodelling expatriate Australian Frank Ifield with 'I Remember You', or The Bachelors with 'I Believe', or Ken Dodd's soupy 'Tears for Souvenirs'.

It's hard now, when you can stream any sort of music at will, to explain what pop meant in the early 1960s. It had been lurking for a while, but something massive was changing. I remember listening to the radio in the summer holidays of 1962, when everyone seemed to be called Bobby: Bobby Vee, Bobby Rydell, Bobby Vinton, Bobby Darin. The Bobbies all seemed to have near-identical neat pompadours and near-identical shiny white teeth, and crooned near-identical high-school love songs of near-identical blandness. The wild boys of 1950s rock'n'roll were roaming free no more: Elvis was drafted into the army, then into schlock Hollywood movies; Little Richard got religion in Australia, threw his diamond rings into the Hunter River, and became a gospel singer; Jerry Lee Lewis was sidelined after marrying his thirteen-year-old cousin; and Chuck Berry was jailed for 'transporting a fourteen-year-old girl across a State line'. The bad boys were out of the picture, and the record industry, keen to woo Middle America, was back in control.

Then, just when complacency was setting in, came the British invasion, inspired by exactly the artists the record industry and the radio stations had tried to tame. Kids like John Lennon in Liverpool, Keith Richards south of London and Eric Burdon in Newcastle-on-Tyne had been buying American record imports, from Muddy Waters to Elvis and beyond, and soaking them up. What they'd heard was the roots of rock in rhythm and blues, all the way back to Chicago and the Mississippi Delta, and that raw power was what they were determined to make their own.

Imprisoned at school, I didn't just *want* rock'n'roll, I needed it. The Beatles and The Rolling Stones were proof that it didn't have to be like this: that the virtual jail I lived in, a world of short-back-and-sides haircuts and being punished for talking back, was subject to challenge. Look back at their early press conferences. The Beatles respond with snappy backchat and surreal gags to questions from middle-aged reporters. 'What do you call that haircut?' asks one journalist. 'Arthur,' Ringo replies. The Stones, for their part, were all sneer. Either way, both groups were made up of people only a few years older than me who were prepared to challenge the retired majors and wing-commanders for whom the War had never really ended, and who had held sway almost unchallenged since 1945.

From track one of the first Beatles album, 'I Saw Her Standing There', there was no crooning, no orchestral strings, no 'teen angels', no messing around. Paul McCartney had the vocal power turned up to max as he began to yell, 'Well, she was just seventeen; you know what I mean', and even if you were a pre-pubertal eleven-year-old, with no certainty about what he meant, you could have a damn good guess.

Besides, in those sheltered years, eleven was the age that I first remember finding out anything about sex. In a piece I wrote on the ABC website a few years ago, I put it this way:

> I owe my sex education to Christine Keeler.
>
> Not directly of course: I was eleven years old at the time the Profumo scandal convulsed Britain in 1963. I was on a fishing holiday with my father, in a big house in the north of Scotland shared with two other families, including several teenage boys and girls. In between tying flies and tramping across the heather, everyone—the adults and the teenagers—seemed to have only one topic of conversation, and Christine Keeler was it. My seven-year-old sister and I were the only ones unable to keep up.
>
> I remember chiefly the frustration of hearing jokes and not being able to understand the punchlines. But over the course of a week, and especially later when we got back to London and I was able to sneak a look at the newspapers, I started to get the gist.
>
> Keeler was a call-girl. Once I'd worked out what that meant, I could start to piece together the rest. She'd been sleeping with a man called John Profumo. He was the Secretary of State for War in the Conservative Government of Harold Macmillan. But Christine had also been sleeping with the Soviet military attaché in London, Yevgeny Ivanov.
>
> Was he using her to prise Britain's nuclear secrets out of the Minister as pillow-talk? The possibility was high in the minds of Britain's security

agency MI5. The affair led to the suicide of Christine Keeler's friend, and society pimp, Stephen Ward. He died in St Stephen's Hospital in London's Fulham Road: it was at the end of our street, and I remember seeing the pack of Fleet Street reporters and photographers gathered outside.

Sex sounded interesting. If rather dangerous.

It wasn't just the Profumo affair that started to open my eleven-year-old mind to the outside world in 1963. On 22 November, I was doing 'prep' (the English boarding school term for compulsory group homework) in the main hall, on a wooden bench scored with the initials of boys long gone, when I heard that US President Kennedy had been shot. Someone with an illicit pocket transistor radio had been listening on an earphone when the newsflash broke in, and he couldn't keep it to himself. The whisper went round the school within minutes.

For all the grubby details we've discovered about JFK since, at the time he seemed to represent a chance for youth, and hope under the shadow of The Bomb. The fear of atomic warfare, even for the young, was then pervasive. If you hadn't heard Bob Dylan's 'Talking World War III Blues', 'Masters of War' or 'Hard Rain', you'd certainly heard Peter, Paul and Mary's cover of 'Blowin' in the Wind'. Campaign for Nuclear Disarmament marchers carrying 'Ban The Bomb' placards were on television, led by Canon John Collins, a gentle man who stayed with his family in the same hotel as mine one holiday in Cornwall. The nuclear shadow seemed to loom inescapably over everything. So the killing of Kennedy seemed not just the death of a president, but also the removal of someone whose steady hand had staved off possible Armageddon during the Cuban Missile Crisis. Even at eleven, I read a paper every day and I had some inkling of that.

That year brought me other big changes. For the first couple of years at Summer Fields, I spent the longer school holidays back in Malaysia. It meant solo journeys on BOAC Comets, adding air miles to my logbook as a member of the BOAC Junior Jet Club, whose privileges included being asked up to the cockpit to sit behind the captain and watch him fly the plane. By eleven, I had a lot of air miles. But now my mother was back in England, while my father stayed on in Kuala Lumpur.

Professor Richard Aldrich of Warwick University, who knew my father, wrote to me that 'he ran the MI6 secret war against Indonesia in 1963'. This refers to the first year of Konfrontasi, President Sukarno's attempt to destroy the Federation of Malaysia, in which Malaysian, British and Australian forces ran guerrilla and propaganda operations in Borneo, including across Indonesian borders. Later, when Dad was back in the London station, the secret war would eventually succeed in blocking Sukarno's strategy, leading to his ousting, and indirectly freeing the military who led the coup against him to massacre as many as half a million communists.

My father never told me of his role in Konfrontasi in Borneo, though he did send me letters and postcards from Irian Jaya/West Papua, which was briefly under UN control in 1962–63, after being ceded by the Dutch. He told me later in life that he was not proud of the role he and the SIS had played in the handover of West Papua to Indonesia, but he died before telling me exactly why.

Apart from his letters and postcards, however, and that summer holiday in Scotland, we saw little of Dad at the time, and almost nothing of him and my mother together as parents. Although we were not yet aware of it, his job was one factor in the disintegration of my parents' marriage. It didn't help that he had also become infatuated with a married woman in Kuala Lumpur. My mother, understandably, had had enough, but did an admirable job of keeping the news from us. Whether in London or at school, I had no inkling of anything being wrong: soon, I thought, my parents would be back together at home, and all would return to normal.

I can't remember exactly when my parents broke the news to me and my sister Zoë that they were going to get a divorce, but they did it as gently as they could. We would stay with Mum in the same house, and Dad was going to move to a flat around the corner. My sister's memory of that day is clearer. In a letter to me, she writes:

> It was a Saturday afternoon. Dad had already taken you round to see the flat and then you came home and I was told. It was already dark and someone said, 'Oh look the circus is on the television' and I looked and saw a miserable elephant plodding around the ring and sensed that I should pretend to be thrilled and to have already forgotten what I'd been told. My chief concern was Daddy's flat—the only flats I knew of nearby were grimy Peabody [London Housing Association] ones & I thought he'd be unhappy there.

Our parents were very determined to do as little as possible that would embroil us in their troubles. While staying with Mum, we could visit Dad whenever we wanted, and they remained on friendly terms: I never remember them arguing in front of us. It was a shock, though, and hit me harder than I let on. My school reports for the time showed me suddenly dropping from near the top of the class in most subjects to the lower middle. I just felt the need to endure.

* * *

Whatever he'd been doing in Borneo, Dad was back in London at the end of 1963. I know because you don't forget seeing The Beatles. Dad and my godfather John Villiers took me and John's daughter Ann to see the group's Christmas concert at the Finsbury Park Astoria.

I often tell people that I *saw* The Beatles in concert twice. I have to be careful never to say that I really *heard* them. The Christmas concerts were more variety events than rock concerts as we know them today. The bill before the second half when The Beatles came on included a whole line-up of Brian Epstein's other managerial protégés, from Billy J Kramer and the Dakotas to Cilla Black, and you could mostly hear them, even though a substantial part of the audience was already in a state of screaming excitement. But this was before the invention of the Marshall Stack, the amplifier combination which made it possible for rock groups to be heard over even the loudest yelling. That meant that when The Beatles came on, you could hardly distinguish one song from another. I'm pretty sure they did 'Roll over Beethoven', 'Money' and 'Twist and Shout', because those were belters. But 'All My Loving'? 'Till There Was You'? History says they played them, but no-one in that audience would have known. It was wall-to-wall white noise from the dress circle to the stalls, and I give my father full credit, not only for taking me that year, but for braving the whole experience again the following Christmas.

A peculiar postscript: the 1963 Beatles-led bill was compered by Rolf Harris, the 1964 one by Jimmy Savile. The group that changed the 1960s, introduced by two of the twentieth century's most notorious British-based paedophiles.

Back at Summer Fields, some relief was in sight. The school got a new, young English and Latin teacher named Nick Aldridge. Tall and skinny, with a quiff, he was quite different from all the other masters, with their leather-elbowed tweed jackets, snuffboxes and pipes. Most of them had 'done something in the war'. Mr Aldridge was too young for that, still in his mid-twenties. And he was a livewire. He liked the same music we liked, introduced us to Buddy Holly, started a school pop group, unearthed a dusty old printing machine and taught interested boys (including me) how to set lead type and even print a magazine, talked to us almost as equals, and—most miraculously of all—as far as I know, never hit anyone.

And the end was at least in view. In 1965, I knew, would come the exams that would decide my next destination. When not lost in reading, I buried myself in intensive Latin and Greek study and memorised swathes of poetry which I regurgitated in school verse-reading competitions. That included a massive chunk of Oscar Wilde's *The Ballad of Reading Gaol*: 'He did not wear his scarlet cloak/For blood and wine are red'. My rendering caused the school chaplain, Reverend White, to take me aside and tell me that Wilde had been a Very Bad Man. No amount of questioning, however, would make him tell me how or why.

Summer Fields prided itself on cramming boys with the elements required to get into some of the most prestigious schools in Britain—Eton, Harrow, and Winchester in particular—and there was huge pressure from the school to do well in the Common Entrance Examination, taken at thirteen. I was good at Latin, fair at Greek, excelled in English, was passable at French and not good at maths. History I could manage by memorising, but mostly because it was taught by rote as a succession of dates: there being no context, it took me years before I could really see the point.

I also took the separate Westminster School Entrance Examination, and on being taken there for an interview, was almost sick with anticipation: at last, a school in the middle of a city, a place where I'd be able to walk outside and get on a bus or stroll up the street to a coffee bar. Freedom.

I was accepted at Eton, which I hadn't liked on my one visit, and then the acceptance from Westminster came through. My five years of durance vile were soon to end. Summer Fields, you not-so-Elysian Fields, goodbye.

Chapter 12

The First Turn of the Screw

MY PARENTS HANDLED the end of their marriage well, especially by the standards of that era, before no-fault divorce. The way divorce law was then framed had created a sordid little industry of 'private detectives' hired to take a staged photograph of the 'guilty' party in a Brighton hotel room with someone procured for the occasion to provide the necessary evidence to produce in court. Mum and Dad simply told us that sometimes parents just couldn't get on with each other anymore, but in their case, they could still be friends and it would make no difference to the way they loved us.

And it was true. The fact is that the three years after the divorce, from 1964 to 1966, may have been the ones when Dad was less of an 'absent father' to me than at any other time. He was based in London, with few trips away that I remember, and the promises our parents had made, including that we'd have free access to Dad in his flat around the corner, were kept. My mother had made new friends, like the Halls, with whom we often stayed at their big house in Oxfordshire, and even their ski chalet in France, and later the Bryants, in whose grounds in the hills near Oxford we actually rented a cottage for a while, where we went for weekends and holidays.

And during the holidays from Summer Fields, I had free rein to an extent that might shock modern 'helicopter parents'. I was allowed to take Zoë with me, unsupervised, on the bus to various destinations. We were strictly forbidden to put sixpence in the Pepsi machine outside the no. 31 bus depot at the end of the road, but it was an interdiction we routinely defied. As Zoë says, 'I've always been amused by the way we were fearful of Mum smelling it on our breath, as if we were drunks rolling home from the pub.'

We spent a huge amount of time in the Science Museum, with its vast array of interactive exhibits for children, and the Natural History Museum. I was allowed to go to Earl's Court for the Boat Show, the Motor Show and the Ideal Home Exhibition. I took Zoë in consecutive years to the Daily Mail Boys' & Girls' Exhibition—she reminds me now that the best year was the one when there were Daleks. We went to St Paul's together, trying out the Whispering Gallery and clambering up the ladder to peer out of the very top of Christopher Wren's great dome. Zoë says I told her that a threepenny bit dropped from that height would go straight through a man's skull, an urban myth she claims to have believed for decades. (To save you looking it up, air resistance explains why it doesn't happen.) I was full of stuff like that, from incessant reading of books like *Ripley's Believe It or Not* and *The Guinness Book of Records*.

I explored London on my red Dawes three-speed bicycle. At eleven, I still had the wooden toy sailing boat, named after Captain Cook's *Endeavour*, that I'd been given when I was six, and I'd go to Kensington Gardens to sail it on the Round Pond and admire the vast radio-controlled sloops and motor-torpedo-boats that adult nerds raced across the waters. Mum got our first car, a Mini station wagon with wood panels, and we sat in tailbacks on the road to Cornish holidays, having long stupid conversations as characters called Nigel and Daphne, inspired by BBC Radio's *Round the Horne*.

Australia was never far from my mind, for various reasons, including our regular visits to the Prince's Gate flat of my mother's great-aunt Ethel and her husband, the former Australian prime minister Stanley Bruce. 'Uncle S', as we called him, had stood in for my grandfather and given Mum away at the altar in 1948. The Bruces were childless themselves, and they'd taken my mother with them around war-ravaged Europe when she'd arrived in London from Victoria in the late 1940s.

Uncle S died when I was fifteen, still just too young to appreciate all his stories about Churchill, Earle Page and Billy Hughes, but old enough to appreciate his warm and engaging personality. Far from the caricature spats-wearing toff who lost his own seat when he lost government in 1929, he was a raconteur and a charmer: a fund of stories about sport, food, wine and Australian and international history. I remember that it was not always the political achievements that he relished in old age, or at least he showed appreciation for the things he thought might interest a small boy: among them, his trophy cabinet, made out of a piece of his winning Cambridge boat, and the silver tasting-cup, on a silver chain, of the exclusive Burgundy wine society, the Chevaliers du Tastevin.

But his post-political career, as an international diplomat and statesman, was no swan song: if anything, it was more substantial than his time in the Australian Parliament. He renegotiated the country's crippling loans with Britain, became president of the Montreux conference of the League of Nations, advised on the British abdication crisis, and constantly tried to ensure that Britain would give cast-iron guarantees to come to Australia's aid in the event of attack by Japan.

Stanley Bruce had been seriously wounded at Gallipoli, and his most surprising friendship was with Kemal Ataturk, who had commanded the troops on the other side. They negotiated a difficult League of Nations treaty together in the 1930s, and one of Uncle S' prized possessions was a solid-gold cigarette case that Ataturk had made for him, with their engraved initials interlaced, which now resides in the National Archives in Canberra: the Turkish ambassador and I were filmed holding it carefully in gloved hands for the Anzac anniversary in 2015.

As high commissioner and a member of Churchill's War Cabinet, Uncle S was the principal conduit between Britain and Australia throughout World War II. And after the war, pursuing his interest in eradicating starvation and poverty, he played a key part in the foundation of the United Nations' Food and Agriculture Organization, and became chairman of its World Food Council. I feel privileged to have known him.

The house my mother bought in 1955 had been on the outer edge of a decaying and deeply unfashionable neighbourhood. But as the 1960s became the Swinging Sixties, it was (though the word had not then been invented) 'gentrifying' fast, and King's Road, Chelsea was the place to be. Local shops were being replaced by record stores and 'men's boutiques', which the jazzman George Melly defined at the time by saying that in the latter, the salesman would ask: 'Shirt, sir? Measure your inside leg, sir?'

But much of the old remained. There was the Chelsea Public Library opposite the Fire Station, where my mother took us at least every week. And the Chelsea Bookshop, where we would go with the book tokens we were given by relatives at Christmas or on birthdays. The two middle-aged ladies who ran it—one was some sort of exiled Polish countess, I believe—were an odd combination of stern and indulgent, but they usually had recommendations for books just right for us. Mother would treat us to occasional lunches at Le Reve, a little, inexpensive French bistro. Afterwards, we'd go up the road to browse in a large and copiously stocked toyshop called Laffeaty's, either to gawp and think hopeful thoughts about Christmas, or to spend all our pocket money. On the way home, we'd walk past the magnificent blue-and-white-tiled Art-Deco Bluebird Garage, before passing the Ming Yuan Chinese restaurant, directly opposite my father's first-floor flat in Alexandra Mansions.

Apart from the looming dread of school as the end of holidays approached, and despite the divorce, life in Chelsea was good.

* * *

Christmas 1964, the year of *Beatles for Sale*, is spent at my aunt and uncle's house in Hampshire. I have 'Eight Days a Week' in my head as I sit in the bedroom I share with my father, trying to master the most abstruse tense in ancient Greek, the aorist, with the crucial Common Entrance Exam only months away. I'm not alone. My father is working his way through a pile of economics textbooks. And neither of us is enjoying it.

That's literally the only thing I know about Dad's role in the SIS from 1964 to late 1966: that he was on some sort of economics desk. But it was clear that if economics is, as the old line goes, 'The Dismal Science', it didn't suit Dad at all.

If I've given an Ian Fleming or John le Carré impression of John Colvin as a man, I've done him a disservice, because he was neither a square-jawed action hero by nature, nor a taciturn George Smiley. Being with him was usually a lot of fun. He was an extrovert—too extroverted, his colleague Alexis Forter told me much later in life, ever to rise to the very top of the SIS—and a party animal. He came alive in company, was witty and flirtatious, drank too much, smoked too much, and was never happier than when talking at length about politics, literature (he was almost obsessive about Proust) and whatever else caught his eye. Riding around London on the top of buses—the smoking deck—what caught his eye was often a 'verrrry pretty girl, look, over there'.

Where did we go on those double-deckers? Quite often to the movies. I remember the hilarity of *Cat Ballou* with Jane Fonda and Lee Marvin, a Laurel and Hardy/Harold Lloyd double bill, and a couple of Jack Lemmon films, along with *Let's Make Love*, in which Marilyn Monroe's rendition of 'My Heart Belongs to Daddy' should have had an X-rating all of its own: certainly an eye-opener for a twelve-year-old.

One night in the winter of 1964–65, Dad took me to see Spike Milligan in *Son of Oblomov*. It had started as *Oblomov*, a fairly turgid nineteenth-century Russian play about a man undergoing an existential crisis who decides to spend his whole life in bed. But it quickly became the hottest ticket in town when the producers changed the name and reworked the show because Spike was incapable of sticking to the script. He forbade the rest of the cast to stray from their lines, while he ad-libbed throughout. It must have been terrifying for the supporting cast, but for the audience, especially me, it was a glimpse of utter comic anarchy. Spike heckled the audience mercilessly. One of his tricks was to get a couple of minutes in, pick on a latecomer by chiding them for missing the beginning, then start the play again, ripping through the lines in a high-pitched voice like a tape at double-speed. And he constantly 'corpsed' (provoked) his fellow actors, leaving them either open-mouthed and goldfishing for a line or doubled up with laughter. Some of them didn't like it much—there was reputedly a very high cast turnover—and eventually Spike's swings between manic and depressive became too wild for the show to continue.

We also made trips to the East End to eat great Chinese food. Dad's experience in Malaysia, and later Saigon, meant that he had little time for the standard sweet-and-sour-pork/chow mein menus which local places like the Ming Yuan served up to Westerners. So we took the bus out to Limehouse, London's original Chinatown, to eat at the Old Friends and the New Friends, the best Chinese places in the city at the time. He taught me to use chopsticks, drink jasmine tea, and appreciate flavours I'd never encountered, such as ginger and garlic and coriander, and the texture of jellyfish and chicken feet and black tree-fungi. On the way,

I saw a side of London I'd not known before: twenty years after the war, whole blocks of empty space and rubble, the East End, still mostly unbuilt after the Luftwaffe bombed it.

On birthdays, however, my parents would get together in the most civilised fashion to take us to La Poule au Pot, a French restaurant in Pimlico started by a friend, David Hall, where I ate my first avocado and my first artichoke, among other rarities then almost unheard of in the British kitchen.

At Dad's flat, Zoë and I listened to comedy records. The genius of Shelley Berman, bits of whose stand-up monologues about hangovers ('My teeth itch', 'Stop fizzing, Alka-Seltzer'), or trying to navigate a department store switchboard to alert them to a woman hanging by her fingertips from their window ('Hullo, you don't know me but I work in the building across the street and I was looking out my window … Yes, lovely day isn't it … when I saw …'), my sister and I can still recite impromptu. And the deadpan joy of discovering Peter Cook's man in a raincoat on a park bench, EL Wisty: 'I could have been a judge, but I never 'ad the Latin,' and 'I'll tell you the interesting fact about the Arab. The interesting fact about the Arab is that he can go for a whole year on one grain of rice … No, that's the mosquito. I get those muddled up because they're next door to each other in the dictionary: mosquitos and mosques.' Thanks to EL Wisty, whose voice his resembled, I was never able to take John Major entirely seriously as the Prime Minister of the United Kingdom of Britain and Northern Ireland, no doubt a sign of my lifelong tendency to facetiousness, largely nurtured by Cook and Dudley Moore.

What's now called 'cool' was then called 'with-it', and my father was alarmingly with-it for a man in his forties. At a time when standard office wear was a white shirt and a suit, he was the first parent I ever saw in a pink shirt under his pinstripe worsted. Zoë and I and our cousins will never forget the hilarity of watching him, on the rear deck of a fishing smack off Cornwall in 1962, singing Chubby Checker's 'Let's Twist Again' while doing the dance. One day in 1965, he put a 45 on the turntable in the flat and played me The Who's new single, 'My Generation'. It was a bit disconcerting: by definition, that was supposed to be my thing. It was the *attitude* he liked: 'Why don't you all f-f-f-f-f-fade away'. It could be a bit difficult to start a teenage rebellion against a man like that.

Years later, after Dad died, his old friend and shipmate Rowan Ayers told me a story about how my father, aged eighteen, had put on a surrealist play in the wardroom of a Royal Navy cruiser in Scapa Flow, part of which involved standing with one foot in a bucket of water tearing up ten-shilling notes. I often wonder what sort of life he would have led if not for the navy and the war. Actor? Writer? Artistic enfant terrible?

Not that life with Dad was all idyllic. We spent one ghastly holiday in England's Lake District, in a village called, unprepossessingly, Boot. It was as bad as it sounds. We were supposed to be trout-fishing, but few trout seemed willing to cooperate. I can't do better in describing that holiday than to quote my sister Zoë, blogging in 2010:

> My father did once manage to catch my brother when hurling out his line. Instead of hitting the water, his hook plunged right through the flesh between thumb and forefinger on my brother's right hand. My father reacted with an uncharacteristic display of Edwardian outrage when my brother quite naturally let out a loud yell of pain. 'No son of mine should ever admit to pain', he shouted, an outburst that must surely have been the product of frustration after so many wasted, fish-free hours.
>
> My father was in the grip of one of his periodic bouts of hypochondria—centring, on this occasion, on his digestive system—so instead of going anywhere we stayed at 'home' and listened to him groan.
>
> Perhaps it was the food that did it—it turned out to be unspeakable (far worse even than school). It was provided in the upstairs dining-room of the pub across the road from our cottage, but after a day or two of being faced with dishes that played variations on the colour khaki and always arrived cold and covered by a slick of something that looked very like the stuff filling the Gulf of Mexico at the moment, we gave up going.
>
> There was an alternative—the one and only edible item offered for sale by the village shop. It was a locally made substance called Kendall's Mint Cake and, according to its wrapper, it was exceptionally nutritious. How lucky it was, since we ate it for breakfast, lunch and dinner every day until we were released—I mean, until it was time to go home. At least my brother and I did. My father ate nothing. Progressively more convinced that his days were numbered, he would sit on the front step

in the weak afternoon sunshine, holding his head, sighing, very close to tears. My brother and I, clutching our slabs of Kendall's, would sit on each side of him, munching steadily, trying, always unsuccessfully, to think of something that might cheer him up.

I should point out that I am not being heartless about my father's sufferings—he really was all right. When the 'holiday' was over and we returned down south, he consulted a number of Harley Street specialists and not one of them could find anything wrong at all. Eventually, dispirited and still deep in the clutches of his symptoms, he stepped out of yet another great man's consulting rooms and into a nearby pub. 'You look rough, guv', the landlord informed him, by way of greeting. Once again my father unfurled his tale of woe. The landlord listened and then reached behind him for a packet of tablets. 'These should fix you up', he said. 'They're made in Switzerland and they worked wonders for me.' And they did—my father took one that day and never had to take another. He had to have them in the house though. That was all that mattered. If he didn't have them in the bathroom cupboard, the wracking pains returned.

I believe that was the summer of 1965, when I was thirteen and my sister nearly ten. It must have been early the next year when my mother and sister went to visit relatives in Australia, leaving me in London: I was due back at Westminster for the spring term, and so was unable to join them. As a consolation prize, my father took me to Paris for a long weekend, my first proper introduction to the city. We ate in good small restaurants, where I was allowed to drink a little wine. It snowed, but we walked along the Left Bank anyway, and browsed the bookstalls, visited the Louvre and the Jeu de Paume Gallery (the vastly superior forerunner of the Musée d'Orsay), and went one night to an extraordinary, smoky basement nightclub which I believe was called Le Canari, run by an old Gitanes-smoking ruffian who had certainly done something secret with my dad during or after the war. There were no half-naked ladies or other signs of outright vice, but there was something fantastically, as the French say, *louche*, about the place, and my father, though not always louche himself, somehow fitted right in. He had something of the chameleon about him, obviously, whether by nature or by training: the spy's ability to be at home in, or fade into the background of, wherever he was.

The next summer was very different. It was hot, for one thing. We went to the Algarve, a stretch of Portuguese coastline then almost undiscovered by tourists. The SIS had an earlier retirement age than the Foreign Office—fifty-five—and Dad's old colleague Christopher Wren had retired to the Algarve with his French wife, Marciane, an acidulous woman who took a fairly instant dislike to me and Zoë. She described me, my father told me later, as 'ingrat', and made plain that she understood the French word to mean both ungrateful and ungracious. I was a pasty, resentful, fourteen-year-old, sure enough, but probably no more so than the average. I feel I was more shy and gawky than obstreperous, but to a childless couple like the Wrens I probably seemed an excrescence.

I was admittedly, by this time, already steeped in the attitudes of what pop had become—a new wave, now called rock, in which lyrics were suddenly as often about contempt and dislike as about love. John Lennon had written 'Nowhere Man', The Kinks were doing social criticism with 'Well-Respected Man' and 'Dedicated Follower of Fashion', The Who released 'Substitute', full of anger about class and money, and 'I'm a Boy', which seemed to be an early exploration of transgender issues. And Dylan's songs had turned merciless, mocking the clueless Mr Jones, or bitterly telling false friends what a drag it was to see them. The curled lip was everywhere: on the white laminate front of the raised demonstration desk in one of the Westminster School science labs, someone had written in large letters in indelible ink 'Hey! You! Get Offa My Cloud!' directly below where the master stood. We were the baby boomers, though I don't think I knew the phrase then, and we were out to show that we were not our parents' generation. But we were also, I'm sure, just another bunch of obnoxious teenagers.

An added reason for feeling inadequate and resentful was puberty itself. Also staying in the Wren's place in Portugal was Helen Chavchavadze, divorced wife of an exiled Georgian prince who just happened to be a senior CIA man. Helen was a beautiful and intelligent woman who, it has emerged in recent years, had been one of the many lovers of US President Kennedy. She and my father conducted a fairly consistent flirtation throughout our stay. His evident ease with women could hardly have been a starker contrast to my tongue-tied, single-sex-schooled inability to know how to talk to her daughter Maria, or Moussie, who was my age and staying there too.

There was a pool, and a beach, and I got sunstroke and retreated into my room. There I discovered that someone had left an enormous collection of science fiction, time-honoured retreat of the tongue-tied, shoe-gazing geek. So that was the summer I discovered Isaac Asimov, Ray Bradbury and Kurt Vonnegut, to the soundtrack of the only record in the place I thought worth listening to, an album of Nat King Cole.

Roll on those lazy, hazy, crazy days of summer.

* * *

My father was unquestionably a man of enormous physical courage, but he had been brought up in a hard school, and much as he undoubtedly loved his children, he didn't always have the sense that that love had to be consistently expressed by actually being with them—after all, his own parents had sailed to Australia when he was fourteen, leaving him at Dartmouth for the next five years. The holiday in the Algarve sun was the last time we were going to be seeing him for a while. He had accepted a new posting, and, his memoir *Twice around the World* later revealed, he had accepted it over a lunch a full year before.

My father was going to be the British 'consul-general' in Hanoi, the capital of North Vietnam, a country then under heavy bombardment by the USA, and one to which no-one else in his family could possibly go. It was not only dangerous and unhealthy in every way: there could, from the point of view of a teenager who read about Vietnam in the papers every day, be no possible guarantee that he would survive it and return to be our dad again. Quoted in an academic paper about the consulate-general, one retired holder of the post wrote to the academic Simon Kear in 1996 that 'it was known in the office as the worst post in the world at least ten years before I got there (that is in terms of acute discomfort, health risks, limitations, isolation and general beastliness)'.

If my feelings about my father's actions at this time may seem a little jaundiced, it's because his memoir contains a number of what are too easy to interpret as references to the delight with which he left his family behind. When offered the job, he 'hesitated for no more than 24 hours: the factors [of fascination with the job itself] described earlier—and some regard for married colleagues—made agreement inevitable. The decision became a liberating one'. And, he wrote, 'As usual, "with the first turn of the screw, all debts are paid", the sailor's adage here referring less to financial than sentimental dues, to commitments joylessly and for too long endured.'

It was hard not to feel, reading that years later, that his children were those joylessly endured commitments, and that he left, in other words, without a backward glance, no doubt as he and his father and his father's father, servants of Empire all, had been trained to do—as I suppose I was being trained to do, although the Empire-builder treatment wasn't really working in my case. My sister Zoë, however, once bearded him about this passage, and says that he was genuinely shocked when he realised how it read to us.

What was worst about Hanoi in practice, though, from the perspective of those he left behind, was that for more than a year, we would never be quite sure if he was safe and well, or a victim of a stray American bomb (not unusual) or a misfiring Vietnamese surface-to-air missile (also far more common than the North liked to admit). Letters were limited to once a month: any reply I sent might be received up to three months after his original missive had been dispatched. From having two loving—albeit separated—parents, Zoë and I were, suddenly and without much warning, virtually the children of a one-parent family. That was hard on us, and hard on my mother, but Dad was up and away.

Chapter 13

Faux Diplomacy

DESPITE THE UBIQUITY of the Vietnam War in the media, my sister and I could only really guess at the dangers Dad was undergoing in Hanoi. His letters were descriptive but jocular, and gave little hint of the reality of life in a city under massive, and more or less continuous, bomber attack. It wasn't till the publication of his memoir, years later, that I read this vivid description of one raid in the US operation known as 'Rolling Thunder':

> The air-raid sirens sounded, and we walked out onto the balcony. As we stood there seven or eight United States Thunderchief jet fighter-bombers, flying at scarcely more than roof-top height and no more, it seemed, than 100 yards away, shot across our vision at what appeared—so tight was the space in which the whole incident was framed between houses and sky—enormous speed. They had come on us suddenly out of nowhere, the hard, grey, sleek aircraft, in superb formation at 600 mph, disappearing for an instant behind the trees and buildings that lay between us and the thermal power plant less than one mile to the south, and then quickly climbing clear and away. As they had hurtled past, so close it seemed we could almost touch them or call to the pilots, we had seen the rockets fired from the pods under their

> wings. Almost simultaneously, such lights as were on in the apartment went out, the fan stopped turning, and a column of dust, smoke and flame rose from the direction of the power station. (As the planes had penetrated the city's defences by coming in under the radar screen, the first anti-aircraft batteries opened up only when the raiders had not only departed but were probably twenty miles away.) As we were shortly to observe, the performance of this squadron disposed of every Communist or other illusion about the laxity of American bombing or the imprecision of U.S. bombing techniques.
>
> The all-clear wailed: stillness descended. The apartment, without the touch of air from the revolving fan, was already crushingly hot. 'I wonder what the strong-room will feel like in mid-August? A bit warm, I should think.' 'Not very nice. I hope you've got your Right Guard, Geoffrey.'

Although I didn't know until the mid-1970s that my father was a member of MI6, I was never under any illusion in the late 1960s that his duties as consul-general in Hanoi were actually consular. Consuls and consuls-general occupy themselves with the issuing of visas and matters of trade. During the Vietnam War, very few North Vietnamese travelled to the UK, and vice versa, so the traffic in visas and the job of looking after expats in trouble was minuscule, and trade was similarly negligible. What I was told was that, having had a series of jobs with the title of third, then second, then first secretary (political) in the Foreign Office, he would now be doing a similar job of political reporting from Hanoi. Even years later, after he told me of his real affiliation, he maintained that it was only because of the particular conditions of the war, especially the intensified bombing of the North, that an SIS officer had been appointed to the post. Now, however, even this has emerged as a cover story.

In his biography of Daphne Park, *Queen of Spies*, one of my father's successors in the post, Paddy Hayes, puts it baldly.

> The British consulate-general in Hanoi was no ordinary diplomatic outpost. Though described as a consulate-general, it was in fact an SIS spy station. Described even more accurately, it was an intelligence outpost concealed inside a barely functioning faux diplomatic mission in the capital city of a country at war.

From the very beginning of its operation, the SIS paid for half the mission's budget, and at least one member of the two-person consulate was a trained full-time spy. But what could such a person achieve in a city where he was not even permitted to ride a bicycle, and where his ability to go on foot was heavily circumscribed? Because of Britain's non-recognition of North Vietnam, my father's position as consul-general was not formally recognised by the host country. 'The post was not accredited to anyone,' my father wrote in his memoir. 'Even the Mayor of Hanoi would refuse to receive me if I attempted to arrange a meeting; my predecessor had never had official dealings with him during his stay in Hanoi.'

Back in London, in my second year at Westminster, I received letters from Dad, sent from Hanoi through the diplomatic bag, but even these were necessarily infrequent. Indeed, the very first of them made clear why the correspondence would be so sparse. It described how my father, along with the diplomatic bag itself, had entered the country in an ancient and battered 1930s Stratoliner run by the International Control Commission, an organisation that was the one link between North Vietnam and the West. He spared me some of the details, such as that one previous flight had been shot down 'in error' by North Vietnamese anti-aircraft fire, while another had crashed, killing all on board. What he did mention was the presence in the cabin of a large live goose named Alice, which was being flown in for the French ambassador's Christmas dinner. His letter also laid out the route to Saigon, with stops in Cambodia and Laos, but omitted the story of how the ICC flight, deprived of fuel because of a coup attempt in Vientiane, had sat on the tarmac under threat of attack if it didn't take off within three hours.

It's a story he told later, with characteristic dry wit, in print:

> The air crew, gallant but hysterical, reminded their audience of occasions on which they had been forced to land at Hanoi in the middle of American air raids or subjected to direct DRV [Democratic Republic of Vietnam, the North] surface-to-air missiles or, once, forced down by United States aircraft, dangers now increased by the temporary restriction of the beacon to three, not fifteen minutes. One would have preferred, as so often, ignorance, but the audience was captive. As we lolled among the bushes ten yards from the aircraft, a co-passenger,

> elegant in white silk suit, pointed in immaculate French to the dangers of our position: 'We should sit in the airport building'. 'What airport building?' 'There, of course', he replied, indicating a rattan hut gaping with holes and leaning to one side. 'But what dangers do you fear?' 'Dangers! My dear, there are communists', the word spoken with fear and loathing, 'on the other side of that hedge'. My interlocutor was, it emerged, a senior Polish delegate of the commission.

Poland, need I add, was a member of the Soviet Bloc, and thus a communist country, at the time.

It was no doubt considerate of my father to spare his teenage son the worst of the details, but there was no escaping a constant nagging sense of fear. The Vietnam War was almost inescapable, from newspapers and TV bulletins and discussion shows, to the pop charts. This was the time when 'escalation' became a buzzword, as the American troop presence in the country went from 185 000 to 385 000 over the course of 1966. What had been a team of US 'advisers' under President Kennedy was now a full-scale war-fighting army under President Lyndon Baines Johnson.

Vietnam had seemed a small cloud on the horizon during my first year at Westminster School, where I arrived in the autumn of 1965, but it was already growing closer and darker by the summer of 1966, even before Dad told us he was going to Hanoi. It was the year of Country Joe's 'I Feel Like I'm Fixin' to Die Rag' and Donovan's 'Universal Soldier'. But even the pop charts battlefield was contested. On the other side of the argument, to the disgust of the anti-war movement, the dirge-like 'Ballad of the Green Berets', by Staff Sergeant Barry Sadler, a hymn to US militarism, managed five weeks at number one in the USA.

There were no British troops in Vietnam, but Britain was still a nuclear-armed superpower, in its own eyes at least. The threat of nuclear war was still ever-present in the culture, in the form, to take one of many examples, of Barry McGuire's bleak and strident song 'Eve of Destruction'. At the end of 1965, during my first term at Westminster School, the BBC banned a film it had commissioned from the director Peter Watkins, *The War Game*, a drama made to look like a quasi-documentary about the UK in the aftermath of a Soviet nuclear strike. It was the classic censorship own-goal, drawing far more attention to the issue than it might otherwise have received, and ensuring that the film, which was a justifiably frightening piece of work, would for decades be a sought-after rarity at film clubs and festivals overseas. (It would not actually be shown on the BBC until 1985.)

At school, the tolling of Big Ben every quarter of an hour, just a couple of hundred metres away, day and night, could seem a macabre reminder: maps of where a nuclear holocaust might strike in London always put the Houses of Parliament at ground zero. I'd be exaggerating to suggest it was a constant preoccupation, but in a school where debate and engagement with current affairs were encouraged from the moment you arrived, it had a tendency to lurk in your mind.

Still, life went on, and I could already feel that my next five years were bound to be happier than my last.

* * *

Westminster was such a reprieve, after Summer Fields, that the relative privations of being a new boy had been easy to take. The overriding feeling at the beginning was simple relief that I would never be beaten again. I might conceivably be expelled, but never beaten. Westminster had abolished all corporal punishment several years before, along with its archaic top-hat-and-tails uniform—you wore a grey suit, a white or pale-blue shirt, and a black or blue tie: anonymous enough, in an area which housed many Civil Service departments as well as the parliament, to prevent you from standing out. Many other major schools still practised corporal punishment at the time. Some of them still let seventeen- and eighteen-year old boys, as well as masters, carry it out. When I saw Lindsay Anderson's *If...* in 1968, with its depiction of just such a place, at which armed revolt breaks out against its gross sadism and the enforcement of absolute discipline, I knew people at other Great Public Schools for whom it was practically a documentary.

Westminster, under the laissez-faire and amiably distant leadership of headmaster John Carleton, was, for its time, probably the most liberal and free-thinking of the major public schools of the 1960s. There was technically something called 'fagging', but it was nothing like the licensed abuses practised elsewhere. At other schools, a first-year would 'fag'—run errands, make tea or coffee, toast crumpets over the fire—for a boy in his last year, a role which could also, depending on the senior boy, involve floggings for stepping out of line; some senior boys were also reputed to sexually abuse their fags. This kind of individual fagging had been abolished at Westminster in favour of a collective system: manning the toasters for your school house at mealtimes for a week, washing up the milk bottles, or being on wake-up duty, which just meant going round the dormitories and studies in the morning rousing people out of their beds.

There was a compulsory Combined Cadet Corps, the prospect of entering which in my second year I frankly dreaded. Boys serving in it seemed to spend all their free time blacking their boots or applying pipe-clay to their belts. I also, with my broken arm getting more deformed as I grew, feared a repeat of the humiliations of gym class at Summer Fields. But my timing was lucky: before that could happen, 'Corps' became voluntary, and was eventually phased out altogether.

I was placed in a house called Liddell's, named after the father of Alice Liddell, she of *Alice in Wonderland*. Before becoming dean of Christ Church at Oxford, where CL Dodgson (who used the pen-name Lewis Carroll) taught mathematics and had a photographic studio, Liddell had been headmaster of Westminster. The house named after him, however, had only been founded in 1956. It was put together as an afterthought out of existing school property, rather than being purpose-built, so that physically it was not so much a house as a higgledy-piggledy collection of houses, full of awkward little staircases, tiny, almost secret rooms, and narrow passageways. In its centre was the arch by which you entered Little Dean's Yard, the school's quadrangle, from Dean's Yard proper, the administrative centre of the great medieval abbey in whose shadow we all lived, worked and studied. Our daily lives were mostly lived within the Westminster Abbey grounds, and we walked to morning service in the abbey's South Transept through its ancient cloisters. Before my voice broke, I sang in the abbey, just one small treble somewhere up the back in a Westminster Choral Society performance of Bach's *St Matthew Passion*.

Meals were taken in College Hall, a medieval refectory which had once belonged to the abbot of Westminster. 'Up School' was where assemblies were held, the film society screened movies, and plays were staged. The 'School' of 'Up School' was a long, high-ceilinged building which had been the monks' dormitory as far back as the eleventh century, and, more recently, had been restored after German incendiary bombing in the Blitz. It was here, acting in school plays, that I was taught to 'project' my voice: if the director, standing at the back wall of this vast room, couldn't hear you, you weren't doing it right. Later, elocution, emphasis and projection were skills I didn't really have to learn as a broadcast journalist: acting and poetry readings had prepared me from an early age.

The housemaster at Liddell's, Charles Keeley, was, like my father, a man in his mid-forties, but he seemed much older. He smoked a pipe almost constantly, and perhaps because of the effect of smoke on his vocal chords, spoke in a near-whisper. He was certainly not a harsh man, though I had my run-ins with him over time, but compared to his predecessor, Stephen Lushington, he was regarded by some of the older boys in Liddell's as almost tyrannical. This was because Lushington had had a reputation as being astonishingly lax. In this all-male school, he was rumoured to have walked into a boy's study to find him having sex with a girl. Lushington quietly withdrew, saying only 'Lock the door next time.' During his tenure, Liddell's had also acquired a reputation for marijuana use.

Charles Keeley was made of slightly sterner stuff, in that he did at least try to impose some discipline, but he was an ineffectual man, and besides, it was a difficult time and place to be a disciplinarian. This was, after all, in the middle of London at the beginning of the youth revolution.

If our movements during the school day were largely confined to the abbey grounds, weekends and the late afternoon and early evening were pretty free. Among my more salubrious pursuits, I spent a lot of time browsing in Charing Cross Road bookshops, looking at pictures in the Tate and National Galleries, and, when I could get Keeley's permission, which was generally not hard, going to Sadler's Wells to see if I liked operas (I found after three or four visits that I didn't), and to the Royal Court and National theatres, both of which sold extremely cheap tickets to school students. There was also a lot of sitting and talking about poetry, politics and sex with friends over cappuccinos in a grubby Italian café in Tothill Street.

Further away there was a café in Strutton Ground, but boys with slightly feminine looks, as I had at the time, tended to avoid that because 'everybody knew' that a couple of men there were in the habit of trying to pick up Westminster boys. There's an old joke about the London Tube—'Is this Cockfosters?' 'No, it's mine'—which reflected an unpleasant reality. Being felt up by older men on the Underground was a regular hazard. I am never particularly surprised by stories in the British papers about 1960s paedophile rings in Dolphin Square, because I knew a couple of boys who were lured back there for a coffee, only to beat a hasty retreat when presented with a pile of pornographic magazines.

When I went to see *The Graduate* at a fairly empty afternoon showing in a cinema in Victoria, aged fifteen, I moved seats because a middle-aged man had sat down next to me and was running his hand up my thigh. I moved again, twice, and each time he followed me and did it again. I was about to tell him loudly to leave me alone when an usher, alerted by my movements around the theatre, came over and demanded to see my ticket. I went through my pockets but couldn't find it. The usher took me out to the foyer to see the manager, who threatened to call the police. In a cold sweat, I tried repeatedly to explain what had happened, to stony disbelief: failure to produce the ticket had convinced the manager that I must be lying. After several panicky minutes, a final check yielded the crucial ticket stub among schoolboy pocket-detritus, and only then was I off the hook. By now I had missed a good quarter of an hour of the movie, so their offer to let me back in (not a hint of an apology or a free ticket to another showing) seemed paltry.

To make matters worse, they demanded I go back in with them to identify the molester. By now, in addition to the cold sweat, I was shaking—I suppose I was in mild shock, from the real fear, before I found the ticket, that the police would be called. The last thing I wanted was further confrontation. The manager was insistent, saying he needed to know who the man was to stop him doing it again, but I refused and fled. It was a small enough incident, but I think of it whenever I hear of a woman being blamed for not reporting sexual abuse, or not reporting it soon enough.

My friends and I worked out fairly quickly which pubs to avoid because masters drank there, and which pubs outside that radius would turn a blind eye to the fact that we were blatantly under-age. If you were desperate for a pint out of hours (most pubs in those days had to shut for a few hours in the afternoon), there was even a bar on the westbound platform of Sloane Square Tube station which not only asked no questions about your age but had an all-day licence. This usually involved a double misdemeanour: under-age drinking *and* fare evasion.

In the evenings, in prep time, there was also the trick of getting Keeley's permission to go and see a play, but going to see Jimi Hendrix or Eric Clapton instead. For all my transgressions, I did not, however, start smoking cigarettes until I was sixteen (still horribly early, and something I'll always regret), and I never got offered either grass or hash, let alone anything stronger, until well after I'd left Westminster, so in that regard presumably the school would have counted Charles Keeley a success.

My passion at the school, and the area in which I excelled, was English. I had not one but two inspiring English masters: Jim Cogan and John Field. They could hardly have been more different.

Jim Cogan was calm and uncompromising, a phlegmatic man who had picked up the habit, while teaching at the University of Kingston, Jamaica, of calling you 'man' while critiquing your work. Asked whether he thought *The Lord of the Rings* could be classified as literature, he replied, 'I've got no time for whimsy, man,' which indicated clearly how uninterested he was in ingratiating himself with a bunch of fifteen- and sixteen-year-olds, but which somehow seemed to increase our respect for him. Almost everyone Jim taught tended to be infected with the 'man' virus, somewhat in the way that the word 'dude' spread through youth culture in the 1990s and early 2000s. But he was highly analytical and extremely rigorous, particularly about Shakespeare. By insisting we read aloud, constantly taking each line apart and explicating archaic words, he brought the Elizabethan and Jacobean eras alive in the high, book-lined library/classroom in which he taught us through the second half of the 1960s.

John Field, by contrast, was energised and full of enthusiasm, whether for Classicists like Milton or Romantics like Keats, always pushing, pushing, pushing to find the emotion and sensibility behind a poem or a piece of prose. One of the most inspiring hours of my school life was spent discussing one of Blake's *Songs of Innocence and Experience*: 'The Sick Rose'.

O rose, thou art sick.
The invisible worm,
That flies in the night
In the howling storm,

Has found out thy bed
Of crimson joy:
And his dark secret love
Does thy life destroy.

Interrogating us each around the table, Field questioned not only every line but every word of this deceptively simple poem. By the end, there was an ambiguity in every line: was the worm the devil? Original sin? Sex? Was the rose a flower? A girl? The barmaid at The Rose and Crown (as Germaine Greer once jokingly suggested)? What does the end of the poem mean? That the inevitable end of childhood brings with it the inevitability of death itself? That sexuality is both 'crimson joy' and destruction? These questions and so many more opened the poem out, appropriately enough, like a flower.

There were some boys who walked out of that class thinking that Field was over-interpreting, that the whole thing was self-indulgent. For me, it was a brain explosion, almost psychedelic in the way it opened up every great poem I read from then on. It was the moment that I first saw the point of literary criticism, and decided that English literature was the subject I wanted to pursue: to university and, if necessary, beyond. I began by immersing myself in Blake, but soon discovered that the way of thinking I had just learned was applicable to anyone from Andrew Marvell to TS Eliot, for that was the year I also first read 'The Love Song of J Alfred Prufrock'. It would be a year or two before I got to 'The Waste Land', and realised what a mass of Western and Eastern culture I would have to absorb before I understood even half of it, but in retrospect, I can see that I was on my way.

John Field was also the driving force behind the school's drama productions. I had no sporting abilities, but I did like acting, and acting was important at Westminster. The sons of Richard Attenborough and Jack Hawkins were both there, and I recall spotting their fathers' faces, so familiar from films like *The League of Gentlemen* and *Guns at Batasi*, beyond the footlights during a performance of—was it Max Frisch's *The Fire Raisers*, or Ben Jonson's *Bartholomew Fayre*? I was in both, as well as Richard Brinsley Sheridan's *The School for Scandal*, and a play called *The Happiest Days of Your Life*, in which I was given the part played by Margaret Rutherford in the film. I enjoyed it all up to a point, but I was late to puberty, and by 1968, when my slightly girlish features and still half-unbroken voice meant I was getting only female parts, I think I was getting sick of it. This expressed itself in increasing attacks of stage fright which eventually made up my mind to stop auditioning. I was prone to this fear for the next thirty or more years, though oddly never on radio: only on stage or on camera with a live audience. Then, some time around my fiftieth birthday, for no apparent reason, it just stopped. I do public speaking engagements and TV talk shows now without a qualm or even a raised heartbeat. After decades of anxiety, the quality of not giving a damn, after so many years, is strangely liberating.

* * *

Almost throughout 1967, Dad was in Hanoi. At that time, even in Britain, which was giving the USA tacit support but making it clear there was no question of sending troops, opposition to the war was growing. Our elders saw us as a generation who felt more kinship with our age group—particularly in the USA—than with our own nationality, and maybe they were right.

Personally, I felt divided about Vietnam. Plenty of my contemporaries had anti-war and even pro-Viet Cong posters on their walls, but I had heard far too much, from my own reading and from my father's table talk, to have any illusions about Ho Chi Minh and his government in Hanoi. On the other hand, I didn't think much of the government in the South, and enough had already been revealed about American involvement in the 1963 coup against President Diem to make me doubt any US claims of supporting democracy and the rule of law. It seemed far too much like a war between one kind of dictatorship and another. My father wasn't there for me to argue these questions with. He was being bombed, or watching others being bombed, every day. Would he come back? Or would one of those rockets go astray, leaving him to be buried in a foreign field? On one level, I just wished the war would be over, almost regardless of how.

The occasional letter from my father didn't always help. One of the early ones described how he'd been walking back to his residence one day when the air-raid sirens sounded. He had heeded the instructions of a Vietnamese air-raid warden and jumped into an 'air-raid shelter'. This, in his description, consisted of a cylinder set just over a metre deep into the ground. As he was 185 centimetres tall, this required considerably more contortions than for Vietnamese men at this impoverished time, who were on average a good 30 centimetres shorter. Once you were in the shelter, Dad wrote, the warden would cover it with a heavy concrete lid, and you were stuck. There was usually water in the bottom of the cylinders, they were frequently infested with frogs and mosquitoes, and there was an occasional snake. That one time Dad obeyed the order to get in, the warden failed to return on his rounds and remove the lid until an hour or more after the all-clear had sounded. There and then, my father told me, he resolved to react to air-raid sirens by ignoring all instructions and walking home as fast as possible. In practical terms, his residence was probably not really any safer than the street, because the North Vietnamese had refused the British permission to erect their own air-raid shelter, but he was determined never to get into one of those holes again.

I knew also that he had had severe dental problems, and had been unable to go to Saigon to get them fixed, so he ended up having the work done in difficult circumstances in Hanoi. I didn't know until much later that this involved the removal of two abscessed teeth without anaesthetic—all anaesthetics were reserved for the war effort. He described the process in his memoir:

> I took a bottle of Haig Gold Label whisky from the reserves and, seated in the squalid gloom of the dining room, began gradually from a tumbler to reduce its level until, at 11 o'clock, about three-quarters—or such was my misty estimate—had been consumed. Arms on the shoulders of Dong and the blind gardener, I was then escorted, feet somewhat at the trail, to the Ford Escort, the driver's mouth agape. The pain of the subsequent proceedings must have been sensibly diminished by this measure. It did not seem so at the time, and the aftermath was even worse than recovery from the older type of general anaesthetic. But the business was, after all, over.

Hanoi was a city of bicycles, but my father was denied permission to import or buy a bicycle. His movements, and those of most diplomats, were constrained to walking, except on the monthly visits to the airport, for which the consulate's Ford Escort was allowed just enough of a petrol ration for the return journey, sometimes hardly even that. In a secret despatch in late 1966, he wrote that the consulate was down to its last 18 litres of petrol, and that neither he nor the French (normally in a better position) had any immediate prospect of a refill.

How does a spy operate within these extremely tight constraints? Dad's memoir, tightly vetted as it was by the SIS, nowhere acknowledges that spying was his business, but it gives quite a few clues to how he worked. His diplomatic status was anomalous and officially non-existent as far as the Vietnamese were concerned, but access was not entirely blocked: 'At the DRV National Day celebrations, we were customarily accorded the status of foreign journalists, in parallel with that of the two DRV journalists in London, although included with ambassadors, Ho Chi Minh and the Politburo at the top table.'

Thus, he not only saw, but occasionally had short conversations with, 'Uncle Ho'. In one letter, he entertained me with an account of a reception for the Soviet cosmonaut Gherman Titov, the second man into space. There were so many toasts and counter-toasts, he said, that Ho Chi Minh ended up drunkenly sitting on Titov's knee, fondling his face. This part of the story didn't make it into the memoir, but even the version Dad set down over two decades later was entertaining enough:

> Ho's eyes, under the weight of boastful technicalities, closed, opened, intermittently flickered shut but, before he drifted off entirely, caught mine and saw me smiling. He laughed gently and shook himself. 'Who is that man', inquired Titov, 'who is laughing at me?' 'He is not laughing at you', the leader said. 'That is the British Consul-General. He is the only man who smiles in Hanoi, and he smiles all the time.'

But these opportunities for first-hand observation were rare, and communication with the Vietnamese Government mostly very hard. Paddy Hayes' biography of Daphne Park recounts one story I'd never heard which illustrates the difficulty:

> Colvin was directed by London to hand a particularly important message directly to the Foreign Ministry. Unfortunately the DRVN Foreign Ministry refused all contact with the consulate. Colvin's solution was to

> approach the rear of the ministry building which boasted a fine garden tended by a gardener. Colvin attracted the man's attention, then stuck his arm through the barred gate and handed the startled gardener the missive from London, scarpering before the amazed man could do anything about it.

As an aside, 'scarpering' was certainly one of my father's words, along with 'trousering' instead of 'pocketing'. His language ranged from the abstruse—he would dazzle opponents in debate by talking about things like 'irredentism' and 'revanchism', and debate the finer points of Marxism with 'Marxists' who then proved never actually to have read Marx—to the full range of British sailors' swearwords, possibly the richest source of foul language in the world.

So where was intelligence to be found? One answer lay in pure observation. One of the disciplines taught in the SIS tradecraft training centres, my father told me, was a version of what was known as Kim's Game, a series of memory exercises based around the game the young spy is taught in Rudyard Kipling's *Kim*. He was good at it: here's his account of a stroll around The State Department store in Hanoi, which, like all department stores in communist countries at the time, had a stock which could politely be described as minimalist:

> The goods available in November 1966 included footballs, enamelled basins and chamberpots in immense quantity, a guitar or two, Bulgarian watches, Soviet and Chinese radios, hundreds of Chinese thermos flasks, two Czech bicycles and accessories, shelf upon shelf of torch batteries, one pair of Zeiss field-glasses, two crowded counters of foreign drugs (Caffeine, Nivalin, Ematin, Philophran, Adrenaline, Progesterone), soap dishes, two or three showcases of local scent and soap, a few lipsticks, tin pots of face cream, one brand of tooth-paste, Soviet tinned and Chinese powdered milk, gumboots and poor-quality shoes, monocolour gabardine and other cloth, skimpy shirts and vests, face-flannels by the thousand, light-weight trousers.

In circumstances where taking a photograph or writing in a notebook would have attracted instant hostile attention, this is a considerable feat of memory.

But there was also human intelligence, because even without formal access to the Vietnamese Government, the British consul-general was treated as a full colleague by most of the rest of the Diplomatic Corps, including those of the many communist and socialist countries who represented Vietnam's allies and supporters in the war. That said, an exception was a Red Guard chargé d'affaires who, at the height of the Cultural Revolution, used the opportunity of a reception to spit directly into my father's face, addressing him (because of his ambiguous diplomatic/non-diplomatic status) as 'Mister British journalist'. 'To have replied, in these circumstances,' wrote my father in his memoir, 'with a backhander across the chops, would have carried no national consequences. The chargé was, however, surrounded by five beefy colleagues, and retaliation would also have led to unsuccessful brawling.'

The French and Canadian embassies were particularly helpful both socially and regarding material restrictions on a colleague who was denied the normal privileges of diplomatic status, but there also seems to have been a remarkable amount of contact with the Soviets, who were not always happy with the way the Vietnamese treated their aid and advice and sometimes played them off against China. There was also the 'all in it together' factor, because neither supporters nor opponents of the Hanoi government were immune to the endless bombing. My father illustrated it thus:

> One of [the Soviet] senior officials converted from straight vodka to gin and tonic in the course of repeated visits to my house ... Another, with previous service in London, laid maddening emphasis on his acquaintance with [former Conservative minister] Reggie Maudling, pronounced by him 'Moddling'. A Soviet military attaché, in the time he could spare from complaining about DRV mismanagement of SAMs [surface-to-air missiles] or from chasing Tonkinese waitresses, recounted interminable dirty stories in an English which few could grasp.

Plying a military attaché with booze to loosen his tongue about the way the Vietnamese mishandled their Russian missiles: that's Intelligence Collection, Level 1.

My father also had a long-held interest, and some expertise, in East Asian ceramics, and he soon found the shop of Monsieur Dong, whose sign claimed 'De Grande Valeur' ('Of Great Value'), but who was inevitably known as 'Le Grand Voleur' ('The Great Thief'). He described it as one of the social rendezvous of the capital. And, he believed, it was a relatively safe place to make contacts:

> On arrival at Hanoi, I had assumed that if Le Grand Voleur were not working directly for the State, he must be under close official supervision. I discovered, or think that I discovered, that this was a false impression of an omnipresent state. I never saw anyone remotely like an official, or even informant, in his shop.

He would, however, have assumed the presence of bugging devices throughout. He always did in countries in the communist sphere.

There were also occasional visiting reporters, some of whom appeared to my father to be excessively gullible in the face of North Vietnamese propaganda, but one of whom (unnamed) gave him a panoramic account of his escorted travels, including the state of bombed bridges, roads and villages, and many other significant details, which were of undoubted intelligence use but would be unlikely to get into print in the reporter's articles. What was in it for the journalist? Presumably the analysis of an astute observer and resident of the Viet Cong capital who liked to talk, and who understood the ground rules of talking to the press.

Even within the restricted zone within which my father was allowed to walk, there was the evidence he could gather with his eyes and ears. After the massive raid referred to at the beginning of the chapter, he walked around Hanoi to inspect the damage. The power plant was, to Dad's eye, a wreck, with collapsed chimneys, and the whole structure listing drunkenly to one side. The city's electricity, shut down by the attack, remained out that night, and the next morning my father began composing a telegram to the effect that Hanoi's power system would probably be crippled for a long, long time:

> I concluded that there was no possibility known to me of restoring any electric services. Hanoi, my last paragraph would have read, must now be finished as a functioning industrial and economic city. Geoffrey [Geoffrey Livesey, his second-in-charge] had started to work on the

> accounts ... I handed him my finished telegram for encypherment and dispatch ... At that moment the lights went on, the fans started to turn, and the rattle of the box air conditioner began. Across the street, the repair factory was once more brightly lit.

Halfway around the world, I had had to learn to push Dad's welfare to the back of my mind for the duration of his posting. I had The Beatles' 'Strawberry Fields Forever' rigged up on endless repeat on my record player for what seems in retrospect like weeks. On television, Patrick McGoohan wrapped up *Danger Man* and began *The Prisoner*, a brilliant, mysterious psychological thriller set in a fantasy world but shot in Clough Williams-Ellis' glorious folly, the village of Portmeirion: 'I will not be pushed, filed, stamped, indexed, briefed, debriefed or numbered. My life is my own. I resign.' My mother, my sister and I all watched that together.

Peter Cook and Dudley Moore's *Not Only ... But Also* had just left our screens, but *At Last the 1948 Show* gave us Marty Feldman, John Cleese and Graham Chapman. These last two, like a lot of adults, became fans of a surreal comedy for children and teenagers, *Do Not Adjust Your Set*, which my sister and I were both glued to. It starred Michael Palin, Eric Idle and Terry Jones. The two outfits combined, of course, would eventually produce Monty Python's Flying Circus. *Do Not Adjust Your Set* also introduced me to The Bonzo Dog Doo-Dah Band, later just The Bonzos, fronted by one of the great English eccentrics of the century, Viv Stanshall. If nothing else, you might know him as the spoken-voice artist on Mike Oldfield's *Tubular Bells*, but he was also one of the funniest people in England. The Bonzos' album *Gorilla* was on high rotation on my turntable that year, along with *The Who Sell Out*, Spencer Davis, and The Small Faces' second album. I was listening to more soul music too. Like half the teenagers of my era, I had a thing for Dusty Springfield, and her material helped lead me to The Supremes, Jackie Wilson's 'Your Love (Is Lifting Me Higher)', The Four Tops' 'Standing in the Shadow of Love', and many more which helped form the soundtrack to my 1967.

On other tracks of my life, this was the year of my first kiss, at a dance at my aunt and uncle's house. If I attempted a fashion style (and I couldn't afford much of one), it was probably closer to mod than anything else.

And I had my father's Lord's membership card while he was away, so I went to watch Wes Hall and Charlie Griffiths bowl for the West Indies against England, a display of awe-inspiring speed and intimidation I would not witness again until I saw Dennis Lillee and Jeff Thomson bowl at the SCG.

The Beatles, whose records had been burned on American bonfires the year before, ended the year with *Sergeant Pepper's*, redefining what an album could be. The Rolling Stones responded with *Their Satanic Majesties Request*. Distant voices were telling of flower people in San Francisco, and a hippie revolution, but London still seemed, to a London teenager, like the centre of the universe. Pink Floyd put out 'See Emily Play', and their spring 1967 poster for Games for May—a concert I couldn't persuade either my housemaster or my mother to let me go to—was the first time I remember seeing a piece of psychedelia in printed form. No-one I knew had taken acid, but the word 'trippy' had entered the lexicon: everyone was now talking the language of mind-altering substances.

The beat went on, but thousands of miles away, where GIs were smoking heroin through the barrels of their rifles, so did the war.

* * *

There are repeated denials in my father's heavily vetted memoir that he had a direct line to the US State Department, then headed by Dean Rusk, but the reality, I understand, is that the *indirect* line, whether through the British embassy in Saigon or the British Government in London, was swift and reliable. Indeed, I've been told by people who should know that Dad's key despatches were read not only at CIA headquarters in Langley, Virginia, but in the Oval Office of the White House. Coming as they did from an ally inside the enemy capital, his descriptions of massive bombing raids like the one described earlier, and his frank reporting of North Vietnamese resilience in the face of Operation Rolling Thunder—the US campaign of sustained aerial bombardment—may well have undermined the morale of President Johnson, much as determined media reporting of US losses and blunders was doing among the wider public.

Late in 1967, the consulate-general met a serious setback, revealed for the first time in Paddy Hayes' Daphne Park biography. Based on an interview with another now-dead SIS colleague, Brian Stewart, Hayes writes:

> He [John Colvin] submitted a report in code to London on the aftermath of a particularly severe bombing raid by the USAF. In a follow-up report which he sent en clair [not encrypted] he referred to the contents of the previous coded message in such a way that it was clear he had been secretly reporting on the effect of the US bombing. The DRVN authorities reacted predictably by banning all future outbound coded messages. It was a bad mistake by Colvin and the result was a serious drawback; secure coded two-way communications are the lifeblood of any intelligence outpost, and diplomatic ones for that matter.

As my father's successor in the post, Stewart had every reason to be annoyed at the restriction on his ability to communicate, but it's possible both that he had his chronology wrong and that the reason for the action may not have been quite so clear-cut.

I have read a series of once-secret telegrams about this incident, released through the Public Records Office. A message from an official in London, Richard Fyjis-Walker, does suggest that Vietnamese sensitivities 'may have been heightened by Hanoi's telegrams Nos 504 and 505. The North Vietnamese could have inferred from the remark about "alleged" U.S. bombing appearing in the telegram that the confidential reporting in the *following* [my emphasis] cypher telegram was unfavourable to themselves.' My father replies: 'I do not think they made this deduction. There have been similar instances without incident.'

There is, over several weeks, a lengthy correspondence about the cutting off of the cypher 'privilege', in which it is clear that the North Vietnamese at no time specified any reason for their actions other than the long-held official line that the British consulate-general held no official diplomatic status, was therefore a 'commercial' enterprise, and hence had no reason for enciphered telegram facilities. Vietnamese officials claimed the decision had been taken autonomously by the PTT—the postal and telegraph office—but this was clearly a fiction in a centrally planned communist state. Asked why the decision was being taken now, after thirteen years in which in practice the PTT had allowed ciphered telegrams, they were unresponsive.

My father told London in a series of messages that he believed that the reason for the cut-off was in fact heightened North Vietnamese Government paranoia about espionage. As evidence, he included anecdotes about new difficulties the French, Canadian and Indian missions had all been having at the time. Contrary to Stewart's impression, in a telegram to Hanoi sent the day after Fyjis-Walker's, London says, 'We agree that the most likely reason for North Vietnamese action is "espionage psychosis".' This is, in its own way, pretty rich, since my father was indeed a senior intelligence officer using all means possible to commit espionage, so in point of plain fact the 'paranoia' had some justification. However, the whole set-up—a British diplomatic mission with no actual diplomatic recognition, a game of potential tit-for-tat being played out involving two North Vietnamese 'journalists' in London and a four-person North Vietnamese 'trade delegation' in Hong Kong—was such that a degree of comic irony was probably to be expected on both sides.

What the secret correspondence does make very clear is that, even without enciphered telegram facilities, the Hanoi mission remained extremely important to London (and presumably Washington). London weighs up in the telegrams the possibility of threatening the North Vietnamese with withdrawal of their London and Hong Kong personnel, or even to close the consulate, but comes down heavily against making any such overt threat. Regardless, there was still a slower backstop alternative in communicating with London: the Canadian mission had a weekly diplomatic bag in which reports could be sent in physical form to Saigon. But this in itself was vulnerable: my father, asked to make more use of this, points out in one telegram that

> The carriage by Canadians of our bags is itself (repeat itself) secret, or at least not declared to North Vietnamese, and we act accordingly. There is an elaborate cover procedure to avoid any indication of 'carrying bags to the Canadians'. I am trying to avoid among other things exposure of the system.

Earlier in the year, he had described one small part of this cover procedure, which had just been closed off by the North Vietnamese: a door from the kitchens of the Indian mission into the Canadian compound. However, via enciphered messages in the weekly Canadian diplomatic bags, and with occasional use of radio facilities provided by friendly embassies, one way or another, the consulate was able to continue to report to London—and through London, often to Washington. But with what consequences?

We know from an opinion piece in *The New York Times* in early 1988, by President Johnson's chief of staff James R Jones, that by September 1967, 'Johnson had begun to doubt our ability to prosecute the war to any clear-cut victory'. That was six months before LBJ announced that he would not run for another term as president, but Jones strongly suggests the decision was as good as made then. Although my father believed when he was in Hanoi—and would continue to believe—that Johnson was wrong, that the US could have won the war, it's hard not to conclude that his own reports on 'facts on the ground', on days like the one on which the power plant attack took place, had their effect at the very highest levels.

Saigon would not fall until 1975, but by the time my father's posting ended, the bombing of the North was already de-escalating, and in March 1968, President Johnson ceased all bombing of North Vietnam north of the 20th parallel. The Vietnam War had, for the Americans, become purely defensive, a question only of protecting South Vietnam. The tide had turned, and the next seven years (even though President Richard Nixon later resumed the bombing of Hanoi) would form a long, humiliating, slow-motion defeat.

Chapter 14

Standing Alone

THE CLOSEST THING I ever had to a Damascene conversion was, paradoxically, when I ceased to be a Christian. I was not on the road to Damascus, or a road to anywhere really: I was walking across Little Dean's Yard at Westminster, on an ordinary day, when a kind of revelation struck.

Summer Fields, in addition to its other educational rote-learning and force-feeding, had provided a constant daily indoctrination into High Anglicanism. This was not the woolly faith sent up in Alan Bennett's *Beyond the Fringe* parody sermon, not the institution referred to in the old joke 'I don't have a religion: I'm a member of the Church of England.' Oxford High Anglicanism was very close to Roman Catholicism. We attended chapel twice a day, there were sung Eucharists, including 'bells and smells'—gorgeously robed clerics with censers of smoking incense—and boys were encouraged to go to confession and be 'confirmed' as young as possible. Roped into being an altar boy partly by the promise of a decent post-service breakfast in the chaplain's house on Sunday mornings, I was also persuaded to study for confirmation. It was a training which placed a huge and oppressive emphasis on Sin, with a capital S.

An eleven-year-old boarding school boy at that time could be sexually innocent in a way that's almost inconceivable now. There was no sex education of any kind until you got the 'talk' or 'pi-jaw' from the headmaster at the end of your last term, aged thirteen. I had heard the 'f' and 'c' words from local kids on holidays in the country, but apart from a few playground rhymes about 'stiff cocks' and the like, I had no real idea about what boys and girls might do together. My mother remembers me asking 'What's a homosexual?' when I was eleven, but it turned out it was only because I'd read the word in a story about a political scandal in a copy of *Private Eye* at my father's flat. Half of what I had to memorise for the catechism, and indeed, the Ten Commandments, seemed meaningless. 'Thou shalt not kill' was easy enough to understand, but what was all that stuff about coveting thy neighbour's wife or his ass? (I was far too young, and too English, to make the well-worn joke about coveting thy neighbour's wife's ass.)

I can't remember exactly what I 'confessed' to the chaplain before I was confirmed, but my worst sins, of deed or thought, would probably have been along the lines of 'I looked over at my neighbour's paper during a maths exam', or 'I got in a fight'. The result was that by the time I reached Westminster I was still very definitely a 'confirmed Christian' in both senses of the word.

It was in 1967, with Dad in Hanoi, that I had my moment in the quad. I'd just read Voltaire's *Candide*, the picaresque black comedy of a young optimist. He begins the book as a follower of a philosopher called Dr Pangloss, who believes that 'everything is for the best in this best of all possible worlds'. Candide's faith in this proposition is tested by every kind of extreme misery the world can bring, short of his own death, until eventually he concludes that the best an individual can do in a world where no God ever intervenes to spare humanity from itself, or Nature, is to 'tend our own garden'.

I'd also been reading Giorgio Vasari's *Lives of the Artists*, I think on the recommendation of a newish young history master called Richard Woollett. It's probably the first book in Western culture that acknowledges the artist—Michelangelo being the prime example—as an individual genius rather than a hired craftsman, and as such makes him (for Vasari it was definitely *him*) a hero.

And I was working my way through EH Gombrich's *The Story of Art*, while haunting the National Gallery, and starting to understand one of the key points about the Renaissance: the emergence of the individual from the medieval thrall of the Holy See. Gradually, first the aristocracy and then the bourgeoisie started to change the nature of art's focus. Christianity was no longer the artist's only subject: Greek and Roman gods entered the pantheon. Where portraiture had previously had to be disguised as images of Jesus or the Virgin Mary, now, princes, dukes and other nobles had their pictures painted, first as figures in Bible scenes, but eventually alone in their secular finery. I had seen reproductions of Albrecht Dürer's 1500 self-portrait, in which, with staggering insolence towards the Church, he painted himself fairly unmistakably as a Christ-figure. And I had returned again and again to Rembrandt's self-portraits, a man in the vigour of his successful prime, seeing himself with unyielding clarity grow older, poorer and closer to death.

All this somehow flowed into what happened that day. I simply remember it as a mental flash, in which I thought a series of simultaneous thoughts which all somehow added up to this: 'If there is a God, he, she or it is not taking the slightest interest in my life or anybody else's. I am a human being, standing on my own feet, and I can and must stand alone.' In short, in that single moment, I became a humanist and an agnostic.

Many people throughout history have lost their faith in God, but most probably gradually, through a slow accretion of doubt. I suspect I'm one of the few to whom it has come as a bolt from the blue, on a sunny day, without a single individual trigger, and in the very shadow of one of the most famous churches in Europe.

I stopped abruptly even being interested in theology. Since that day, I have taken little interest in the arguments for or against God: I regard them as an interruption to and distraction from the business of leading a fully human life. Proselytising atheists hold as little interest for me as those who try earnestly to persuade me of the virtues of Christianity, Buddhism, Islam or Hinduism. Having felt the need for faith at one point in my life, I sympathise with other people's attachment to it: individuals should do what they can to get themselves through this vale of tears. En masse, though, I wish they'd stop hanging, lashing, torturing and invading people to enforce their beliefs on others. Understanding the English Reformation, the Puritan ascendancy under Cromwell, the Thirty Years War and the Counter-Reformation not only reinforced this belief, but still serves as a permanent reminder to me that unspeakable brutality has not always been the trademark only of fundamentalist Islam.

The reference to reading history is deliberate. Before my father's return from Hanoi, I had passed my O-Level exams, and was now studying for the A-Levels. The system meant that you had to specialise: if you wanted to go to university, you had to choose just three subjects.

History had been a genuine choice. A couple of the science masters had been trying to persuade me to go into their stream, because I'd had a strong interest in biology and chemistry for several years, and at one point expressed a wish to be a biochemist. But maths, my perennial Achilles heel, struck again: even differential calculus was a stretch, and without it, my marks weren't good enough for A-Level physics, which you needed if you were going to do any science subject at university. There was no way the system would, for instance, let you do chemistry, biology and English. It was CP Snow's *Two Cultures* theory, ossified in the education system. So I opted for English, French and history, but I already knew what I was aiming for: to read English literature, if possible at Oxford or Cambridge, but if not, then maybe at York or Bristol.

* * *

If the soundtrack to my life when Dad left for Hanoi had been The Beach Boys' 'Good Vibrations' and The Kinks' 'Sunny Afternoon', by the time he got back it was Hendrix' 'All along the Watchtower' and The Rolling Stones' 'Jumpin' Jack Flash'. That year, 1967, had been billed as the 'Summer of Love', but now the mood was darkening. Not long after Dad's return, it became clear that the post-divorce stability my sister and I had enjoyed before he went to Hanoi was never really going to come back. He came round one evening to tell us that he and Moranna Cazenove were getting married at Chelsea Registry Office the next morning. We remembered her, didn't we? A young woman we'd met with him on a train coming back from Hampshire?

My sister and I did indeed remember an occasion when we'd walked up and down the platform at Winchester station for no apparent reason, choosing which of several apparently identical near-empty carriages to get into. Then, once inside, the staged moment of 'Oh hello, what are you doing on this train? Oh, these are my children, Mark and Zoë.' It was like a rather incompetently mounted espionage operation.

We were certainly surprised by the wedding news, and asked if we could come to the ceremony. 'No, I'm afraid not,' my father explained. He was forty-six, Moranna was only in her early twenties, and they feared that her father, an extremely unpredictable alcoholic stockbroker named David Cazenove, would go mad and try to stop the wedding. No, he told us, there would just be a couple of witnesses, and he and Moranna would go straight from the registry to the airport for the honeymoon. By the time they got back in a fortnight's time, the fuss should have died down.

We later found out that for the previous few days he'd been staying with his mother, our Granny Sybil. He'd told her nothing about the impending marriage until that morning, when, having packed the car, he was sitting in the driver's seat preparing to leave. 'Oh, mother,' he said. 'I'm marrying Moranna Cazenove tomorrow,' then wound up the window and sped off in a shower of gravel.

This was even more complicated than it sounds, because Moranna's father had previously been married to my father's first cousin, Barbara. Dad, his sister Prudence and Barbara had all grown up together in my grandparents' household, after the death of Barbara's mother. During her marriage to David, in other words, Barbara had been for a while the very unpopular stepmother of my father's new bride. So there were bound to be massive reverberations on both sides of the family. What the wedding meant for Zoë and me, other than the melodrama of its beginning, was that the days of dropping into Dad's little Chelsea flat were never really going to come back, because he and Moranna were going to buy and renovate an old house near Basingstoke.

The following year, my life changed even more radically. At the beginning of 1968, a Royal Australian Navy officer named Tony Synnot, who my mother had known in Melbourne in the 1940s, arrived in London to do a year-long course at what was then called the Imperial Defence College. He was a captain, and the IDC course was the transitional training ground for the step up to rear-admiral. He and my mother resumed their old friendship, hit it off, and in March they took me out to lunch to tell us they were going to get married.

I liked and respected Tony, and I was happy for my mother, but I can't say in detail what my reaction to the news was that day: all memories were effectively blotted out by what happened directly afterwards. As we left the restaurant, I doubled over in pain, recovered, walked a few more steps, doubled over again, then had to clutch some railings. The agony was excruciating, like a dagger to the stomach. I was rushed to hospital, where a doctor diagnosed acute appendicitis, warned that it could turn to peritonitis at any moment, and put me straight to sleep. I woke up vomiting (it had been too urgent for them to wait the usual six-plus hours for digestion) and with a long row of stitches in my gut. The thing that worried me most was not that I was going to spend my sixteenth birthday in hospital, but that I would miss the school trip to Greece.

I was no longer studying Latin or Greek, but I retained an interest in classical history, and the Greek trip was also known as a kind of rite of passage, with usually minimal supervision when not actually visiting classical sites. Fortunately, teenagers heal fast, and I was out of hospital just in time. Although I wasn't supposed to carry my own suitcase, masters and friends helped, and soon we were rattling across Europe in couchette class, with six hard beds in each compartment—talking, playing cards, reading, drinking wine and eating mortadella bought at station stalls, through France and down to the toe of Italy. The first Italian phrase I ever learned was the one printed under every train window: *E pericoloso sporgersi*—It is dangerous to lean out. Italian is such a musical language that we kept thinking of new tunes to sing it to, cod-opera style, as the countryside sped by.

Waking early on the Brindisi–Piraeus ferry after an uncomfortable half-sleep in a reclining chair, I went on deck to watch, for the first time, the sun come up over the western coast of Greece. I had given up ancient Greek as a subject, but I had read *The Iliad* and *The Odyssey* in the Penguin translation, and there in front of me were the familiar Homeric epithets, turned literal: 'rosy-fingered Dawn' rising over 'the wine-dark sea'. I should not have been entirely surprised to see 'fleet-footed Achilles' running along the hills, as I breakfasted on coffee and a roll, passing through the Gulf of Corinth. Later that day we made landfall in Piraeus, before a bus ride to our hotel in Athens.

It's worth remembering that mass tourism was still in its infancy then. It may have been the year Hollywood was filming *If It's Tuesday, This Must Be Belgium*, but that in itself was an indication of how novel the phenomenon was. We were used to that: tour parties could be seen wandering around Westminster Abbey, a few making it into the cloisters, and a very few managing to reach the school itself. And of course, with the

Houses of Parliament and Whitehall just across the road, our whole area was a tourist destination. But there were as yet no budget airlines, and even the cheap-ticket 'bucket shops' hadn't sprung up: there were few alternatives to paying full price to fly—or to stay in hotels. Westminster was largely ours, for most of the time. I knew from experience that you could wander through the Tate Gallery, for instance, with perhaps only two or three other people in each room, even for the Turners.

As in Britain, so in Greece. Our school party may have been occasionally unruly and often raucous, but we had the ancient Agora in Athens, if not to ourselves, then certainly with plenty of room to move. We wandered largely unsupervised around the Parthenon and through the echoing rooms of its museum, taking in the wonders of ancient Greek sculpture and pottery. I remember sitting in the amphitheatre at Delphi, listening to a master explain the mechanics of Greek theatre, and we were the only group there. I pointed my camera up at a solitary eagle soaring in the thermals around the cliff-edge above, and thought about the Oracle and the clever ambiguities which had misled both Oedipus and his father Laius.

Or perhaps I was thinking about how bad the food was: for most of the fortnight the tour operators scrimped by feeding us on little but rice and cooked tomatoes, and most of us supplemented our diet by discovering the dessert called halva and the resinous Greek wine called retsina. I had an unreasoning and misguided prejudice against Greek food for years afterwards.

Not being a fan of anything that tastes like licorice, I avoided ouzo, but I did succumb to peer pressure and smoke my first cigarette. A packet of Papastratos cost almost nothing: even a schoolboy could afford them. The second day I bought a packet for myself, and by the time I got back to London I was smoking several a day, switching to Rothmans. It was a habit I would escalate for a decade before giving up for the first time. It would be several more years before I kicked that habit once and for all.

Back in London, we moved house. Tony Synnot was a widower with two young daughters, Jane and Amanda, and our Chelsea flat wasn't big enough for an expanded family, so when he and my mother married, we moved in with him, in a big house not far from Harrods. But it was always clear this was temporary: at the end of Tony's course, he and my mother would be going to Canberra. I was halfway through the A-Level

My mother Anne and father John arriving in Australia in early 1949. It was the first time my father had met her parents.

Fotografía

FILIACION

Edad 27 años Estatura 6 pies y 1 pulg.

Cabello castaño Color Blanco

Estado Civil casado

Nacionalidad Britanica

Señas particulares ninguna

3

Nº 1302

MARINA MERCANTE PANAMEÑA
(Certificado de Idoneidad)

El Cónsul de Panamá
en Hull, Inglaterra.-

CERTIFICA

El Sr. John Colvin
hijo de Ragnar y de Sibyl.-
Nacido en Japon el 18-6-1922
Domiciliado en 921, Chelsea Cloisters, Londres S.W.3,
ha comprobado mediante documentos fehacientes, que tiene la capacidad necesaria para ejercer el cargo de Oficial aprendiz
en buques a vapor
hasta de - 5000 - toneladas brutas que se dedican al servicio de alta mar y queda por tanto autorizado para ejercer igual cargo en los buques de la Marina Mercante Nacional de servicio Internacional.
Para constancia sello y firmo el presente en Hull, Inglaterra a los cinco
días del mes de Septiembre de 1949.-

LEOPOLDO ALGUERO. V.
Consul

My father's Panamanian Merchant Navy registration papers, dated September 1949, which describe Lt-Cdr John Colvin, R.N., as a 'trainee'.

My parents on their wedding day.

With my mother, aged 1.

Dining with my mother in Caorle, Italy, 1954.

Clockwise from left:

Aged about 4, with my beloved dog Bamse.

On my 7th birthday in Kuala Lumpur, with the magician or 'gully-gully man'.

With my sister Zoe, arm still in plaster, 1959.

On 'Merah' at Kuala Lumpur racecourse, having a riding lesson.

My father at the Kuala Lumpur family home, 7 Lorong Kuda. The famed Petronas Towers now stand where the racecourse (and the house) used to be.

At the funeral of the head of SIS, Sir Dick White, in 1993. The man in the three-piece suit with the watch chain, someone whispering in his ear, is my father.
Photograph Brian Harris, courtesy *The Independent*

At Double J, circa 1976.
Photograph courtesy ABC Archives

First week on The World Today.
Photograph courtesy ABC Archives

With my eldest son Nicolas in Brussels, 1985.

In Brussels in 1985 with the ABC's chief political correspondent Barrie Cassidy, who was travelling with Prime Minister Bob Hawke.

With producer Sally Wiadrowski, camera operator Dave Maguire and sound recordist Eric Briggs, on the edge of the vast Namib Desert, Namibia in 1989.

In 1990 during the run-up to the First Gulf War at the multi-million dollar building in Baghdad promised as a memorial to the hundreds of thousands of dead of the Iran–Iraq war, but in fact a museum of the life of Saddam Hussein.

Already ill but still undiagnosed, with Archbishop Desmond Tutu, 1994.

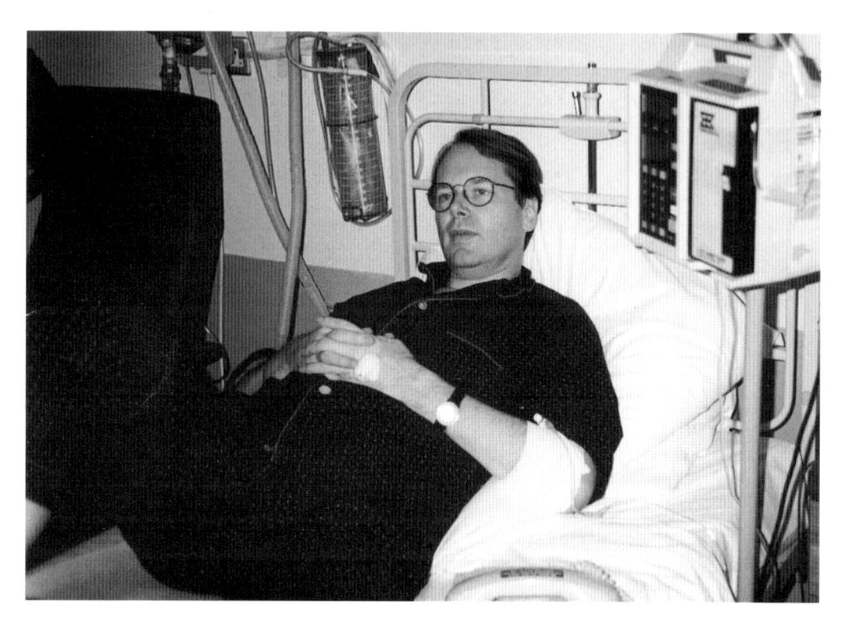

In Charing Cross Hospital, London, 1994. It was to be the beginning of a stay of several months and a chronic illness that affected me for more than two decades.

With my son William.

course: should I go back to Australia with them, moving into a completely different educational system, or stay in London?

There were negotiations between my parents about what would happen when Mum and Tony left England. Zoë, who was then happy and doing well at the highly academic St Paul's Girls' School, was nevertheless not at the academic hinge-point I faced, and could transfer from one system to the other. She would go with Mum, a blow in itself, because although three and a half years separated us in age, we had always been very close in affection. I was to stay with Dad: to finish my A-Levels, and on the clear understanding that if I then got a place at Oxford he would not take any postings that would leave me stranded for three years without a home to go to in the holidays. He made this solemn undertaking to my mother, and the thing was decided.

Even so, the whole business was a wrench. I had been a weekly boarder at Westminster, spending every weekend with one parent or another (depending on whether Dad was in the country). More significantly for me, Mum lived a fifteen-minute bus ride away from school, and I often popped over in the afternoon to say hello and spend some time with her and Zoë. In some ways I felt almost more like a day-boy than a boarder. Now it was clear that from 1969, I was to board pretty much full-time, with only occasional weekend trips down to Dad and Moranna's place.

At the end of 1968, I said goodbye to what was now my Australian family with sadness, but also with the knowledge that I would see them again in less than a year. My relationship with Dad became more volatile and difficult during this time, as I worked towards A-Levels and, in the winter term, the Oxford Entrance Exam. Moranna gave birth to a daughter, Joanna, which meant there was understandably less time for anyone else. Dad was commuting up to London every morning on the train from Basingstoke, so when I did see him it was usually when he took me for lunch at his club, the (now-defunct) St James'.

My father's intelligence expertise, when it came to me, was sometimes artfully deployed: never more so than the day Westminster got itself into the *Daily Express* over a student demonstration. This was late-ish 1968, the year of the Paris riots and the Czech uprising, and the spirit of rebellion was everywhere. I printed out a series of what I thought were fairly mild requests for more consultation with students—an early plea for student democracy—and went round Liddell's collecting signatures.

My housemaster, Charles Keeley, in an uncharacteristic rage, got wind of this from somebody, descended on me, refused to listen to my arguments, seized all the signed copies, tore them up in front of me, and told me I was grounded.

I wasn't the only one: similar petitions were going around other houses. One of the others involved was an American boy called Robbie Fields, and the next day he was called in to see the headmaster, John Carleton. It was then that Westminster experienced its first sit-in: a crowd of boys sitting on the ground in Dean's Yard, shouting 'Free him, free him.' With photographs, and in the aftermath of Lindsay Anderson's *If...*, this story of a Top Public School In Revolt was a tabloid dream. I probably would have been in those photos myself, but my father had already spoken to Keeley, got him to suspend my grounding temporarily, and descended in the late morning, just before the ruckus began, to take me to a very urbane lunch at his club, where we had a reasonably civilised argument about generational change and what he regarded as the need to be patient. I wasn't entirely convinced, and said so, but arrived back at school to find I'd missed all the action, including, allegedly, the hanging of an anarchist black flag from a window of historic Ashburnham House, by the heir presumptive to a barony, no less.

My career as a student revolutionary, craftily nipped in the bud.

Chapter 15

Night Tripping

IN 1969, I knuckled down just enough to get through A-Levels with no great distinction: I believe that my last exam was on the day that Neil Armstrong walked on the moon. Then I flew out to Australia for the (northern) summer holidays, and to wait for the results. After so long in grey England, this return to Australia was welcome in its way, though I missed the theatres and rock concerts in London. My mother and Tony had bought a house in the Canberra suburb of Deakin, less than a kilometre from the prime minister's Lodge.

The air was so different, so clean and eucalyptus-smelling. My mother fed a family of magpies who would come to the back door and sing to her. We had a lemon tree in the back garden, covered with sacking in winter to keep off the Canberra frost. One day a baby possum fell down the ventilator of the kitchen extractor fan, and its fiercely protective mother made clear I wasn't welcome when I climbed up a ladder to help—we eventually managed to push the baby up to safety with a broom handle. And in contrast to the underpowered small and mid-sized cars that were common on English roads, we had a long, spacious, white Holden station wagon, in which we drove on the long switchback road down Brown Mountain for NSW South Coast beach holidays.

My music was The Doors, early Led Zeppelin, The Band, Joni Mitchell, The Stones' *Let It Bleed*, and—what we didn't know was going to be The Beatles' swan song—*Abbey Road*. The biggest Australian hit that year was Russell Morris' brilliant and epically produced 'The Real Thing'. I also remember seeing *Midnight Cowboy* at the cinema in Manuka, not only an extraordinary film, but the first time I'd heard the voice of the great Harry Nilsson.

Even in Canberra's winter and spring, Australia seemed more expansive and easy, and I was tempted to stay, but I went back to Westminster for one final winter term, to prepare for the Oxford Entrance Exam. Those last three months were more like university learning than school days: we had seminars rather than lessons, including a number from the headmaster's wife, the historian Janet Adam-Smith. We were treated like adults, and expected to behave as such, an atmosphere in which I found it considerably easier to work.

At the beginning of the term, Charles Keeley had sat me down and told me apologetically that he'd decided not to make me a monitor (prefect), to which I replied politely that I should have refused if he had, because I had no taste whatsoever for wielding authority—a line in my Twitter bio, 'Lifetime Lance-Corporal in the Awkward Squad', reflects a long history. Keeley accepted this with equanimity—his deputy housemaster, Jim Cogan, had always been in the habit of calling me 'Colvin, you truculent youth'—and I got on with my life.

Although I was aiming to read English, everyone wanting to enter Oxford had to take a 'general paper', in which you were expected to write essays on philosophical questions or current affairs: 'Is it possible to learn lessons from history? Discuss'; or 'Empires rise and fall: Britain is to the US as Greece was to Rome. Discuss.' This was meat and drink to me, and I performed well enough in the exams to get invited to an interview at Christ Church, Oxford, where I must have been plausible enough to impress someone, because they offered me a place. Then it was farewell to my life at Westminster and back to Canberra for my first Australian Christmas since my maternal grandfather had died a decade before, and to work out how to fill the time before 'going up' to Oxford in September 1970.

Because I'd learned how to develop and print photographs in the Westminster School Photographic Society, I answered an ad in *The*

Canberra Times for a junior darkroom worker at the Research School of Biological Science at the Australian National University. They hired me, and I spent most of 1970 there, learning eventually how to produce pin-sharp prints of shots taken by the school's electron microscope. I had little idea what the images I was printing—mostly viruses—represented, and instead of concentrating on the negative print image on the paper, I had to learn how to focus with a sort of small adjustable periscope onto the grain of the glass negative itself. It was quiet and repetitive work, but I had the most congenial of companions in the form of an Englishwoman called Maureen, the senior darkroom technician, who was patient enough to help me learn, and being extremely well read herself, a delightful conversationalist about books and other subjects. We had ABC Radio on most of the time, Anne Deveson's talk show and *Ellis Blain's Guest*, and so I began to get a picture of Australian public life which I hadn't absorbed naturally, growing up elsewhere.

I had little awareness of politics at first, beyond the burning issue for people of my age of conscription. My sister Zoë had a schoolfriend called Sally Burns. Sally's father was a professor of political science called Arthur Burns, a vigorously free thinker and vocal anti-communist, and her mother, Netta Burns, was a senior policy adviser to a string of leading Labor Party figures, up to and including Bill Hayden. They and their children kept open house, and Arthur in particular was always keen to stir up debate among his children's friends, an intellectual atmosphere which I relished. Their son Jonathan would soon challenge his own army call-up on the grounds that he was a genuine pacifist: when it came to court, he had so many witnesses to his lifelong gentleness and peaceful nature that his was one of the rare so-called 'conchy' cases that succeeded.

When it came to conscription, I thought I'd be OK for a while: I wouldn't turn eighteen until I was studying at Oxford, a valid reason for deferral. But who knew in 1969 whether conscription would still be in force by 1973, when I was due to graduate? The Liberals had just won the 1969 election, albeit with a much reduced majority, and although the conservative coalition was apparently riven by infighting, the surge that swept Labor under Gough Whitlam into power in 1972 was only just beginning.

It may seem odd, but not wanting to fight in Vietnam was no barrier to a harmonious home life, even though my stepfather was now a rear-admiral in the RAN. Tony Synnot was an equable and tolerant man, though he had an occasional barrack-square yell that could freeze your blood when he needed it. He was extremely intelligent but chose not to flaunt this: you just became aware of his brainpower by degrees. He also had an exceptionally good way with people: former sailors who had served under him inevitably remembered him fondly, and more than once, ex-RAN traffic cops let him off speeding fines when they saw the face behind the wheel.

In his naval role, he was a man of complete integrity. In 1970 his job involved buying ships and their equipment for the navy, so he was constantly besieged by manufacturers who tried to shower him with gifts: gold pens, cases of wine and more. There were very few formal guidelines in public life about this at the time, certainly no compulsory gift registers, but Tony set his own rule, which was to accept nothing more valuable than a few dollars: a perspex paperweight, a set of branded pencils, a calendar, that sort of thing. Even these he only accepted so as not to offend, and brought them home for the kids. This absolute determination to play straight and resist corruption became over time the gold standard for me.

As did his resolute sense of duty. In the Christmas holidays of 1974, we scarcely saw him because he was coordinating the Defence response to the great disaster of Cyclone Tracy: he dropped in at home for about an hour, for Christmas lunch, then went straight back to his offices in Russell Hill. Tony worked on the Tracy response almost without interruption for ten days, then came back hoping for a long sleep, having decided things were now sufficiently well coordinated to leave it briefly in the hands of others. I think he was having a well-deserved whisky that evening, 5 January 1975, when news came through that a bulk ore carrier had crashed into the Tasman Bridge, killing twelve people and dividing Hobart in two. With hardly a murmur, he went straight back to work.

Later, in journalism, I would come to regard Tony Synnot as the finest role model I could have had for any form of public life. Among other things, I've always tried to follow his example and refuse freebies and junkets, which in my view can hardly fail to sway even the most determined reporter's work.

I've never been particularly good with my hands, but Tony was also a patient teacher as we built together an aviary on the front porch for a pair of Burke's parrots. He either had astonishing self-control or a very, very high pain threshold: he's the only man I've ever seen hit himself hard on the thumb with a hammer without swearing. I've never emulated that feat myself, but at least trying to live up to that degree of stoicism proved useful to me on occasion in subsequent years.

I liked it in Australia, and I was by no means totally committed to giving it all up and going back to take my Oxford place. I could just as easily have stayed in photography, or applied for a place at the ANU or the University of Sydney. And I had some kind of social life in Canberra, however relatively small the national capital was at the time. My hangout at the time was the garage under John Langtry's house. John was a lanky Canberran on his way to becoming an engineering student, who spent much of his time taking apart and putting together motorcycles while listening to music. John was crazy about Bridgestone motorcycles, the last of the high-performance two-strokes. I started off with no idea even of how an engine worked, but by September 1970, through osmosis if nothing else, I did at least know the difference between a head gasket and a carburettor. I also owned a small and very noisy Bridgestone, which John helped me choose and maintain. And since he'd been to school in Canberra, there was a circle of John's male and female friends with whom I went to see acts like Tully, Jeff St John and Wendy Saddington when they were in town.

John eventually switched from engineering to Japanese, went to live in Japan, combined his interests by racing motorcycles there, then joined the Department of Foreign Affairs. At the time of writing he is Australia's first-ever resident ambassador in Mongolia, a country I had barely heard of in late 1970 (it was more commonly known as Outer Mongolia then) when I returned to the UK to begin my time at Oxford. I was soon to get a crash course.

Not long after I began my first term at Christ Church, eating my meals in the hall you would almost certainly recognise from the Harry Potter films, drinking in one of Britain's oldest pubs, The Bear, and reading set texts in the glorious Radcliffe Camera extension of the Bodleian Library, my father, true to form, announced another move. Despite his solemn promise to see me through university, he had instead accepted *another* posting in one of the world's most inaccessible places. He was to be Her Majesty's Ambassador in Ulaanbaatar, then better known as Ulan Bator, and would be leaving for Outer Mongolia in a few months. I would be left in the guardianship of my aunt Prudence (or Pooh), his sister, and uncle Colin, who very kindly made a room available for me in their house for holidays, but made it clear that this wouldn't extend to the long summer vacation, when a job would be required.

And so it was that, halfway through my second term, I was sitting prelims, the exams that determine whether you will stay on to complete your Oxford degree, when I looked up from the Anglo-Saxon translation paper (extracts from *Beowulf*, *Sir Gawain and the Green Knight* and *The Dream of the Rood*), noted the time on the clock, and thought, 'Dad, Moranna, Joanna and David [my toddler half-sister and baby half-brother] must be taking off from Heathrow about now.'

* * *

At Christ Church, I lived in Canterbury Quad, on a staircase directly above the college's extraordinary collection of drawings and painters by old masters—Leonardo da Vinci, Giovanni Bellini, Albrecht Dürer—a collection which I discovered years later had first been catalogued in 1902 by Sidney Colvin, nephew of my great-great-grandfather John Russell Colvin. It was so easy to saunter down two flights and spend a few hours hunched in the low light over the glass cases, admiring the extraordinary draughtsmanship, the charcoal and red and white chalk, of people who had seemed to see so clearly into the lives of contemporaries. And yet there was so much else to do: lectures in which JRR Tolkien's son Christopher talked about the finer points of Old English, or where the great Richard Ellmann could be equally inspiring talking off-the-cuff about James Joyce or Oscar Wilde.

There was the famed Oxbridge tutorial system, in which you wrote an essay (often scribbling through the night), then went, half-drunk with fatigue, to read it to your tutor and another student, both of whose duty it then was to tear it apart. The sting was taken out of the process by the knowledge that, next week, it would be you trying to pick holes in your colleagues' work. If nothing else, it got me used to the process of editing early on, and the idea that my prose was never going to be sacrosanct however much passion or effort I had put into it: a useful lesson in journalism.

I remember coming out early on one of those mornings, having been up writing an essay all night, to find the great expanse of Tom Quad filled with a thick white mist, to a height of about a metre. The raised walkway around the quad, originally planned as a cloister by Cardinal Thomas Wolsey but never covered because Henry VIII decided he had grown too powerful, was entirely free of the soft cotton-wool cloud: the mist was all in the lower, grassed area. Only the statue of Mercury in the middle of the quad floated above it, seemingly flying free with its bow and arrow. It was a perfect, once-in-a-lifetime shot, and I rushed back to my room to get my camera. But by the time I returned—a matter of two or three minutes—the mist, the moment, and the picture, were gone.

There were also afternoons, evenings, nights spent drifting away smoking dope, mostly in the rooms of one accommodating friend who had an open-door policy for all, listening to Neil Young, Joni Mitchell, Floyd, The Stones' *Sticky Fingers*, Leonard Cohen. And next door at Corpus Christi, in Peter Saugman's rooms, something similar, only with Dr John the Night Tripper on the turntable, New Orleans rhythms with a voodoo backbeat, and James Taylor's *Sweet Baby James*. One afternoon in summer, someone rigged up big speakers on either side of Christ Church's Georgian Peckwater Quad and blasted out Terry Riley's seminal minimalist work *A Rainbow in Curved Air*. I sat on the steps of the Christ Church Library for forty-five minutes and soaked it up in the sunshine. No-one complained. That was the kind of year it was, 1971. And if that didn't suit, you could wander down to Folly Bridge and hire a punt for a picnic on the river. Time slid away like mercury skittering across a floor.

In the summer vacation I went to Cornwall and worked as a photographer on the *Falmouth Packet*, a harbour-town newspaper which also published editions for the villages of Helston, Camborne and Redruth. I travelled there under the impression that I was going as what we would now call an intern, expecting to shadow the paper's main photographer, Denis Jory, for most of the summer, but I arrived to find that Denis was soon going on holiday and I was supposed to be stepping into his shoes. This was a tall order, because I had no press experience, and perhaps more importantly, no driver's licence. I did my best, cadging lifts, taking public transport and doing whatever I could to get to jobs. By the end of the summer, I was perhaps approaching somewhere close to halfway competent, but certainly no more.

The strongest lesson that time instilled in me was that accuracy in journalism really matters. In local papers, even if you're photographing someone's prize vegetable marrow or the carriage clock they were given after forty years' loyal service, they really care that you get their name and age right, because that photo and that caption are going to stay in their scrapbook for a lifetime. And as an aside, having been quite savagely bitten by a farm dog when I was invited to photograph a man's prize bull, I learned the value of wearing a pair of stout boots, preferably quite high-sided ones, when out on jobs in the country.

I made a significant mistake towards the end of my first year at Christ Church: the college told me that due to lack of space, I could not remain in my rooms the next year, and I was too disorganised and perhaps fatalistic to appeal the decision. I'm almost sure in retrospect that, had I appealed to them on the grounds that both branches of my family were overseas, they would have relented and let me stay. But I let things slide too long, and when a friend named Charles Lillis told me he was going to rent a tiny fifteenth-century cottage in the village of Stanton St John, time had run out and I had few choices left but to join him.

I'd reckoned without a number of things, my own lack of a driving licence being one of them. Charles had a licence and a car, but I couldn't rely on him for all my transport. The second thing was the infrequency of buses to and from the village into Oxford. The third—which I could not have foreseen, to be fair—was that this was to be a winter of rolling power blackouts. Edward Heath, as Conservative prime minister, was engaged in a running battle with the unions, and while what we went through was nothing like the later and far more serious Three-Day Week (where commercial electricity users could only switch on for three consecutive days each week), there were eight-hour periods—sometimes in the day, sometimes in the evening—when we had no electricity. The cottage, which had once housed a family that left for America on the *Mayflower*, was pretty but very cold in winter, and on the days when there was no power for the heaters or the stove, even colder. It was a damp, chilly year, and towards the end of it, I began spending more time on the sofas of friends in Oxford, having missed the last bus home.

My favourite of these overnight stops was River House, a brick place on the towpath of the River Isis, where I had a number of friends and there was a constantly shifting flow of visitors. It belonged to the artist Nikki Greswell, daughter of friends of my parents, and the other inhabitants included Amit Pandya, son of exiled Ugandan Indians and an intellectual powerhouse with interests spanning politics, history, literature and more; Ken Hylton, then pursuing a thesis on Ezra Pound, whose eclectic musical tastes ranged from Herbie Hancock to Mahavishnu John McLaughlin, with huge doses of Hendrix and Captain Beefheart in the mix; and Mike Grieve, who was doing his thesis on the philosophy of David Hume. Another friend, Alex Monnas, was an English-educated Greek quantum chemist with an extraordinary gift for explaining subjects like black holes and Einstein's theory of special relativity, and whose hobby was post-Wittgenstein philosophy. I often say that I gained as much of my general intellectual education talking to friends like these as I did in any lecture, seminar or tutorial. The atmosphere, despite the reasonably frequent ingestion of hashish, was as often one of fairly rigorous intellectual debate as it was of all-night games of Monopoly or chess, though sometimes the two things happened simultaneously.

When my second year at Oxford came to an end, and Amit was leaving to go to the USA (where he eventually became a lawyer and an international humanitarian aid specialist), the others offered to let me have his room for my third year, and I gladly accepted. In the meantime, I was packing to spend my second summer vacation in the most exotic way possible: I was going to join my father in Outer Mongolia.

Chapter 16

Foreign Devil

MY ROUTE TO Ulan Bator was not the most direct or obvious one, which would have been through Moscow. Ten months before, Britain had expelled ninety diplomats for spying, and UK–Soviet relations were at one of their many lows: going through the Soviet capital was not considered a safe option. The way in was therefore through China. I flew to Hong Kong, was met at the airport by a junior Foreign Office official, spent a night in a hotel, and was taken to the station for the train journey to what we now know as Guangzhou but was then, in its much less expanded form, called Canton.

The first part of the trip—to the border of communist China—was short and uneventful. My long hair, fair skin, height (192 centimetres) and King's Road–fashionable wide-lapelled lightweight suit had drawn no particular interest in British-ruled Hong Kong, where gwai lo (Western ghosts/foreign devils) were commonplace. On the mainland, though, I was soon going to experience what it was like to be utterly foreign—an object of scorn, curiosity, even disbelief. But first I had to get across the frontier. The Hong Kong train stopped there, and all the passengers had to get off. I was faced with a no-man's-land—from memory about 200 metres—across which I had to lug my suitcases.

Since I had brought my Oxford set-list summer reading, including Edmund Spenser's *The Faerie Queene*, half of Dickens, George Eliot's *Middlemarch* and *Daniel Deronda*, and a few other massive tomes, and since there were then no wheeled suitcases on the market, this was no mean feat. In fact, I recall lugging one bag 20 or 30 metres, then going back for the next, repeatedly, until I reached the Chinese Customs shed on the other side. Four blank-faced People's Liberation Army soldiers, automatic rifles slung forward for easy use, if necessary, watched this spectacle without apparent emotion: they may for all I know have been trying to conceal their contempt or stifle their laughter at this gangling, decadent, imperialist running-dog. Inside the shed, there was at least a trolley, and I endured the thorough rifling of my cases before boarding the train to Canton.

Here it was that I first encountered the two middle-aged Queen's Messengers—special diplomatic couriers—who were to be my travelling companions all the way to Ulan Bator. My diary of the trip is long-lost, so I regret that I can no longer remember their names, but I believe one was a retired colonel, and the other a former Colonial Special Branch officer. Both wore the official Queen's Messenger's tie, carrying the service's symbol: the silver greyhound. Both carried red diplomatic passports, and told me that they always had several of these on the go, though not on their persons: usually two or three were in various foreign embassies in London, waiting for new sets of visas. They were stolid, brave men, in a service where those qualities were needed. Their job was to carry the sacrosanct, heavily sealed diplomatic bags, big off-white canvas sacks made by prisoners in the UK, containing the despatches and ciphers considered too secret to entrust to any more-insecure means, along with other embassy necessities. They were never, under any circumstances, to leave the bags unattended: if possible, both should be with the bags at all times, and if one needed to use the bathroom, the other would have to take extra precautions—they used handcuffs or shackles, if necessary, to ensure the bags could not be taken away from them.

This was not always hypothetical: not long before, they told me, at the hysterical height of Mao's Cultural Revolution, two Queen's Messengers had had to drag the bags bodily through a screaming mob of young revolutionaries who kicked and punched them all the way onto the train.

One of them had been in the British embassy in Beijing in 1967 when it was besieged and much of it set on fire by Red Guards, who then manhandled the diplomats and frog-marched them around for over an hour before the idly watching People's Liberation Army soldiers could be persuaded to intervene.

So my two companions took their jobs very seriously, and they warned me that, although things were now far less intense than at the peak of the Cultural Revolution, this was still a potentially dangerous journey. They were not, perhaps, imaginative men, but they were both immensely experienced: they'd carried bags to every country in the world where there was a British diplomatic mission, and despite my self-described membership of the 'counterculture', I took these greying short-back-and-sides veterans with proper seriousness.

I remember the train journey from the border to Canton as a series of vistas of paddy fields, dotted with bent figures in conical hats: all that landscape is now pretty much one vast city of concrete, steel and glass. We arrived in Canton itself by late afternoon and checked into our hotel. The Queen's Messengers advised me very strongly not to leave the building, not only because I spoke no Cantonese, but because I would be the immediate object of large and possibly hostile crowds. There was no air-conditioning, and it was both swelteringly hot and extremely humid, so confinement to a hotel room was irksome, but was at least relieved by the view from my window.

From about five floors up, I sat and watched the activity on the Pearl River as the sun went down. An extraordinary menagerie of shipping crowded the waterway, from pole-driven sampans to elderly steam-driven tugs, newer motorboats, and junks—large and small—under their lateen sails. They moved in such profusion that it was hard to understand how they never seemed to collide. Dusk fell, and the power failed at about 9 p.m., so even the single small fan that had been struggling to cool my room was now out of action, and I spent a sweat-soaked night sleeping intermittently before rising early to get the plane to Peking (now called Beijing).

Chinese airlines in the 1970s were still part of the Chinese Air Force, and the service was accordingly basic. We boarded a British-built Trident jet in CAAC livery at about 11 a.m., with the temperature and humidity both still extremely high. Unfortunately, China still had only rudimentary abilities in airline engineering—most of their planes had to be serviced outside the country—and this aircraft was malfunctioning; in what way, neither the flight crew nor the cabin crew seemed able to tell us. The Queen's Messengers, each with a diplomatic bag occupying a full seat beside him, were phlegmatic: not only were they probably the world's most frequent flyers, they'd had plenty of prior experience on CAAC. It wasn't too hard to try to imitate their air of calm, but what did become more difficult was not to expire from the sheer heat. The plane's auxiliary motors appeared to be out of commission, so the crew simply opened every available door in the hope that a draught would blow through. It did, but it was a hot draught carrying more hot moisture. After some hours on the tarmac, the effect was something like sitting in a toothpaste tube over a Bunsen burner turned to high.

For the first few hours, this being a totalitarian state, there was hardly a murmur from the other passengers. Eventually we could hear some grumbling, to which the neatly dressed women of the cabin crew reacted by handing out consolatory packets of Chinese cigarettes. Even I, by then a regular smoker, found these particularly disgusting, especially when the breeze through the aircraft proved insufficient to dispel the heavy fug that then ensued. By the end of the afternoon, the crew were doling out unlimited glasses of Moutai, a Chinese liquor, and a number of our fellow passengers decided to anaesthetise themselves against the whole experience. It was early evening before the jets coughed into action, and the air-conditioning finally started to suck out some of the choking smog we'd managed to build up inside our metal prison. I'd also spent some of the afternoon trying very hard not to think too much about the BOAC Trident—the same model as this plane—which had crashed only a couple of weeks before, near Heathrow, in Britain's worst ever air disaster. But finally we made it into the air and headed north, arriving at Peking Airport at about 9 p.m.

An hour passed before we were loaded into the British embassy's van for the trip into the Chinese capital. As we drove through the dark, we saw the city's inhabitants everywhere by the roadside, making use of the streetlights to read, play chess, or talk. Power to ordinary homes was restricted in 1972, in what was still an extremely backward economy despite all Mao Zedong's attempts to persuade the world of the virtues of his disastrous Five-Year Plans and Great Leaps Forward. The Beijing I see on TV screens now is almost completely unrecognisable from the low-rise, bicycle-teeming city I remember: only the vastness of Tiananmen Square seems unchanged, in an urban horizon which otherwise seems to consist of massive skyscrapers.

As a guest in the home of the British deputy head of mission in Peking, I had three days to fill before the Queen's Messengers and I would board the train to Ulan Bator. With the Cultural Revolution still in full swing, there was simply no tourism industry in China then: the Gang of Four were near the height of their power, and Chinese rhetoric about foreign, decadent, imperialist lackeys was still rife. The upside was that the privileged few, and they were very few, had the run of the tourist sites.

On the first day, an embassy driver took me to the Forbidden City, and I walked the steps up to the inner sanctum almost alone, hearing how only the emperor himself had been allowed to use the middle of the staircase. The vast compound seemed inhabited only by sweepers and janitors and a few other diplomatic visitors. There I also saw for the first time the treasure that had been dug up in Gansu only three years before, and was now on display for the first time: an extraordinary collection of bronze horsemen, and nobles in horse-drawn chariots, carrying parasols of the most delicately worked bronze.

But nothing could compare with the centrepiece of the exhibition, the 'Gansu Flying Horse', which I still regard as one of the greatest works of sculpture in Eastern or Western art. Poised with one hoof on a bird in flight, the horse is pure liquid motion turned to metal, and it struck me with the force of revelation. Because of my father's interest in Chinese ceramics, I had seen a great deal of blue-and-white and Celadon pottery, and I had learned to associate ancient Chinese art with a degree of stillness, simplicity, purity. Here instead was a creature whose coiled energy would have inspired or even intimidated Michelangelo, but which had been cast over a thousand years before he was born.

At that point, despite US President Richard Nixon's visit to China early in the year, there was no way of knowing that the Cultural Revolution still had four years to run, no way of knowing for how long China would seal itself off against the world. I had a sense of extreme good fortune, of knowing that I was seeing things totally closed to the rest of the world, for the moment and perhaps for much longer.

I had the same sense, but tinged with shock and disgust, at Beijing's Summer Palace the next morning. The palace is more than a building or even a series of buildings. It was built as an aristocrats' resort, a place of beautifully landscaped hills, lakes and high, tiered pagodas, where the Imperial Court would pass the time in the eighteenth and nineteenth centuries. Buildings were linked by long covered walkways, open at the sides, or 'breezeways', their ceilings gorgeously decorated with painted scenes of pastoral or court life. But when I was there, it was the scene of some of the most extensive official vandalism I have ever seen. In every case where the paintings depicted a person, which was most of them, that person's face had been systematically painted over, or worse, scratched out, seemingly by chisels hacking into the plaster. This had been done by the Red Guards at the height of the Cultural Revolution, and even though it involved no torture, public humiliation or bloodshed, seeing it in person somehow brought home, more starkly than any TV news clip, the brutal fanaticism of the time.

It reminded me of a school trip to Ely Cathedral in East Anglia, when I was fifteen, where we had seen the results of another bout of fanaticism, 400 years before, during the orgy of iconoclasm after the dissolution of the monasteries. We were led into the elegant, airy, Gothic Lady-Chapel, whose hundreds of alcoves had once each held a statue. After Henry VIII's campaign wrought its destruction, many of the statues were completely reduced to dust, but even those whose bodies had been spared had one thing in common: they were headless.

Something about the human face—its individuality, the implication it contains of others' humanity, the possibility of compassion—has the ability to enrage fundamentalists, whether Protestant, Islamist or, in the case of the Summer Palace, Maoist. We know now that Mao's rule caused the deaths of up to 70 million people. I discount none of them in noting this act of vandalism, but observe that the two things are linked. Before you commit mass murder, you first have to turn the people into a *mass*, and you can only do that by taking away their humanity, their individuality, their face.

But the Summer Palace also contained a reminder that human folly was hardly confined to the Red Guard or its mad leaders. A huge boat made of marble—shimmeringly beautiful but forever unable to float—seems like the perfect metaphor for Imperial extravagance, and indeed, the Empress Dowager Cixi, in the mid-nineteenth century, had diverted much of the tax money raised to fund the Chinese Navy into having this extraordinarily paradoxical symbol of her dynasty's power enlarged and restored.

So far, I had seen few Chinese crowds: the Summer Palace and Forbidden City were largely off-limits to most of Mao's proletariat. But that afternoon, there was shopping: first at the big State Department Store, which, as was usual in communist societies, had very little to sell. I bought alarm clocks in which a Red Guard waving Mao's *Little Red Book* ticked off the seconds: my sister Zoë still has hers. Then I was taken to 'Antique Street', the street where a few state-licensed shops were allowed to sell trinkets of dubious provenance, mostly to foreigners. On a student budget, I had little money, but enough to buy some gifts and souvenirs. I was let out of the van and told I could walk down this street, going into shops, but on no account to stray off it. Immediately, I was surrounded by a large and growing crowd.

Everyone in Beijing then dressed almost identically, either in blue or khaki Mao suits. The figures milling around me, some reaching out to touch my Western clothes, seemed identical from the neck down, mostly very thin, wiry, scrawny. Only their faces distinguished them: some hollow-eyed from the long-lasting effect of the famine years in the first Great Leap Forward, others, younger, with more-unlined faces. Some looked more like city people; others had the bewildered look of peasants just up from the country for the first time. I walked slowly and carefully up the street, smiling and trying to speak very quietly and reassuringly while quite aware that no-one around me spoke English, and ducked into the first shop I reached. It was all so intimidating that I only managed perhaps four shops before going back to the van and safety. I had bought a couple of scroll paintings, a little piece of jade for my sister, and some small thing for my father and stepmother in Ulan Bator.

It had felt like being ejected by a time machine into the Middle Ages. This was a society which had deliberately exiled, imprisoned, 're-educated' or killed a huge percentage of its most cultured and educated population. Mao's revolution, aimed at lifting the country out of peasantry, had instead made a cult out of peasant ignorance. It was impossible, at the beginning of the 1970s, to imagine China as the emerging superpower of the twenty-first century.

That night, we went out to eat at the Little Duck, a place off Tiananmen Square, where we ate in a booth upstairs and I experienced Peking Duck for the first time.

If all this sounds like the standard tourist itinerary *you* were taken through on *your* visit to Beijing in recent years, I can only reiterate that at the time it was utterly exotic and, for me, completely new. And if you've walked among the vast throngs along the Great Wall, or jostled among the crowds around the Ming Tombs, just imagine doing it alone: having all that history to yourself. I had that good fortune: few others have, and probably few ever will.

On the appointed morning, I rejoined my comrades, the Queen's Messengers, at the train station, and, farewelling my kind diplomatic hosts, boarded the branch-line of the Trans-Siberian Railway which took passengers from the Chinese capital to Ulan Bator. For someone accustomed at the time to the grime and discomfort of British Railways, the first-class carriages we travelled in seemed magnificent. I have seldom taken a journey of such comfort and splendour since.

My carriage appeared to have been built before World War I but had been immaculately maintained. Each compartment was outfitted with an armchair, complete with antimacassar (presumably in case you had pomaded your hair); a small writing table; and a massive and yielding velvet sofa, convertible at night into a comfortable bed. Between compartments was an ancient but workable flushing lavatory, bearing the imprint of Thomas Crapper and Company, of London: I believe the model was called The Venerable.

Both the train and the track were elderly. The result was that the speed never exceeded a sedate 50 to 60 kilometres an hour, and in areas of track subsidence was sometimes as low as 20 or 30. Far from being a problem, this was a luxury. It meant that from your magnificently large picture window, you could watch the Chinese countryside roll by as you approached the Great Wall. Then, as you moved regally out towards Inner Mongolia (the northern region of China that borders what is now the Mongolian republic), you could see that what you had thought was *the* Great Wall was instead the last of a series of Great Walls, the innermost engineering triumph of a civilisation which had earlier tried to protect itself with walls further out from the mountains—walls which were not strong or high enough, so that as the first signs of desert showed themselves, you could see the remains of the very earliest earthwork walls, almost entirely worn away by time and erosion. And after that, before dusk shaded into night and took away all views, the endless monotony of the dunes of the Gobi Desert.

Conductors came around with constant supplies of tea and Tsingtao beer, there was beef and black-bean sauce with green peppers and rice for dinner, and as night fell, I fell asleep over my copy of *Middlemarch*, thinking about seeing my father the next day for the first time in eighteen months.

Chapter 17

Dear God, the Ear

I HAD FORGOTTEN, AS I drifted off, about Er-Lian. Someone had told me, I'm sure, but the reality of being ousted from my well-sprung, gently rocking bed at a chilly frontier post at 1 a.m. was still a shock. Er-Lian, the border station between China and Outer Mongolia, was also the place where the railway gauge changed. We would be continuing in the same comfortable carriage, but not until it had been lifted off its Chinese-gauge bogies and onto ones built for the Russian system. That meant sitting in a station waiting room, drinking gunpowder tea from a samovar, for a couple of hours.

It was there that a member of the People's Liberation Army sat down next to me and asked if he could practise his English. Sure, I said, and we talked—about how he was here in this remote border post but his wife was in Shanghai, and how I was going to visit my father who I hadn't seen for such a long time. And then he started talking to me about someone called Lin Biao.

The name didn't really mean much to me. I was naive and largely apolitical at the time, with no journalistic ambitions and little recent Chinese current affairs knowledge. So the man explained to me that Lin Biao had been a marshal in the PLA, very close to Mao, and that in September the previous year, 1971, he had tried to mount a coup, which failed, then boarded a plane and took off to defect to Moscow. I believe, but this may be a false memory—at this distance I can't be absolutely sure—that he also told me that the Chinese Air Force had shot down Lin Biao's plane and thereby prevented a potential Russian coup. (This claim has certainly been made since, but mystery still surrounds exactly how Lin, Mao's deputy and designated successor, really did die.)

I thought the story was interesting, but I didn't know enough to ask any penetrating questions: I had little idea of Lin Biao's significance. And besides, I thought, if a junior soldier is telling some travelling student this story, it must be common knowledge. He must have read it in the party propaganda sheets.

The transfer of the carriage to the Mongolian gauge completed, I shook hands with my new friend, boarded and went back to sleep. I woke to fields of rolling grassland, my first real sight of one of the strangest, wildest, emptiest countries I've ever seen. Here I was to spend the next six weeks.

Dad met us at the station with the embassy Range Rover, then a novelty issued to diplomats in some far-flung places as an advertisement for British technology, while his deputy, Phillip Shaw, had brought the thoroughly utilitarian Land Rover. The Queen's Messengers loaded the diplomatic bags in the Land Rover, their task now almost complete. I lugged my cases to Dad's car and we proceeded to the embassy. This was a large 1930s building on Peace Street with a neoclassical front portico which was seldom used. Instead, you entered the compound through the less-imposing rear gate, which revealed a tennis court, a cottage where my toddler half-sister and brother, Joanna and David, lived with their nanny, the redoubtable Mrs Taylor, and the back of the embassy and residence itself.

Home was upstairs, to the right at the top of the landing. Dad's office was to the left, behind a heavily locked door through which, it became gradually clear, I would never be allowed to go. My father told me at the time that this was because there was code machinery in there, which I was not allowed to see, but in retrospect that was a serious understatement.

In his memoir, *Twice around the World*, my father claimed that 'The value of a British presence in Mongolia' lay 'in the visible witness we afford of a different civilization'. But his book was a sanitised version of the truth, vetted by the SIS and scrubbed of anything that would hint at the reality of the embassy's role—principally that of a spying station. The espionage expert Professor Richard Aldrich wrote to me during research for this book that electronic eavesdropping was at the centre of the operation, that the 'main role' of the British embassy in Outer Mongolia 'was protecting the GCHQ listening site there'.

It's now clear from a number of sources that the embassy in Outer Mongolia, like the consulate-general in Hanoi, was maintained by the SIS budget and was therefore 'their' station. As Professor Aldrich suggests, this meant that a large part of the premises concealed a Government Communications Headquarters (GCHQ) Signals Intelligence (SigInt) station whose principal purpose was to monitor communications between China and the Soviet Union, and, where possible, the internal communications of each regarding the other.

Mao, once something of a protégé of Stalin's, had if anything outdone his mentor in bloodthirsty extremism, shrugging off some of Moscow's influence in the process. Especially after the mysterious death of Lin Biao, there were real fears in some quarters that the two communist superpowers might go to war, and any signs of that would first be reflected on the borders, notably that between the Soviet satellite state of Outer Mongolia and the Chinese province of Inner Mongolia. SigInt for the period remains closely guarded, no doubt to protect 'systems and methods', but I have read a number of confidential and secret documents written by my father, now declassified, which confirm, among other things, that one of his central preoccupations was the number and placement of Soviet troops in Mongolia, which ranged from 20 000 to 200 000 depending on his source.

In my own observation of his activities during the summer I spent there, 'protecting' GCHQ's SigInt was only part of the job: he was constantly using his eyes, his ears and his contacts to gather human intelligence (HumInt) as well. His sources ranged widely among the diplomatic community, both overt and covert: there are references to conversations with ambassadors of friendly states such as India and France, and an intriguing suggestion of an informant in the Romanian embassy. But he ranged far wider than the diplomatic circuit. In fact, his whole method was to get out of the embassy, and out of Ulan Bator, as much as possible.

Two days after I arrived, the Er-Lian anecdote about Lin Biao cropped up over dinner. I only hadn't mentioned it before because there'd been so much personal catching up to do, about Oxford, friends and family, and it just wasn't at the top of my mind. I told the story as a throwaway, and was shocked at Dad's furious reaction. He went straight to his office and filed a report.

It had not been common knowledge at all. It was the first ever Chinese account of the circumstances of Lin Biao's death, and I'd clearly been meant to pass it on. How did my father know that? Because in the past twelve to twenty-four hours, in a couple of other ambiguous encounters in countries in Eastern and Western Europe, the Chinese had 'let it be known' that this was their official version. But my vagueness had seen him beaten to the intelligence scoop of the year by a whole thirty-six hours. Not my finest hour, but then again, I was his son, not his agent, and he didn't hold a grudge, at least not for more than a day.

Dad used to get up very early, walk across the landing through the safe-like office doors, and usually finish his official work by lunchtime. I would spend the morning talking to my stepmother, Moranna, playing with the children, and otherwise trying not to get in the way. I had plenty of reading to do, anyway, so it was no problem to have a few hours a day alone with my books.

Mongolia is, I believe, after Kyrgyzstan, the country furthest from the sea in the whole world: a high, dry, climate where it seldom rains in summer but which experiences extreme cold in winter. I was there in high summer, so almost every day Dad and I would pile into the Range Rover with fishing rods and drive into the steppe. There was a theoretical limit on our travels of a 40-kilometre radius around the capital, but this did not seem to be policed in any systematic fashion. The whole country was said to have no more than 200 kilometres of tarmac roads, most of them in and directly around the capital, with the rest built for Soviet transport. Once we got on the dirt, there was never any sign of being followed.

We explored rivers and streams, fishing on dry fly, wet fly and spinners, for grayling, char and trout. The world's largest trout, a massive beast called the taimen, is native to Mongolia, and we had some heavier tackle on hand just in case: one day I did see a huge creature break the water about 200 metres downstream, but I cast for about two hours in vain. Dad fished mostly from the banks, while in the dry heat, I liked getting into the water, waist-deep if necessary, to cast. I had no waders, but the smooth pebbles of the riverbed were easy under my plimsolls or bare feet, and the rivers seldom too fast-flowing for safety. They were idyllic days, fishing and talking. And, on the way home at the end of the afternoon, observing.

One day we drove back on a dirt track past a small army installation, where a Soviet military officer was trying to drill a Mongolian platoon. They were not actively rebellious (though in my father's despatches he records numerous instances of Mongolians deliberately spitting to show contempt for a Soviet colonial overlord). They were simply pretending not to understand what the officer was saying. The command of 'Halt' would be ignored, for example, or on 'Left turn', half of them would turn right or about-turn. Whole groups of them would march blithely off the parade ground, pretending they couldn't hear the officer's yells. I was reminded of *The Good Soldier Schweik*, Jaroslav Hašek's side-splitting novel of Czech 'dumb insolence' under the Austro-Hungarian Empire.

One thing my father was on the lookout for was the survival of Mongolia's religion under Soviet rule, which had done its best to suppress the creed. Essentially similar to Tibetan Buddhism, but with strong animist overtones, its signs, when you got out into the country, were everywhere if you knew where to look: every spring and every stream running into a brook or river sported a branch, planted in the ground and decorated with fluttering prayer-flags to the gods or spirits of water and land. In order to uphold the fiction that it was not trying to impose atheism on a religious population, the Soviet Union allowed the Mongols to maintain the Lamaist Gandan Monastery in Ulan Bator. But they also set up, close by, a lurid museum of the atrocities committed by monks before the country was 'liberated' by Sukh Baatar in 1921, allowing it to boast of being the world's second communist country.

Dad's insistence on getting out and seeing for himself was not confined to the summer months. In the winter, he would go shooting grouse and sand partridge for the pot, usually in company with the Yugoslav ambassador, Vladimir Milovanovic, a Serb former World War II Partisan. Who could say what exactly these two knew of each other's activities during and after the war, but they were, strangely, friends.

Mongolian winters are very, very cold, with temperatures as low as minus 40 degrees Celsius at night, often exacerbated by wind chill. While we were out fishing one summer afternoon, Dad told me the story of a shooting expedition seven months earlier, in deep midwinter, when

Milovanovic's Russian-built Gazik broke down. This, from his memoir, is pretty much how I remember him telling it then:

> The Ambassador's only method of repair was to warm the carburettor with the flame of a petrol cigarette-lighter. The temperature was minus 35°C. It was getting dark. The nearest village, from which we were separated by a river, was ten kilometres away. But unless we were to dance together all night, or sleep in one another's arms, even fur-coats and hats and five woollen layers below the coats, would not prevent us, if we stayed by the car, from freezing to death before morning.
>
> We set off down the hill. The faster stretches of the river, despite the terrible cold, were still flowing. We moved downstream until we found the stream frozen over. We could not, however, gauge the thickness of the ice nor the weight it would bear. If it broke, we should die quite soon. We looked at each other and stepped out, laden with guns and game, hand—incomprehensibly—in hand, across the ten-yard section, and reached the other side. 'That wasn't too difficult', said Milovanovic. As he spoke, the ice broke up behind us.
>
> We walked up the valley, all vehicles resolutely ignoring our signals. In the village Post Office, lit by guttering candles, an aged crone refused to allow us to use the telephone until Milovanovic distracted her with a bottle of Yugoslav brandy. I was then able to get through to the British Embassy and a Landrover arrived an hour later. The experience gave a firm foundation for friendship.

I always had the impression that it was a friendship of mixed suspicion and trust, with each probing the other for clues about the intentions of their respective power blocs. But one thing they certainly agreed on—given that Tito's Yugoslavia was the most maverick of the Iron Curtain nations—was that the Soviet experiment in Mongolia was not working, and that the country was only even partly viable because about 80 per cent of its economy consisted of subsidies from Moscow.

The population of Mongolia then was about the size of Adelaide now, one and a quarter million, but spread over an area half the size of India. Notoriously, the Mongolian people were greatly outnumbered by animals, of which there were about twenty million. The majority of those were sheep, which constituted most of the national diet, provided tallow for lighting, and whose wool clothed the Mongols and made the rugs which insulated their gers, the round white-frame tents (called yurts by the Russians) in which this nomadic people had lived for centuries. Most of the other animals were horses, the short sturdy beasts on which the Mongols under Genghis Khan had conquered China, whose milk the Mongols relied on, and which (along with camels) were still the foundation of nomadic life and transport.

As the colonial power, the Soviet Union had tried everything possible to eliminate nomadism, insisting that the Mongols create collective farms instead of moving from place to place according to the season and their knowledge of the land. But the collective farms had largely failed: the 'national herd' and its output were actually smaller than before Stalin began to impose Russian systems on Mongolian agriculture. And in Ulan Bator, my father said, there was copious evidence from all foreign observers that Mongols forced by the Soviets to live in concrete apartment blocks would instead slip away each night to their own gers, dotted around the outskirts of the city. Colonialism and communism had combined to form a remarkably dysfunctional country, both as a society and an economy.

I discovered during research for this book that my father's confidential 1973 annual review was now declassified, though hitherto unpublished. It begins:

> Ulan Bator's only dry-cleaner recently informed one of my colleagues that the concern had fulfilled its 1973 Plan, and no more clothes would therefore be accepted until April 1974. This seemed a goodish joke, but it later emerged that, far from fulfilling the plan, the cleaners had run out of equipment, and forgotten to order more. Shifty incompetence remains the characteristic of this Marxist State.

I should emphasise that, while he disliked Mongolia's Soviet overlords and their puppets in government very much, my father genuinely loved the country and its people. The normal length of an ambassador's posting in Ulan Bator was two years: he chose to extend his to almost four. After the fall of communism, he did everything possible to help Mongolia open up trade and diplomatic links to Britain, and at his funeral in 2003, the Mongolian ambassador was conspicuous among the mourners.

* * *

During his tour of duty, my father set out to visit every corner of the country that he could. This was only partly a question of 'flying the flag' or gathering routine political intelligence about the state of the place: it was also a calculated attempt to find out where he was and was not allowed to go, on the principle that the forbidden zones must be forbidden for a reason and that reason was probably military. In the summer of 1972, I accompanied him and my stepmother Moranna on one of these long trips, to the country's remote west and north-west.

The airborne sections of this journey around four aimags (provinces) were undertaken with Mongolian Airways, in Soviet-built copies of the wartime Douglas DC-3 Dakota. An aviation workhorse in its original version, the Dakota's Russian-built Lisunov and Ilyushin knock-offs were if anything even more spartan than the original. Flying was neither luxurious nor reassuring: Mongols who travelled with us tended to vomit copiously during flights, and rush out praying to forbidden gods and kissing the ground in gratitude on landing. As diplomatic VIPs, we were generally seated at the front of the cabin; towards the rear, clucking could be heard, indicating the presence in the cabin of caged or tied chickens.

We arrived in Hovd, the capital of an aimag on the border with the Chinese region of Xinjiang, and were driven to the town's guesthouse, a whitewashed, mudbrick, two-storey building whose rooms provided little more than a hard bed, a table, a bowl and a ewer. My father was just remarking that we were almost certainly the first Westerners in these parts since the 1920s when a tall white man in a Loden coat and Tyrolean hat, complete with feather, came down the stairs carrying a hunting rifle. He and my father struck up a conversation in German. It turned out that he was an Austrian and either a first or second cousin of my sister's godmother, a friend from the Vienna days. They conversed for some time about mutual friends and acquaintances before the man departed on his mission: he had paid a large sum to the Mongolian Government for one of the few annual licences to hunt ibex (wild goat) and argal (wild sheep) in the nearby Altai Mountains. I have never encountered a better practical proof of the truism that 'It's a small world'.

If I do not recall every detail of this lengthy trip, I have an excuse: we were all either quite drunk or quite hung-over—sometimes both—most of the time. To quote my father's memoir describing one morning of our expedition, 'When I said to the somon Chairman that we did not usually drink more than three glasses of vodka for breakfast in England, he correctly commented, "You are not in England now."' Or this, from a letter he wrote to British Foreign Secretary (and former prime minister) Sir Alec Douglas-Home on another trip: 'It falls to few to be drunk on the Mongolian steppe at nine o'clock in the morning. Such was my fortune, in a Land Rover, after a gruelling tour of this province.'

This sottishness was emphatically not of our choosing. Mongolian society, being nomadic, has extremely strong hospitality rituals, born of necessity. If a horseman arrives at your ger at midnight, in a blizzard, you do not turn him away. You give him and his animal shelter, and you ply him with food and drink, knowing that you may someday need the same hospitality in return.

To quote from the same letter to Douglas-Home,

> without encroaching on you again, Sir, about the sanitary arrangements, the most distressing feature of travel in Mongolia remains the nomad requirement to eat a full and displeasing meal, not only between destinations, but also on departure from one centre and arrival at the next. As the centres these days may be as little as two hours apart, and each repast involves a great deal of arkhi (vodka), strain is imposed. Lies about one's liver, vegetarian habits and that, are just no use. A Chinese phrase for travel, 'Eating Bitterness', is apt at such times.

I do have memories of the collective farms we biliously visited, the agricultural research stations we inspected, and the tiny provincial museums where we were expected to admire local handicrafts. But they are somewhat blurred, and in any case, I might do better to give you a series of travelling impressions.

First to those 'full and displeasing' meals. There were no menus, but if there had been, they would have read as follows:

Mutton soup.
Mutton.
Mutton dumplings.
Mutton-fat.

Mutton pancakes.
Pickled carrots.
Mutton.

And if you were lucky, for variety, there was sweetened sheep's cream (quite delicious, to be fair) to follow. The mutton dumplings were sometimes very good, once you worked out how to eat them, which was to take a small bite of the outer casing, releasing the hot mutton, onion and herb juices in a hot spurt into your mouth before biting into the contents.

The worst of all these meals occurred close to the border with Kazakhstan, at a collective farm where we arrived, in the dark, after a ten-hour jounce across the steppe, a drive I thought would never end. The natural inclination was to wash and sleep till the morning, but no. As my father recorded in his memoir, there was to be a welcoming dinner featuring the Kazakh national dish:

> half-boiled legs of mutton reposing in a tin wash-basin, surmounted by a sheep's head, the teeth jauntily protruding. It is the privilege, and duty, of the honoured guest to slice, and eat, from this memento mori, the gristly lips, cheeks and, dear God, the ear.

Dear God, the ear. The scene is graven on my memory. The 'tin wash-basin' was chipped pale-blue enamel, brought in proudly by a young woman who held it above her head before plonking it down with a flourish. Only then did we see the meal in its full horror. The late sheep seemed to stare accusingly at us all. The 'honoured guest' on slicing duty was my father, who got the cheek as by right; my stepmother had the lips, while I was left with the ear.

What was it like? A stewed Goodyear tyre, with added gristle but without the flavour, might be one answer. Forty minutes of solid chewing with no discernible result, might be another. Eventually, as surreptitiously as I could, I stowed the remnants in a plant pot.

To drink, there was always gunpowder (or caravan) tea boiled with salted water and copious quantities of yak's butter, Tibetan-style. Otherwise, the basic beverage was koumiss, a lightly fermented mare's-milk concoction of low alcohol by volume, which tasted like slightly fizzy yoghurt. It was not the koumiss, however, but the arkhi that did the damage. Arkhi is a type of vodka, but to say that is to sell it short. It is distilled milk, usually mare's milk, and to me it tasted like a cocktail of pure surgical spirit and milk left in the Australian sun for a week. The gag reflex kicked in almost every time I saw it, let alone put it to my lips, and it was only the consciousness that I was, however peripherally, part of a diplomatic mission that allowed me to force it down.

Force it down you had to, though. First, the local chairman would toast the British ambassador for honouring his region with a visit, then my father would reply with a toast of thanks, then there would be a toast to the beauty and elegance of my stepmother, and perhaps a few words from her and another shot glass downed in return, then 'Amity between our peoples', then 'Peace among nations', and so on. There was no mercy, and each toast demanded the next, until everyone was more or less under the table. I was twenty and still had a young man's powers of recovery, but my father was fifty that year, and it was no wonder that as the tour progressed he began to look a bit grey. On the other hand, he had always been a hard drinker: he had the spy's training of out-drinking his opponent while still remembering and noting everything that happened. We all survived somehow, but in a sort of bleary fog.

Much of the ground in our four-province journey was covered in Gaziks, a far cry in comfort or reliability from the embassy Range Rover. My father and stepmother were always in the lead vehicle with the driver and translator, while I followed behind in the second Gazik, with little idea of what was happening or where we were going. The hangovers, combined with the Gaziks' extremely uncomfortable seats and heavy leaf-sprung suspension, made these long drives, always across almost trackless steppes and stretches of Gobi (desert-like terrain), supremely tedious. The monotony was usually broken only by mechanical failure, followed by an hour or two of argument between the drivers about which spanner to use to get the vehicle going again.

On the other hand, this made the highlights seem even more remarkable, such as going across a pass in the Altai Mountains and stopping at the highest point of the road, where there was a tall cairn of stones. Atop it, looking west out to one grand expanse of steppe, the skull of an ibex, and gazing east, towards the valley from which we had come, the bleached skull of an argal, and with prayer-flags fluttering in the stiff, cold mountain breeze. And driving along a line of hills on what was obviously a very old and well-worn track, we met a camel train coming the other way, the great beasts loaded with dismantled gers, rugs, kettles, saucepans and all the apparatus of nomadic life: thinking 'Marco Polo must have seen something like this, as must all those who travelled the Silk Road, for hundreds of years.' Elsewhere, we came across a camel market in the middle of nowhere: hundreds of the creatures were tethered or wandered with hobbled feet, moaning and keening at extraordinary volume, while their owners haggled and lied like animal dealers everywhere.

Driving across a vast stretch of uninhabited plain towards a line of cliffs, we saw a pair of eagles on tree stumps, a kilometre or so from a village under the hill. Diverting to get closer, we were puzzled to note that the birds didn't fly away. Then we saw why: they were chained to the stumps. Someone was dispatched to the village and returned with a wizened old Mongol, who said he owned them. 'What did he use them for?' my father asked through the translator. 'Hunting.' 'Hunting what?' A shrug. 'Foxes. Wolves.' It seemed the eagle would swoop on the wolf, take its pelt in her claws, then fly laboriously up with this considerable load, before dropping it from a great height. The Mongol told us that every year at hatching time, the villagers would gather at the foot of the cliffs and make a great racket, leading the parent birds to swoop angrily. Meanwhile, young men would be lowered down to steal one or two of the eaglets from the nest. Each stolen bird would then be reared to adolescence, when it would be bent to its master's will. This was done by tying it to a perch, then keeping it awake by shouting at it for up to seventy-two hours. After that, the villager said, it would be ready to train.

These were hard people in a hard terrain. In Uvs province in the country's north-western corner, after breakfasting on rice pudding and vodka (grain spirit this time, not arkhi, which was a small comfort), we were taken out for a day of traditional activities. There was a large herd of unbroken horses, and first we saw a Mongol rider on his high wooden saddle cutting one animal out from the rest and lassoing it. When the horse bolted, the rider leapt off his mount, still holding the rope, and allowed himself to be dragged by it, though digging in his heels: an effect that resembled watching a waterskier on dry land. He simply wore the beast out and led it back to a pen. Then we watched aghast as he took a second horse from the pens—one which had been caught the day before—and subdued it to the bridle by first tying a rope painfully around its nose and upper lip and dragging it around: treatment which would have appalled animal lovers anywhere. Finally, there was a demonstration of breaking a horse caught three days ago to the saddle, again a process in which the horse's fury and fear were to absolutely no avail: the ruthlessness of Mongol horsemen was clearly matched only by their skill.

Much of the rest of the afternoon was spent watching displays of Mongol wrestling, and feats of horsemanship which included accurate archery by men actually hanging off the side of their horses, held apparently only by the grip of their thighs. A late-afternoon meal was served in a ger in which goats and calves came and went, and more and more vodka was drunk. In addition to the toasts this time, there was singing: the local chairman demonstrated the Homi, something akin to Tuvan throat-singing, in which the singer seems to emit two tones, nasal and bronchial, simultaneously. Songs were demanded from us in return. I remember my father bellowing 'Old MacDonald had a farm', while I contributed the whole of 'Waltzing Matilda'.

Drunk though we were, that day at the top of a low slope looking out on the great Central Asian plains was not just memorable but often hilarious: proof that despite all differences of language, ideology and nationality, totally disparate people can still occasionally form some kind of bond.

The final leg of our journey was intended to take us to Hovsgol, in the Mongolian north, but we were diverted by blizzards and had to fly south instead to the forbidden province of GoviAltai (rough translation: 'Desert/Mountain'). If previous flights had seemed merely unpleasant, this one was genuinely frightening. We climbed and climbed, but still the Altai Mountains towered above us. Unable to surmount them, we flew through a pass so narrow that the wingtips almost seemed to be in touching distance of the rocks on either side. The winds were so strong that the aircraft was being blown from side to side and up and down in the currents. Above the entrance to the cockpit was a considerately placed altimeter, its dial registering from nought to 20 000 feet. The needle climbed inexorably towards 20 000, where it stuck in the vertical position while the plane continued to climb. I tried to focus on my copy of George Orwell's *Homage to Catalonia* but succeeded only in reading the same page about thirty times, with not a single word registering.

We survived, but this time on landing we felt very much like joining the Mongol passengers in a spot of grateful ground-kissing.

The local bureaucrats, completely unprepared for our visit, nevertheless managed to put together a program. I remember an experimental livestock station where a scientist was trying to interbreed wild sheep and goats with the domestic variety, and Mongol horses with donkeys, in innovative ways, but can recall little else. Our requests to visit the southern half of GoviAltai, bordering on Xinjiang and Inner Mongolia, were flatly refused, presumably because of Russian troop movements. There was not a lot of rhyme or reason to this, because as my return trip to Peking in daytime would later prove, there were plenty of large and elaborate Soviet military installations near the Chinese border, clearly visible from the train window.

No flight could ever match the horror trip to GoviAltai, and our return to Ulan Bator seemed almost luxurious by comparison. I remember looking out the window down to the faintly visible ruins of Karakorum, the historic capital of Genghis Khan, now little more than an outline in the desert. Look on my works, ye mighty, and despair.

* * *

A while after we got back to the embassy from GoviAltai, there was a diplomatic incident. What it was wasn't clear to me till dinner one night, when we sat down to eat and my father motioned us to silence.

I knew already that the walls had ears. I'd been told the story of how, every year, the de-buggers—tech-heads from London—came and removed all the hidden microphones and wires. Then, predictably within days, a team from the Ulan Bator central heating department turned up, always in the middle of summer, by the way, declaring that they'd detected a fault and needed to service the radiators. 'Servicing' meant dismantling them entirely and reinstalling them, including removal and replacement of half the plaster in the walls. Of course.

I could also see with my own eyes that the embassy's phone lines weren't connected to the nearest telegraph pole. They all went through the blockish, windowless brick sentry post just outside the compound. Why on earth would that be?

I hadn't really let these bugging warnings bother me too much, except to notice that my father only ever really opened up when we were out fishing. Then he talked freely about all kinds of things, including the fact that one of his predecessors was so obsessed by the bugging that he went mad, imagining that cameras were following him everywhere, even on long walks on the Mongolian steppe—so mad, in fact, that he had to be recalled to England.

But tonight was the evening when the reality sank in. My father, astonishingly, wanted to talk shop in the dining room. And he didn't want a conversation either. This was going to be a monologue, and Moranna and I were not the intended audience. He leaned back in his chair at the head of the table and began to talk very loudly … to the ceiling. He was very angry, he said, almost more angry than he could express. And Her Majesty's Government was angry too. Diplomatic bags had arrived from London on a plane via Moscow, and they'd been tampered with. The wax seals had been broken, the padlocks had been smashed, and the contents had been rifled.

Now I happened to know this was not in itself a deeply serious security breach, because all the really sensitive material came in by land across China, the way I'd come with the Queen's Messengers. But I had just enough sense to keep my mouth shut about that, because my father was talking about a point of principle. Diplomatic bags of any kind are sacrosanct under the Vienna Conventions, and what the Mongolians or maybe the Russians had done was a casual insult at best, and at worst a deliberate provocation.

All these points my father made, loudly, to the walls and ceiling, while saying that his repeated protests to the country's foreign ministry had been blandly ignored. Now, he said, he'd had enough. He'd decided to cable London the following morning to recommend they begin proceedings to break off diplomatic relations with Outer Mongolia, close the embassy and return him home. Which would have been huge, as big a diplomatic breach as they come—enough to make headlines from *The Washington Post* to *Pravda*. It was quite a speech, probably about ten minutes long, and delivered with exceptional dramatic vehemence. It took real effort, when Dad gave us the sign that it was all over, to resume the charade of normal dinner-table conversation.

This would have been about nine o'clock of a Thursday evening. Promptly at eight o'clock the next morning, there was an obsequious call from the Mongolian Foreign Ministry. They were sending an official car to collect the ambassador for a face-to-face meeting with the minister, who wanted to apologise profusely for an incident which had only just been brought to his personal attention, and which should never have happened.

As I've already written, I didn't then know that my father was actually a spy. That kind of bugging was normal for conventional diplomats in every embassy, every residence, every staff flat and often every car in every country where the KGB and its sister organisations like the Stasi held sway.

* * *

It had been a beautiful and fascinating summer, but at the end of August it was time to go home—and also time for one more little adventure—after saying goodbye. Dad always wore sunglasses for farewells, to hide the possibility of tears. On this day he wore his darkest pair. We would not, as it turned out, meet again for another five years. We hugged, and I boarded the train with a small task to perform.

To test the degree of thaw in the Cultural Revolution, the UK embassy in Peking had hatched a plan to have me travel to Hong Kong overland, rather than by another potentially nightmarish CAAC flight, something no Westerner had been able to do since 1966. Rather than book me direct from Ulan Bator to the southern border, Dad had bought an Ulan Bator–Peking ticket, and, to fool the system, the Peking embassy had bought a ticket in my name for the rest of the journey. A British embassy staffer met me at the station in Peking and escorted me onto the train. The authorities might, or might not, notice the subterfuge. If they did, I would presumably spend another night in Peking before being put on a plane. If they noticed while the train was well underway, there was probably nothing they could or would do about it.

With the confidence or ignorance of youth, I remember feeling excited rather than nervous. This train was faster but far less luxurious than the Ulan Bator service, and with the added disadvantage of loudspeakers in every corridor blaring out incessant renditions of Maoist revolutionary operas like *The White-Haired Girl* and *The Red Detachment of Women*. The compensation was the view from my sleeper cabin window: the Chinese landscape spooling by, like a scroll-painting unrolling, and especially waking in the morning to views of what I think was the edge of the famous Wulingyuan National Park, with its plunging peaks, dramatic cliffs and grottoes among dense forest.

And so, after twenty-four hours, I arrived at Hong Kong as the first Westerner to have travelled overland from China's north to its south since the Cultural Revolution had begun. It was no feat of mine, merely a little embassy experiment, but one which marked its own tiny little moment in history.

Emerging into the high-energy hustle of mercantile Hong Kong, I had also, after a summer spent travelling through one communist country and living in another, received a thorough lifetime inoculation—not by propaganda but lived experience—against any form of Marxist-Leninist thought.

Chapter 18

Five Lines of Copy

When I graduated in 1973, I had, really, nowhere in England to go, but my last year had been so much fun that I didn't want to leave Oxford. I hung around for a few months while my circle of friends gradually scattered. I did bar jobs and washed up in restaurants, and slept on people's sofas. But soon the fun was fading, it was getting cold, and I signed on for the dole. There wasn't enough work around. Not having got a First, I was told not to bother applying for a BBC traineeship, and not yet having discovered a vocation for journalism, it didn't occur to me to start applying for junior reporting jobs on provincial papers—easily the fastest track to Fleet Street in those days. I felt I had no long-term prospects, and Dad would not be back in England for more than a year. There was less and less to keep me, and when my mother sent me a ticket back to Canberra, I accepted gratefully.

I described in the preface how I was accepted as a cadet (trainee) journalist at the ABC in William Street, Sydney, starting in February 1974. There being no journalism schools then, let alone journalism degrees, the first few weeks were basic training: how to write a news lead, how to arrange a story in a sort of pyramid order of importance, how to keep your sentences simple, declarative, active and short. We were ABC News trainees, starting by learning how to do radio news: that meant that mostly we would be trying to distil whatever we needed to say into ten sentences at most, with the likelihood that they'd be cut down to five, or even three.

ABC News had stringent standards: we were not to assume that anything that had been published in a newspaper was true without making phone calls or consulting authoritative sources to check. There was to be no opinion, no analysis, no comment. A young journalist was rumoured to have been sacked a couple of years before for wearing a badge supporting the Moratorium (against the Vietnam War). If you were on camera, beards and moustaches were strongly discouraged and jackets and ties were mandatory.

Radio Current Affairs, down the road in another building, seemed tacitly to be the enemy, much more so than the newspapers or other TV and radio stations. This was partly because they had different rules: their reporters were freer to analyse, had more time to ask sharp questions, and were even occasionally encouraged to inject some satire. But it was also partly a literally sectarian rivalry: News' leadership was said to have been historically Catholic, while Current Affairs was thought of as Protestant.

The soon-to-retire head of News, Keith Fraser, was a former policeman from Joh Bjelke-Petersen's Queensland, with a temperament that matched the stereotype. His deputy and designated successor, Russ Handley, a kindly but vague man, was famous for once having emerged from the toilets, walked up to the chief sub-editor, and said 'G'day chiefer, what's happening?' unaware that he was trailing a long roll of lavatory paper from the back of his trousers. The cadet counsellor, Don Gordon, was usually known as 'Spring-heeled Jack' because of his peculiar bouncing gait. He was a decent man, and not a bad tutor, but it wasn't hard to pick up the notion that he was in this job because his career as a reporter or sub-editor had reached about as high as it was ever going to.

Our leaders all seemed very old. I think people in their late fifties and sixties really did look older then, faces cured by sun and tobacco smoke and lined with ten thousand hangovers.

The newsroom I joined was a clattery, cluttery place full of typewriters, big rotary-dial phones, and lots and lots of paper. Newspaper, typing paper, carbon paper. Fresh paper, scrumpled-up, discarded paper. Occasionally paper on fire, in a rubbish bin, when someone had carelessly stubbed out a cigarette. If you wanted to make an interstate call, you had to go through the ABC switchboard; if (a rare event) you needed to make an international call, the ABC switchboard had to ring the international switchboard, and they had to ring a switchboard in the country you were ringing, and as often as not the person you were ringing would be out. News came in from overseas on telex machines, so noisy that they had to be housed in a soundproof room at the back. 'Research' was a cuttings library of fading photocopied or Roneo-ed ABC News stories, the collected volumes of old ABC News bulletins, some battered encyclopaedias, and a *Who's Who*.

We learned to use tape recorders, microphone technique, how to cut tape by 'dubbing' (transferring from one machine to another) or cutting with a razor and sticky tape. We went up to the ABC Training Centre in Darlinghurst Road to learn the rudiments of how to direct a television news story on the road and how to work in a TV studio. Back in William Street, there were exercises in how to turn a press release and a sheaf of cuttings into a story at speed, and how to build up a contact book. But we were told above all to be curious: not to rely on handouts but to see the stories in the events we experienced.

On the other hand, it was obvious that some of the things we saw, or were 'common knowledge', were not reportable. The newsroom was three blocks from King's Cross: just up the road, you could sometimes see a prostitute or a pimp step out of a shop doorway to hand a brown envelope through the window of a police car.

Across the road from the newsroom, in Forbes Street, was the Forbes Club, a notorious illegal gambling joint. ABC TV Current Affairs' *This Day Tonight* once set up its camera on the roof of the building next door and told viewers, in innocent tones, that the program had phoned the police hours earlier to alert them that the place was hosting gambling without a licence, but that no-one, so far, had turned up to raid the place. The program kept crossing back to the camera for the next half-hour, but no police ever came. This provocation so enraged the NSW premier, Sir Robert Askin, that the next day he went into parliament to announce that there would be police raids on all of Sydney's illegal gambling dens at six o'clock that evening. Given that kind of notice, it was hardly surprising that when the cops arrived, TV cameras in tow, nothing untoward was happening at any of these fine establishments.

Privately, most people in journalism believed that NSW was corrupt from top to bottom, and the corruption began around the corner from our office, with two people only ever referred to as 'Mr Big' and 'Mr Sin'. Mr Big was a thug and organised crime figure called Lenny McPherson. Mr Sin was Abe Saffron, a former sly-grog seller who'd accumulated a gambling and prostitution empire. Years later, in a book called *Gentle Satan*, Abe Saffron's son Alan said his father paid Premier Sir Robert Askin, as well as two successive NSW police commissioners, Norm Allan and Fred Hanson, huge sums in bribes over the years.

Everyone in Sydney journalism 'knew' most of this, but the barriers to publication were huge. Juanita Nielsen, who ran a little crusading newspaper in King's Cross, crossed someone powerful and disappeared—kidnapped and murdered, presumably, though nobody knew that for certain at the time. And where intimidation didn't work, there were the defamation laws. At ABC News, it was unthinkable that these kinds of stories would get into our bulletins, not least because the ABC's legal department at the time was thought by most journalists to be cravenly cautious. Its teetering, almost-ceiling-high piles of dusty old files and briefs tied with pink tape gave a Dickensian impression, and its default setting seemed to be 'If in doubt, don't publish.' Our job, it was clear, was bread-and-butter news. Campaigns, crusades and investigation were largely off-limits.

In any case, I was completely wet behind the ears. I knew we cadets had to start small, and that meant doing routine minor assignments handed out by the chief of staff, shadowing 'rounds' correspondents, going to Miss Hale's Secretarial College in the CBD twice a week for shorthand lessons, and keeping your eyes peeled for stories.

I had found a shared house in Coogee through friends of my Canberra mate John Langtry, and one steamy night almost a month after I joined up, John got us tickets to see the great blues guitarist BB King in concert at the Hordern Pavilion. All went well until, an hour or so in, King collapsed on stage while playing 'Sweet Sixteen' and had to be carried off. I left the Hordern in search of a phone box. The first one was broken. Finding one that worked, I stuffed some money in, rang one of the copytakers at ABC News and dictated five lines of copy. I got on a bus and got home in time to hear those lines being delivered on the hourly ABC Radio News: 'The blues guitarist BB King collapsed on stage tonight …'

It was the first time anything I'd written ever got to air. It was a thrill at least equal to seeing my first photo in print in the *Falmouth Packet* in 1971.

* * *

The key to getting sent out into the wider world as a cadet was to get through the shorthand course. Tape recorders weren't enough for a radio reporter back then. You needed to be able to take notes at talking speed: at least 100–110 words per minute. Until then, you were stuck in the Sydney newsroom. For some reason, I found Pitman's easy, getting to the requisite number of words in what I was told was a record twelve lessons in six weeks. There was no great secret to it, other than doing a couple of hours' practice every night, and rote-learning—boarding school had given me plenty of experience of that.

Once I'd passed, I was eligible to be sent out to regional offices to fill in for more-senior journalists on leave. I was sent first to the ABC's Canberra newsroom in Northbourne Avenue. There I learned the daily routine of helping fill the local radio bulletins, which involved ringing around a regular circuit of police stations, farm agents, firemen, hospitals, local identities and stringers. Canberra was much smaller then, and in any case its transmitters served places as far afield as Cooma and Cootamundra. I got into the swing of it, and was obviously competent enough: after about three weeks they told me that the chief of staff in the ABC's press gallery bureau, Owen Lloyd, had asked for me to go over there to replace (temporarily) one of the long-time reporters, who was going on leave.

Parliament was broadcast live, but the law then said it was not to be recorded, certainly not for edited rebroadcast. So doing accurate shorthand 'takes' of ten minutes at a time, in relays, was an essential part of the job. It just happened that I was the one doing the 'take' at 8.30 p.m. on 10 April 1974, when Prime Minister Gough Whitlam rose to his feet and said, 'Mr Speaker, I inform the House that I have this evening advised His Excellency the Governor-General that a situation has arisen under section 57 of the Constitution which would entitle him to dissolve both Houses. His Excellency accepted my advice and granted an immediate simultaneous dissolution ...' It was just on two months since I had started as a cadet, and there I was, sitting at a typewriter in the press gallery, with Owen Lloyd standing over my shoulder, bashing out the lead for the nine o'clock news: 'It's official: there's to be a double-dissolution election.'

My little piece was hardly a major achievement in itself: the people telling the story on TV that night—Ken Begg for ABC News and Richard Carleton for *This Day Tonight*—had far bigger parts to play. But it was my own first small introduction to the adrenaline rush of covering a really big national story.

I liked Old Parliament House, despite its cramped and crowded conditions. Or perhaps because of them: there was an intimacy about it, which meant that politicians—especially ministers—couldn't quarantine themselves from journalists, as many do now. Some MPs would just drop into the ABC office for a beer, but even for the others there were few ways to keep away from the media. It was difficult to get quickly around the building without going through King's Hall, at the front, and old hands like the 'Silver Fox', Alan Reid, were famous for lurking behind its pillars to buttonhole their political targets. That said, it was an atmosphere hugely dominated by men and booze. A large portion of some journalists' days was spent in the non-members' bar, which many MPs also frequented, giving the journos the excuse that they were 'cultivating sources'.

The ABC's chief Senate correspondent, Les Love, a tiny, genuinely charming man in his sixties, was very seldom even remotely sober. But somehow he managed to do the job despite his steady intake. Les had been there so long he was generally known as 'Senator Love'. On one famous occasion, he was muttering from the press gallery during a speech by Senator Margaret Guilfoyle about Aboriginal 'trachoma'. 'It's *glaucoma*, you stupid woman,' Les said, rightly or wrongly, but definitely audibly. 'I thank the honourable senator for his correction,' said Senator Guilfoyle, glancing up.

One story about him from before my time concerned the then uncovered walkway that joined the rear of the Senate to the House of Representatives. It was the shortest way back to the ABC office, and late one night, during a snowstorm, Les slipped over and fell unconscious. Parliamentary attendants found him an hour later and an ambulance took him to hospital. The doctor who saw him when he woke the next morning is alleged to have said, 'Mr Love, you are a very lucky man. If not for the quantity of alcohol in your blood, you would probably have died of hypothermia. On the other hand, if not for the extreme cold, which slowed down your metabolism, you would almost certainly have died of alcohol poisoning.'

With parliament dissolved, there was less to do after Whitlam's election announcement, and I spent a few weeks largely following up press releases by far-flung MPs and candidates, for stories which were mainly used on ABC Rural and regional stations. I had returned to Sydney by the time Whitlam beat Billy Snedden in the May 1974 election, but I came back to Canberra for a year in 1978, by which time Malcolm Fraser was prime minister. By then things were slowly—very slowly—starting to change. Women like Niki Savva, Michelle Grattan and Gay Davidson were starting to make much more of a mark in the press, but it would take decades for the male dominance of the gallery to change radically.

* * *

In Sydney in mid-1974, for some absurd reason, my English accent gave someone the mistaken idea that I was the right person to compile and read the finance report on the ABC's breakfast show. This was way outside my area of expertise. A more senior reporter kindly told me the story of how a previous incumbent had made a mistake on air with the price of gold which led to an investor ringing in to say that he had just lost $20 000 on the strength of it. No pressure there, then. To make things worse, the breakfast presenter, Clive Robertson, who could be very funny, had no respect at all for the 'just-the-facts-no-personalities' rules of ABC News, and would keep interrupting, playing sound effects, or asking me questions.

I survived, somehow, for a while, and soon I was down at the NSW Parliament shadowing the state political correspondent, Paul Mullins. 'Mullo' was an ex-boxer whose broad shoulders and slightly crouched posture always reminded you of his ring days: he went on to a long career asking politicians the tough questions on Channel Ten. But in 1974, at the end of every week, he wrote and presented a fifteen-minute radio program, *The Week in State Parliament*, known in the newsroom as 'Twisp'. There I learned the rudiments of radio producing, timing scripts, cutting tapes as needed, and sitting in the control room with a stopwatch making sure it all fitted.

The NSW Parliament press gallery then was a complete anachronism, really not much changed from the kind of press room depicted in Ben Hecht's 1928 Broadway play *The Front Page*. Uniformed parliamentary attendants served ice-cold beer, and meals on crested parliamentary crockery, while the reporters sat around telling all the salacious stories they could never print or broadcast, and playing the card game 500. Meanwhile, the government of Sir Robert Askin was not only corrupt but old and tired. A sharp new ALP leader, Neville Wran, made question time more interesting in the Legislative Assembly usually nicknamed the 'Bear Pit', and Liberal 'law-and-order' (or Laura Norder) slogans seemed to be losing their punch in the face of growing discontent over the state's crumbling transport system.

Towards the end of the year I got another regional posting, this time to Orange. I packed my gear onto my Yamaha 250 motorbike and headed west through the Blue Mountains. The Orange area was a far more traditionally agricultural region then: now known as a food and wine destination, in those days it was known for fruit, cattle, sheep and grain crops. But its ABC radio station covered a huge area of western NSW: Bathurst, Dubbo, Cowra, Forbes, Parkes, Canowindra, and all the way out to Cobar. With local bulletins at breakfast, lunch and dinner, it was far too big to do much coverage on the ground: it was all about the daily round of phone calls to friendly contacts, farmers, the occasional stringer on a retainer, police and so on. Fortunately, the senior reporter, the kindly Amos Bennett, had been there a long time, and the contact book was huge.

I settled into a routine, usually producing enough 'lines' to fill the bulletin with local news, though there was occasional recycling from, say, lunchtime to evening bulletins. Country towns tend to be places where everyone knows each other, and my colleague Chris Masters remembers working at the ABC office in Albury at around this time, when the local news journalist and newsreader was a man called Cleaver Bunton, who also happened to be the town's mayor. Chris swears that one night the bulletin began: 'This is the ABC News, written by Cleaver Bunton and read by Cleaver Bunton. The mayor of Albury, Cleaver Bunton, said today …'

I seem to recall that the most exciting thing to happen in the Orange region one week was an exploding outside dunny in Canowindra, but I have long forgotten the details. I had a room in the Hotel Canobolas, ate a steak or a casserole in the pub most nights, and, knowing no-one of my own age in town, had very little social life other than conversations at the bar. At weekends I buzzed around the district on my bike.

ABC News at this time featured very few reporters' voices. Most stories were read in actorly, English-accented tones by veteran newsreaders like Bruce Menzies (pronounced 'Ming-ies'), Martin Royle and Peter Dawes-Smith. The only other voices that audiences heard in bulletins (as opposed to current affairs programs like *AM* and *PM*) were those of people like federal ministers and their opposition counterparts, the ABC's foreign correspondents, and its federal and state political reporters. But that began to change in 1974, as general and rounds reporters started to be encouraged to file 'voice pieces' and 'actuality' into bulletins.

It was about time. It created a greater incentive for reporters like me to get out into the field with a tape recorder and see and hear for themselves. In Orange, with its thrice-daily round of bulletins, I hadn't yet been able to do that.

In December, a huge bushfire broke out around Cobar, way over to the west of our territory. For about a day I covered it by phone, ringing the fire service in Cobar and anyone else I could find—Cobar is about 450 kilometres from Orange by road, so I thought, being stuck with the bulletins, I didn't have a choice. Then an announcer called Terry Berkrey suggested that we both hire a plane and fly there. He would cover the crisis for the station, and since this was now much more than a local story, I could file for ABC state and national news. This was an astonishing notion to me, but I rang Sydney and they said yes. While ABC local management in Orange organised someone to do the local bulletins, we drove out to the local airfield, got in a single-engine Cessna, and headed out.

It was a hell of a flight (though still small beer compared to the one I'd taken through a Mongolian mountain pass two years earlier), because as the plane got closer to the fire, the thermal currents became more and more turbulent. It felt as though we were being tossed around like a leaf in the wind as we approached the bushfire, the first I'd ever seen. It was a wall of smoke and flame stretching for many kilometres along the ground and hundreds of metres into the air. A fire as big as that sucks in powerful winds at its base and creates a whole microclimate of aerial chaos. It was hard to keep from throwing up as the pilot wrestled to keep us on course and on the level through a series of unpredictable thermals.

I scribbled a description of what we'd seen from the air and filed by phone from the airfield. When I arrived at the emergency centre, people were listening to the ABC bulletin, and my voice piece was there as the national lead. But to send better-quality audio, I needed a line, not a phone. The answer was at the PMG—the Postmaster-General's Department—which was what we had before Telstra or even Telecom. A friendly tech ushered me behind the scenes into a world of switching boxes, cords and plugholes, and I was able to hook up at will for the next few days to send high-quality material to Sydney.

That fire around Cobar burnt out one and a half million hectares. I remember interviewing people who'd seen rabbits and kangaroos with their fur burning running, panicked, across firebreaks and spreading the blaze to new areas. I remember seeing the air over and around a stand of trees—not the trees themselves—explode into flame as a spark hit the halo of evaporated eucalyptus oil they were giving off in the heat.

One evening I filed for the ten o'clock news, and the intake sub Mike Rue told me that I had just become the first ABC reporter ever to have a voice piece in both the national and state bulletins. An incredibly minor achievement in retrospect, but for a cadet approaching the end of his first year, it seemed like something.

I think I was in Cobar for a few days, sleeping on floors and filing around the clock, before the fire was sufficiently under control for Sydney to pull me out. I hitched a ride on an RAAF Hercules back to Sydney. When I got there, I was surprised to see a bunch of other ABC reporters on the tarmac. During the previous few hours, news of Cyclone Tracy flattening Darwin, including all of its communications links, had finally got out to the rest of Australia. When I realised what was going on, I volunteered to go straight there—to switch from one RAAF plane to another and head north.

That was a bridge too far for a cadet, as far as the bosses were concerned. They sent me back to my mum's in Canberra for Christmas. But I was on my way, and I already had hopes of moving out of the ABC newsroom and across the road into the planned new youth station, 2JJ—Double J.

Chapter 19

A Deliberate Middle Finger

LIKE MOST YOUNG Sydneysiders at 11 a.m. on 19 January 1975, I wasn't at the Double J studios for the station's first broadcast. I listened with friends in our share-flat in Coogee. In fact, I was convinced I had missed out altogether on the chance to be in on the station's first year.

As I recall, 2JJ test broadcasts had been ringing through our flat for a couple of days—they'd been playing wall-to-wall music—but this was the launch, the mission statement, and the first time we could hear the station's spoken voice. The minutes leading up to eleven o'clock felt momentous: a complex montage of sound and music, culminating in a Cape Canaveral countdown and the unmistakable opening chords of Skyhooks' 'You Just Like Me 'Cos I'm Good in Bed'. Then the voice of Holger Brockman, admitting he was nervous, something you didn't usually do on the radio in those days, and welcoming the audience. And on to the second record, the Rolling Stones' 'Sympathy for the Devil'.

It may seem quaint now, but at the time, every element of this—every track, everything about the way it was framed—meant something to a generation that felt frustrated and deprived of its own voice. Sydney radio then was dominated by commercial stations, and the most powerful when it came to the youth market was the Catholic Church–owned

2SM. Like all the other commercials, 2SM was limited and conservative in its choice of music: limited in the sense that it had a high-rotation format which only played a certain rota of records; conservative in that a large amount of music was simply banned on moral grounds. They even bleeped out the 'Christ, you know it ain't easy' in John Lennon's 'The Ballad of John and Yoko'.

The opening Skyhooks track was one of those the commercials wouldn't allow you to hear. It came from an album, *Living in the 70's*, that had registered huge sales with the public, but some of its best tracks were on the commercial radio blacklist. Kicking off with a song that was explicitly about sex—especially on the Sabbath—was a deliberate middle finger not only to the rest of the Sydney radio industry, but also to the 'moral majority'. It said a couple of other things, too: its economical length and unforgettable hook said this was not *just* going to be a station that played long, self-indulgent guitar solos or whole sides of Frank Zappa albums, and that this was going to be a station that supported Australian music.

Then there was the significance of Holger Brockman. His voice had long been familiar to 2SM listeners, but not his name. As was common in commercial radio in the 1960s and 1970s, he'd had to broadcast under a pseudonym, because 'Bill Drake' was less likely to put off the audience. Even the nervousness, whether deliberate or not, made a statement of its own: it said this was going to be a station that spoke naturally, not in the pumped-up tones of specially trained announcer-clowns with 'stacks-of-wax-revive-forty-five' slogans, and who introduced records with the same hype that they used to advertise motorbikes or icy poles.

And as for 'Sympathy for the Devil', that was also an obvious up-yours to the wowsers, for its explicitly satanic content alone. Released in 1969, it had never been played on commercial radio: it was six minutes long, and the commercials' rotation formats allowed for nothing longer than three. The choice of a Stones classic also said up-front, 'We're going to be playing the stuff you've been listening to. There's a lot of it, some of which you already know, but even if you've been shopping at import stores, there'll be some you don't. Let us experiment for you.'

It was a great beginning, and it reminded me most of my teens listening to John Peel and Kenny Everett on pirate radio in England. I wanted in, but my cadetship would not formally be over till the passing of a full year, and I was therefore not eligible for the short hop across William Street to the 2JJ offices until mid-February—and even then, a vacancy had to open up. As it turned out, I only had to wait a few weeks. The Double J newsroom on launch day consisted of Ros Lawson, John Arden and Tony Maniaty. John, who I would run across years later in his role as a distinguished Rome correspondent, decided the place wasn't for him, and ABC News management called me in and told me that since my cadetship was officially at an end, I was next in line.

I had just turned twenty-two, and I was now one of just three journalists given the job of bringing some kind of news service to an audience of young people our age—a news service that reflected their interest in music, drug policy, the environment, unemployment and education, as well as the standard fare of traditional ABC journalism: politics, economics, crime, transport. Given that, in the early days, the first bulletin was at 6 a.m. and the last at 10 p.m., there were three shifts: early morning, day and evening. So, effectively, straight out of a year's cadetship, I was producing my own news bulletins every day, though with the invaluable help of the experienced and unflappable production assistant Patti Winter.

Commercial rents were extremely low in the 1970s, and Double J had an enormous amount of office space, much of it half-empty. But otherwise its budget was tiny. It was set up explicitly as an experiment, using the ABC's old standby parliamentary transmitter, and 1975 was effectively a probationary year. Its founding had been a Whitlam initiative, and as ABC Deputy General Manager Clement Semmler made clear on his retirement in 1977 in a *Sydney Morning Herald* interview, he was one of those who had fought against it from within: '2JJ should never have been introduced. Its music is only fit for commercial stations.' Those who opposed the station from outside the ABC ranged from bishops (of more than one denomination) to the Festival of Light's crusading Reverend Fred Nile.

There was an abiding sense of impermanence about the place, reflected in a scarcity of furniture and equipment. The two coordinators, Marius Webb and Ron Moss, had desks by a window in a big room that also served as a meeting place. Then there were desks and chairs dotted around cubicle offices. But in the communal areas, apart from a few old sofas rescued from skips or people's houses, and some beanbags, most people, when we had meetings, sat or lay on the floor. The newsroom was a frosted-glass box in one corner, just big enough to cram in two or three people at a time.

In retrospect, the saddest thing for me about the lack of funding is that the tape budget was so low. As journalists, we edited by 'dubbing'—transferring sound and voice from a tape on one machine onto a tape on another. It not only required real skill to record like this on the fly without your edit points being audible, but in the absence of fresh tapes, it had one gigantic drawback: every edit you did meant you were wiping over another recording. And if there was no money for tapes, there was certainly none for setting up and collating an archive. The result is that very little audio remains from the first few years of Double J.

Another consequence of the lack of budget was the studios. They were tiny and cramped: I believe they'd originally been dug out of the basement of the ABC's tower-block offices in Forbes Street during World War II, for use in emergencies. So basically, we were broadcasting from a bomb shelter. Our offices, meanwhile, were down the hill at 177 William Street.

What did that mean in practice? To get the 6 a.m. bulletin to air, you gathered up your scripts and tapes, dashed to the stairwell, ran at breakneck speed down several flights of stairs, then ran up the sandstone Forbes Street steps. Often enough it was raining, sometimes there was a drunk passed out on the stairs, occasionally a prostitute would be engaging a client against the balustrade, and by 8 or 8.30 a.m., the pavement was regularly blocked by schoolgirls arriving for the day at the adjacent SCEGGS (Sydney Church of England Girls' Grammar School). You then ran up what was known as 'Cardiac Hill'—probably only 30 or 40 metres, but very steep—shot in past the commissionaire, raced down some stairs, swerved down a corridor, and, panting, fell into the studio. Then it was back down the hill to knock out the 6.30 a.m. headlines: Patti took them up while you started preparing a new bulletin for 7 a.m. The same at 7.30, 8 and 8.30 a.m. It was an insane system, given the ease with which someone could have rigged up a line straight from the office to the studio, but this was the 1970s ABC, where even the issue of a stopwatch required forms in triplicate, signed and countersigned, in processes that could take weeks or months.

Taken together, all these factors meant that, effectively, the Double J newsroom was running hard throughout that first year just to keep up.

We had no Canberra correspondent, for instance, in what quickly proved to be one of the most hectic and intense years of Australian federal politics of the twentieth century.

The Whitlam government was by now in a precarious state. Labor had won the double-dissolution election the year before, but its leader had made a series of miscalculations which endangered his ability to govern: notably, assuming that state premiers would follow convention when it came to replacing retiring or deceased senators. And in March 1975, the danger became greater. Billy Snedden, the ineffectual and uncharismatic leader Whitlam had defeated in 1974, fell victim to a leadership challenge from the extremely determined Malcolm Fraser. Snedden might possibly have exercised some compunction about exploiting Whitlam's self-created Senate weakness, but Fraser said, in his first speech as leader of the Opposition, that he had none:

> If we do make up our minds at some stage that the Government is so reprehensible that an Opposition must use whatever power is available to it, then I'd want to find a situation in which Mr Whitlam woke up one morning finding the decision had been made and finding that he had been caught with his pants well and truly down.

Add to this a growing awareness, through a string of media revelations, that Whitlam and a cabal of senior ministers had authorised a massive loan of deeply questionable legality, and rumblings of a sex scandal involving the man who was both deputy prime minister and treasurer, Jim Cairns, and you get a picture of a fast-moving national story which was consuming Canberra, but which we had to cover at a distance.

It helped that by the middle of the year, our complement of journalists increased to four. There were Lee Duffield, Nick Franklin, Jim Middleton and me. I was by far the least experienced. We somehow provided basic coverage of state, federal and international news in terms that 18–30-year-olds could understand, and with the addition of the extra pair of hands, started being able to broaden the scope of what we did. But events in Canberra were magnetic, and it was hardly as if we had no stake in the outcome: the general assumption within the station was that any change of government would almost certainly mean the end of Double J. Not necessarily, as you might assume, because the station was politically left-wing, though some of it was. I prefer to describe it with another epithet: subversive.

If I could take you back in a time machine to that station in that year, it might not strike you instantly as such. The station output that played through the speakers in every office was as likely to consist of Fleetwood Mac or Electric Light Orchestra as it was Frank Zappa or John McLaughlin. I occasionally catch myself listening to a 'classic hits' FM station and thinking how much it sounds like early Double J. But that's the nature of time passing: today's cutting edge is tomorrow's classic. And especially in 1975, there was a huge backlog of great music: Neil Young, Joni Mitchell, the solo work of John Lennon, Paul McCartney and George Harrison, Led Zeppelin, Carole King, David Bowie, Marvin Gaye, Curtis Mayfield, the early, bluesy Rod Stewart, Maria Muldaur, Bob Dylan, Santana, Minnie Ripperton, Stevie Wonder, James Brown, Al Green, Janis Joplin, Jimi Hendrix, Bruce Springsteen, Bob Marley ... some of these artists were just starting out, some were in their prime, some were already dead. But for our audience, even if they'd heard some of these artists' singles, Double J was an album station, and as such most of what they were hearing was new.

That in itself was a subversion of the status quo, but it was the station's attitude that infuriated its opponents. From the casual irreverence of breakfast presenter Alan McGirvan and his companion 'Captain Goodvibes the surfing pig', to the first documentary the station aired, *The Ins and Outs of Love*, this was a station that wasn't going to play by the old rules. It was sex and language as much as politics that had bishops and politicians demanding the station's closure. Yes, those were more likely to be issues that raised the ire of small- and large-'c' conservatives, but they were in essence social, and not political, questions.

This engendered a certain sense of siege. Double J was both a loose-knit organisation, with an almost anarchistic way of self-government, and a very tight social group, with a strong sense of its own identity against the world. And that put me and my immediate colleagues—as journalists seconded from the ABC newsroom, with one other, John Francis, seconded from ABC Current Affairs—in a peculiar situation. We were trying to evolve a form of journalism which reconciled a point of view, that of the young people we were broadcasting to, with the traditional values of balance and 'objectivity' enshrined in ABC journalism. In my view, this was not impossible: it's possible to reach conclusions from a given set of facts, as long as you don't reverse the process, starting with the conclusions and hammering the facts to fit them. Nick Franklin, for instance, was a huge influence on me, with his dogged, combative style of interviewing providing proof that you can be persistent and curious without being rude. And our dealings with the nascent industry of spin-doctoring in our coverage of state politics made us more determined not to take anything or anyone on face value. In that sense, all good journalism is or should be subversive.

But there was also the deliberate choice to cover subjects like sexual health, teenage pregnancy, abortion, feminism, the environment, the then-prevalent autocracy widespread in schools, the appalling state of NSW prisons. Even talking about these things got under some people's skin, to a degree it's difficult to convey today. Where we believed we were getting our contemporaries to talk honestly about birth control, sexually transmitted diseases and homosexuality, the ABC's own deputy general manager said, in his *Sydney Morning Herald* interview, 'Kids think it smart to listen to 2JJ but its programs are filled with smut and innuendo. It exploits the permissive society.'

'The permissive society': even the phrase is redolent of the 1970s. A Google data search shows that its use peaked in the middle of that decade, before falling away steeply in the early 1980s, seldom to be used again. Whether we liked it or not, Double J was seen as the vanguard of the permissive society, which made us a target. Against this background, it was probably not surprising that the constitutional crisis which began in October 1975 was as polarising for the station as it was for the wider community.

* * *

Malcolm Fraser's decision to block the government's supply Bills—effectively its legal authority to pay for the business of government—felt to many at Double J like a death knell. Many, but by no means all, of our audience felt the same way. Whitlam's election in 1972 had been to quite a large extent youth-driven, and not all the gilt had worn off three years later. And it was natural that listeners to a Whitlam-initiated youth station might be friendly to the government that created it. Some at the station felt so strongly that what Fraser was doing was unconstitutional that they wanted to campaign against it. They began planning a 'Day of Rage' in protest, a move which caused the first major rift between the newsroom and the rest of the station. Since everything was decided democratically at big, loose meetings, and since we journalists were vastly outnumbered, we could do nothing but argue that such a sustained and one-sided piece of broadcasting would be unbalanced, unfair and contrary to the ABC charter, and insist that we would have nothing to do with it.

The Day of Rage went ahead. It was a Saturday, a day when due to our lack of budget there was no news service anyway, so our 'boycott' as journalists was, strictly speaking, theoretical. But our fears were realised, as in practice people who wanted to defend Fraser were either blocked from going on air or cut off in mid-conversation. At the post-mortem meeting the following Monday, Holger Brockman questioned whether we really worked for the ABC in the sense of having to obey its charter. Jim Middleton suggested he take a good look at his pay slip, with the ABC's name and logo prominently displayed at the top. Shortly afterwards, Lee Duffield got up, walked across the room and put his hand forcefully on the mouth of the Day of Rage's chief proponent, David Ives, shutting him up in mid-speech. In the shocked silence that followed, Lee said, 'That's exactly what you did to those people on Saturday.' It was a point strongly made, and although there were no backdowns on either side, the fight we put up did help to establish the independence of the newsroom, and to create a (sometimes wary) respect for what we did which would stand us in good stead in the weeks to come.

I was at work early on 11 November 1975, churning out bulletins through the breakfast shift on what was obviously going to be an important day in Australian politics, though few outside Malcolm Fraser's inner circle guessed just how important. As ever, it was frustrating to have to cover a major Canberra story without a dedicated Canberra correspondent: it meant constant runs across busy William Street to get fresh copy and tapes of the ABC's press gallery correspondents, and phone calls to whichever reporters in Parliament House, like Mungo MacCallum, had the time and inclination to speak to a tiny ratbag radio station aimed at teenagers and twenty-somethings. Still, in Sydney I was working alongside Jim Middleton, a razor-sharp political intellect with an encyclopaedic knowledge of Australian political history, who would later, of course, be for many years the ABC's chief political correspondent.

In my recollection, we fully expected the day to play out as a series of purely parliamentary dramas, with Bills moving from the Lower House to the Upper, and everything depending on how the knife-edge Senate numbers would play out—a game of nerves in which the key question might well be whether Malcolm Fraser's steely determination would hold the full backing of every one of his senators, or whether one or more of them might cross the floor. (We have learned since from the men themselves that senators Don Jessop and Neville Bonner considered crossing the floor, and had they done so, Bonner said two decades on, the crisis would have ended 'in a matter of hours'.) We fed constant updates into Keri Phillips' program throughout the morning as best we could, then when parliament broke for lunch, so, with some relief, did we.

And so we were up the road in a tatty Camelot-themed pub called King Arthur's, having a sandwich and a quick drink, when the news broke. It was the publican, a big, cheery bloke, who heard the newsflash on his radio, so it was his voice we heard telling us, 'Kerr's sacked Whitlam'. We all thought, in the first seconds, that he was pulling our leg, but in response, he turned up the radio and there it was: Malcolm Fraser had been to see Governor-General Sir John Kerr at Government House in Yarralumla, and Sir John had agreed to sack Whitlam and appoint Fraser as 'caretaker' PM.

We ran down William Street, up Cardiac Hill and into the studio, from which we broadcast on Mac Cocker's show, almost non-stop, for the next few hours. It was my first major experience of live-broadcasting a major event, and it was like surfing a Hawaii-strength wave of adrenaline. Colleagues were running a more or less permanent relay between the newsroom and our studio with copy and tapes, and we essentially had to riff on what we had.

After the visits to Government House, first by Fraser, then by Whitlam, there was the proclamation on the steps of Parliament House by the governor-general's secretary, David Smith, followed by the now-famous appearance of the newly sacked PM: 'Well may he say "God Save the Queen" ... because nothing will save the governor-general.' On air, Jim astutely, and almost instantly, pointed out a new idea: such were the numbers in the Senate that it was technically possible that Labor could now turn the tables on Fraser, the new caretaker PM, and deny him passage of the supply Bills they'd been working so desperately to pass only hours before.

We were listening to and discussing the audio feed from the Senate, but the law said we were not to broadcast it: the only legal way to broadcast any parliamentary proceedings then was live, uncut, without commentary, and on the designated parliamentary network. After a short while, we collectively took the decision to break this law now, and face the consequences later. We kept talking, interspersed with live crosses to the Senate with explanatory commentary. We got away with it on the day—not surprisingly, given how much else was going on—and forty-something years on, I imagine it's probably too late for us to be brought before the bar of parliament and threatened with the full might of the law. Still, it was, I believe, an Australian broadcasting first, and yet another illustration of how much more controlled the media were at the time.

Whitlam, who had been caught completely by surprise in any case (he was eating lunch), either didn't see the potential should he decide to counter-block supply in the Senate, or decided against it. We can't know if it was rationalisation after the fact or whether he considered it on the day, but he said much later that to do so would have contravened Labor policy never to use the Upper House to block supply.

At any rate, the die was effectively cast. The most divisive and bitter election campaign in Australian history had begun. For the next month, I would be fully immersed in reporting it—the most intense experience of my working life so far.

Chapter 20

Rage and Revelation

THERE WAS NOW a month for Australians to decide their political leadership, and the country was clearly deeply (though not evenly) divided. I think now, with the benefit of long hindsight, that had Fraser left Whitlam to run another twelve to eighteen months, the Coalition would have won anyway, easily and above all legitimately.

The rot had set in nearly a year before when Whitlam toured Europe: 'It was ruins, ruins, ruins all the way,' began one of the reports from the ABC's Ken Begg, on the road with a prime minister who appeared to be pursuing his interest in classical architecture just as Cyclone Tracy flattened the entire Northern Territory capital beyond ruin. The year just went on getting worse for the ALP, as the international oil shock underscored Treasurer Jim Cairns' mishandling of the economy, and, as recession bit, Whitlam gave the increasing impression of believing himself in some way 'above' economics as he pushed through his political agenda. Yet it was economic reality which was starting to put people out of work in increasing numbers. A prime minister who was so uninterested in economics surely could not have survived.

Those were the issues which would have dominated a 'normal' campaign, but instead, this one was filled with fury. On the conservative side, many believed that because the governor-general, a lawyer and judge of long standing, had sacked the prime minister, he had somehow officially confirmed that the Whitlam government was illegitimate. For them, this was confirmation of their suspicions around all the scandals and controversies of recent months. On the left, there was 'Maintain Your Rage', a line in Whitlam's parliament-steps speech which had become *the* slogan. It summed up the fury that blew in the wake of 11 November. It represented a sense among Labor supporters, one certainly widespread among the young listenership of Double J, that Fraser and Sir John Kerr had not only ambushed Whitlam, they had conspired to do so, and in the process breached the letter or the spirit of the Constitution.

I concertinaed half a lifetime's journalistic experience into that intense month. The work became far more than churning out news bulletins, doing a few interviews or covering a demonstration and going home. I remember being at the station for twelve- and fourteen-hour days as we struggled to put together a professional and balanced coverage of the campaign.

We organised a series of debates between federal ministers, who proved surprisingly willing (for the time) to come into our little station, to talk not just about youth issues—schools, universities, apprenticeships, health—but also about foreign policy and economic management. Some of these debates contained talkback from listeners, but not as many as we would have liked. Another major problem for broadcasters at the time was the antiquated legal requirement, imposed by the Postmaster-General's Department, to broadcast a loud beep across every telephone call every few seconds. This made the kind of listener feedback we take for granted now much more rare, because it made for 'bad radio'. Instead, we generally had to gather questions from the audience beforehand and read them out to the politicians.

Outside the office and the studio, though, public opinion was making itself loudly heard—on one side at least. The demonstrations were big, angry and hugely focused on the legitimacy of what had happened. That said, it became more difficult to measure public sentiment. If you judged it by the numbers at public protests, you were in danger of predicting a Whitlam landslide instead of the Fraser avalanche that was, as it turned out, on its way. Coalition voters, by and large, were quietly at home waiting for their chance to vote Whitlam out, so that on the streets and in the TV news bulletins they were relatively invisible. Maintain Your

Rage protesters, on the other hand, were out on Sydney's streets—at rallies in the Domain, Hyde Park and at Town Hall, for example—in large numbers.

This imbalance of visibility, however, was no excuse for understating the vehemence or size of the demonstrations, as Rupert Murdoch's papers—*The Australian*, *The Daily Telegraph* and *The Daily Mirror*—unquestionably did. On several occasions my colleagues and I returned from covering protests and broadcast crowd-size estimates, including those of the always-cautious NSW Police. The Murdoch journalists covering the same demonstrations would have been in the same huddle to agree an estimate, and would have filed the same numbers. That afternoon or the next day, their papers would print a drastically reduced figure: on one occasion, a police estimate of 50 000 was cut down to 10 000 in the next day's *Australian*. You'd run into the same reporter at the next demo and ask what happened. 'Orders from on high. Nothing I could do, mate.'

It was the beginning of a dangerous trend in those papers, in which the separation of news and comment was blurred to the point of non-existence. It wasn't just downplaying crowd numbers: Murdoch journalists complained of a crescendo of management interference in their copy, and the insertion of editorial comment into straight news reporting, as the campaign went on.

This is not some conspiratorial half-memory I've conjured up. The interference was real, and so egregious that it led *The Australian*'s journalists to go on strike from 8–10 December, during the crucial last week of the election campaign. They wrote a letter to management complaining of 'the deliberate and careless slanting of headlines, seemingly blatant imbalance in news presentation, political censorship and, more occasionally, distortion of copy from senior specialist journalists, the political management of news and features, the stifling of dissident and even palatably impartial opinion in the papers' columns'.

What made it somehow worse was that it was so unnecessary—if you accept that Whitlam was actually on a hiding to nothing from day one, and the Fraser victory was a foregone conclusion. But Rupert Murdoch was a belt-and-braces man: he wanted to make doubly sure.

On the night of 13 December 1975, we called the election results live: the station's first ever election-night broadcast. Our political analyst, Denis Altman, the homosexual rights pioneer who is now a professor at La Trobe University, could see within the first hour what the early counting portended—a win for Fraser so big that it ended with one of the most lopsided parliaments in Australia's history: ninety-one seats for the Coalition, just thirty-six for what was left of the tattered ALP.

The ballot-box trouncing did nothing to diminish the rage of the Left. The 'Shame, Fraser, Shame' posters and lapel-pins lingered for years. And the party's remaining MPs refused to make Whitlam shoulder any real immediate blame for the loss: he remained as leader for the whole of the next parliament. The party postponed the soul-searching it might otherwise have begun in favour of a continuing resentment and a sense, both spoken and unspoken, of the illegitimacy of the Fraser government. It was especially prevalent in the age group Double J aimed at, and among many of the people we spoke to. With his whirlwind of health, education, social and welfare spending, Whitlam had captured a large chunk of the youth vote, and with rapidly growing youth unemployment there was real fear of what the Fraser government would bring. A couple of days spent interviewing Year 12 students at a Sydney western-suburbs high school left me with an impression of their deep uncertainty about the future.

Those who had certainty, however, had it in spades. People talk now about the bitterness and abuse of partisan politics today, but that period after the Dismissal remains unmatched, in my memory, for vitriol, partisanship and refusal of dialogue. I can only hope we never see its like again.

* * *

At Double J, we were very aware of one particular story that had been pushed out of the national consciousness by the supply crisis and the Dismissal. Another of the station's founding journalists, Tony Maniaty, had elected to go back to ABC News after a few months' work with the station, and in early October 1975 had been sent to East Timor. From there, he reported for us on the worsening situation of what was still a Portuguese colony, but one from which the Portuguese had abruptly withdrawn. With no transition period, and in the aftermath of direct rule by a military junta in faraway Lisbon, the country quickly spiralled into civil war. It had come down to a battle between the conservative UDT and the Marxist Fretilin, and throughout October, as the supply crisis dominated Australian news, they were fighting it out with guns and machetes.

But Indonesian forces, encouraged by the USA, were getting ready to pounce, marshalling in West Timor and making incursions into East Timor. Tony reported for us from Balibo in mid-October, but was warned to leave because it was becoming too dangerous. On his way out, he met the Channel Seven and Nine crews, who later became known as the Balibo Five, going in. Within days, they were dead, massacred, as we now know for certain, by Indonesian special forces.

Gough Whitlam might have done nothing, unprompted, to intervene in any of this: he was known to have a strong prejudice in favour of large states over small, autonomous or independent ones. And there seems little doubt that it was a nod from US Secretary of State Henry Kissinger that emboldened the Indonesian leader, Suharto, to launch the invasion that finally came on 7 December—six days before Australians went to the polls in the Dismissal election. On a broader scale, there was certainly fear in Western capitals that a communist-led state on Indonesia's border was a dangerous option.

In Sydney, we tried to give Timor as much coverage as we could, but on our little station, with its 18–30-year-olds audience, we were shouting into the gale as far as media influence was concerned. I remain convinced that if Australia had not been so relentlessly focused on itself during that period, the plight of a nation that had done so much to defend us in World War II might have touched a lot more hearts: perhaps, just perhaps, there might have been enough of an outcry to put real heat on Whitlam and his Cabinet to change the course of events. At worst, I sometimes think the hundred thousand or more East Timorese who died over the next quarter-century, and the many more who were tortured and imprisoned, were indirect human victims of Australia's most dramatic political crisis.

At any rate, Australians—and the ABC—now had the Christmas and New Year break to absorb all that had happened. This was probably fortunate, because passions were running nearly as high after the decisive federal election result as they had after the Dismissal itself. I returned to work in January 1976 with trepidation. I wasn't particularly worried about being put out of work myself—I was still substantively an employee of ABC News, to which I would return should Double J be dismantled—but

I had put a year's work and passion into the station, many of my friends were there, and it provided the greatest opportunities for autonomy and adventure that a 23-year-old journalist at the time could possibly ask for.

I had formed close bonds with my newsroom colleagues, and with our increasing excursions into longer work came a warm and creative collaboration with Carl Tyson-Hall, an ex-2SM producer who brought a useful sense of scepticism to any attempt at pretension or long-windedness—in scripts or in interview grabs. He helped us understand that you could do journalism-as-montage, using music tracks and sound recorded in the field as well as the usual fare of script and interview. There was also a realisation, following the whirlwind month of the election campaign, that we could be more productive in terms of how much content we contributed to the station.

I had a really strong interest in broadening our foreign coverage, to try to present international stories that might mean something to our generation. I'd just read George Orwell's *Homage to Catalonia*, and somehow, in November 1975, in the maelstrom of the election coverage, I found time to produce a short documentary on the death of the Spanish dictator Generalissimo Franco; the following year I put one together on the dirty war in Rhodesia, which was still some years away from becoming Zimbabwe. We gave ourselves 'rounds' so as to get a bit more organised and avoid treading on each other's toes: mine included environment and the arts, which meant among other things freedom to interview film directors and write book reviews.

I remember doing a lengthy piece about Vincent Bugliosi's book on the Charles Manson murders, *Helter Skelter*, interspersed with The Beatles' tracks which Manson's crazed mind had told him were secret messages inspiring him to slaughter. He interpreted McCartney's 'Helter-Skelter' in some twisted way as a rallying call for bloody mayhem. To this day, I can't hear the delicately beautiful 'Blackbird' without a mental picture of the word 'Rise!' painted in blood on the living-room wall in the house of two of his cult's victims. In retrospect, we can see 1969, the year of the Manson Family and the murder of a concertgoer by a Hells Angel 'security guard' at a Rolling Stones concert at Altamont, as the year the decade turned sour, but at the time many still found it shocking to read such graphic proof that all the sunny idealism of the Summer of Love had dissipated so quickly, and was gone for good.

During the Manson piece, I reeled off the long list of religions and cults that Manson had embraced before forming his own, including, briefly, Scientology. Immediately, I began receiving abusive and anonymous calls to my office and home numbers, claiming that this was a lie (it wasn't: Manson had dabbled in Dianetics for a few years in the early 1960s). The calls only ended when I rang a Scientology spokesman who'd earlier come in to Double J to try and proselytise his 'religion', and told him in the strongest possible terms that if they didn't stop I'd start doing daily stories about the harassment itself. He flatly denied that Scientology had anything to do with the calls, but—by the strangest coincidence, no doubt—they stopped instantly.

Double J in the early years was something of a magnet for 'alternative', especially Eastern, religions: the Rajneeshis or 'orange people', Ananda Marga, and the guru Sri Chinmoy among others. It had its funny side: you'd occasionally come back sweating from an assignment, Nagra over your shoulder, to find someone in the lotus position under your desk. Our audience age-group was clearly a major target for them, and most of us knew at least someone our age who had made, or wanted to make, a pilgrimage to an ashram somewhere on the Subcontinent. One of the DJs, Sandy McCutcheon, was particularly interested in the Eastern gurus, but in the newsroom, most of their press releases ended up in the wastepaper basket.

I'd moved in mid-1975 to a small rented flat in Rose Bay, which happened to be directly across the road from a beautiful 1920s picture palace, the Wintergarden. It no longer exists, thanks to one of Sydney's many periodic outbursts of architectural vandalism, but back then a relatively austere classical façade led through to a great circular sweep of white, gilt and Dresden blue. I liked sitting at the front-most of the balcony seats, faded and far from their glory days as they were, watching two or three movies there almost every weekend. I'd always liked films, but in youth had thought of them just as 'stories', not in the same critical or analytical spirit university had taught me to bring to literature. It was my ABC News cadet training in directing and editing news footage, rudimentary as it had been, that opened my eyes. Where once I'd watched films for the plots and performances, I now suddenly found myself also seeing the techniques: the lighting, the camera angles, the edit points; the choice of close-up, medium shot, long-shot. I even began noticing something

I'd never really seen, though it was always there: that little dot that appeared in the corner of the screen towards the end of a reel to cue the projectionist to change over.

At the Wintergarden I saw Francis Ford Coppola's *The Conversation*; Robert Altman's *McCabe & Mrs Miller*, *The Long Goodbye* and *California Split*; *All the President's Men*; Claude Chabrol's *Innocents with Dirty Hands*; *Cousin, Cousine*; Yves Robert's *The Tall Blond Man with One Black Shoe*; Michelangelo Antonioni's *The Passenger*; and François Truffaut's *Day for Night*, among many. I became a film autodidact, and started writing (probably very pretentious) reviews. Come June 1976, I put myself on the early shift during the two weeks of the Sydney Film Festival so I could leave at midday every day and sit in the glorious gilded extravaganza of the State Theatre, watching films to talk about on the radio the next day. That year and the next, I interviewed emerging Australian directors like Philip Noyce and Fred Schepisi, and was exceptionally impressed by the passionate tenacity of the visiting Englishman Peter Watkins, whose film about the aftermath of a nuclear war, *The War Game*, the BBC had banned in 1965 but was now being shown for the first time in Australia. It was also in 1976 that I saw *Taxi Driver*, my first exposure to the work of Martin Scorsese and a complete revelation. Its bleak view of a tortured, paranoid, nocturnal New York was deeply controversial, but nonetheless somewhat overshadowed in the press by the controversy surrounding Pier Paolo Pasolini's film *Salo*.

Australian Government censors had been hard at work at least since the 1920s, 'protecting' the public from films that ranged from *All Quiet on the Western Front* in 1930 to Federico Fellini's *Satyricon* in 1969. But *Salo*, a work set in the pariah republic Benito Mussolini set up in northern Italy at the losing end of World War II, was narratively framed around Marquis de Sade's *The 120 Days of Sodom*. The novel was if anything an allegory of the extremes of power, corruption and decadence, and a picture of what happens when people are treated as consumer goods. On screen, it was a horrifying depiction of what happens when all of that is taken to the ultimate conclusion. As such, it was extraordinarily graphic, and in those days before Australian 'censorship' made the transition to 'classification', it was completely banned, not just for public exhibition but also for film societies and festivals, which were usually allowed some leeway. So I found myself not watching the film itself but interviewing an academic and friend of Pasolini's, Gideon Bachmann. He presented the banned work to a packed house at the 1976 Sydney Film Festival, not as a movie—that would have brought in the cops immediately—but in the form of a series of stills, the music soundtrack and a reading of the script.

This represented two things: a bizarre demonstration of the persistence of censorship in this country—despite the reforms introduced several years earlier by the then Liberal Minister for Customs and Excise Don Chipp, reforms intensified under Whitlam—and a unique form of protest. However, the following year, an almost equally confronting Japanese film, *Ai No Corrida* (*In the Realm of the Senses*), was shown at the festival, to protest from the 'moral majority' but without censorship. Slowly, the culture was changing.

Those were insane fortnights, getting up at 4.30 a.m. and 'working', if you can call watching films with a notebook and pen working, till 10 or 11 at night. But I wouldn't have traded them for the world—the 1970s may have been the best decade of all time to plunge into the study of movies as an art form. The next year, 1977, I enjoyed the Sydney premiere of the first *Star Wars* movie without in the least anticipating how its semi-camp, sequel-oriented, action-adventure excess was going to become the new normal.

* * *

As we got more organised as a newsroom at Double J, and established stronger relationships with others at the station, we also gradually got more airtime. Mac Cocker was one key to this.

A big, bearded Yorkshireman with a pronounced Sheffield accent, he and I started at the station in the same week, pretty much at the same time as another Englishman, Tony Barrell, who became one of my closest friends. Mac was an extrovert with a thirst in those days: going to the pub with him usually meant a long session and a lot of yarns. On air, he was not just fearless but positively loved to push at the boundaries of what you were allowed to say. When Mac died recently, an Irish friend of mine told me that Mac's had been the first voice he ever heard on Australian radio, straight off the plane, and definitely the first he'd heard anywhere using the words 'fuck' and 'stoned' on the radio. If Mac liked something enough—one example was Elvis Costello's '(I Don't Want to Go to) Chelsea'—he might say 'Tasty. Very tasty. Very tasty indeed,' and immediately play it again. No-one in 'conventional' broadcasting ever did that. But Mac was also very interested in news and current affairs, and made it clear that he would make room within his drive-time music program for as much material as we could throw at him. This evolved into what might have been the forerunner of Triple J's *Hack*, a fast-moving music and talk program of a type which is common now on ABC Local radio, but which in the mid-1970s had never been done before.

We had plenty to cover. In May 1976, Neville Wran had led Labor to a narrow victory in NSW, ending nineteen years of Coalition government. Increasingly, we were dealing with his spin machine, led by Peter Barron, who later went on to Canberra with Bob Hawke, and who gradually systematised a new method of 'media management' which, as it grew and became more sophisticated, was eventually exported to Britain and underpinned the rise of Tony Blair. Sand mining on Fraser Island and uranium mining in the Northern Territory were big issues for our youth audience. In Queensland, where the police had a particular reputation for violence against hippies and protesters, the first tiny cracks in the Joh Bjelke-Petersen regime were showing: the squeaky-clean Ray Whitrod resigned as police commissioner because of the state government's attempts to block his anti-corruption efforts. That story, of course, still had years to run.

Meanwhile, youth culture itself was changing, not just in Sydney but in big cities like London and New York, from which our generation took a lot of cues. In London, the trigger was mass unemployment amid years of decline under alternating Labour and Tory governments locked in a spiral of inaction and decay. In New York, it was the degeneration of the city into bankruptcy, crime, dirt and squalor. President Gerald Ford's negative reaction to the city's pleas for a bailout (which happened during Australia's supply crisis) had resulted in one of journalism's most famous headlines, 'FORD TO CITY: DROP DEAD', in the feisty *New York Daily News*. The city was also rife with paranoia as David Berkowitz, the 'Son Of Sam', went on a trail of apparently motiveless serial killings which the police seemed powerless to stop.

In sunny Australia, though the problems were far less dramatic, rising youth unemployment and continuing anger about the Dismissal had sown the seeds of punk. It exploded in late 1976 with the Sex Pistols' 'Anarchy in the UK', but New York had been there first, with the Ramones putting out a self-titled album of two-minute thrashers of uncompromising simplicity, like 'Beat on the Brat', 'Judy Is a Punk' and 'Now I Want to Sniff Some Glue'. The Ramones album took a long while to take off, so it is Brisbane's The Saints who are usually credited with the first punk hit single, 'I'm Stranded'.

Musically, this was a generational change as big as the arrival of rock'n'roll in the 1950s or the British invasion of the early 1960s. Rod Stewart, who'd been a rhythm-and-blues man with The Faces but by now had started to morph into a middle-of-the-road pop artist, described it self-satirically years later as a 'well-deserved kick in the harem pants' for him and his generation. Through the 1970s, album stations had encouraged bands to write longer, often more pretentious tracks, filled with virtuoso solos by everyone, including the drummer. There was plenty of great music, but there were also massive and showy concept albums and grandiose collaborations with symphony orchestras. Record companies were spending millions on albums by the likes of Stewart and Fleetwood Mac, much of which was spent on 'fruit and flowers': the A&R man's accounting code for cocaine, booze and women. Now, suddenly, there was a generation of kids who wanted to throw away the flowery shirts and bell-bottomed trousers and jump up and down to extremely loud music made on the cheap, however basic and even badly played. No-one ever played a Ramones song to listen reverently to the guitar solo. Punk was exploding out of gigs in London basements, New York clubs like CBGB & OMFUG and Max's Kansas City, and places like The Funhouse in Sydney's Taylor Square where Radio Birdman were the house band and where I spent a lot of sweaty Friday nights.

A lot of this music was banned on nearly every radio station in the world. Sometimes it was because of the language, sometimes the way the songs treated drugs and violence, but in almost every incarnation, punk, with its ripped clothing, piercings, Mohican haircuts and safety pins, did exactly what it was meant to do: stir up the oldies. Hence Mac Cocker's frequent back-announces of 'Evening, Bishop': a shout-out to the bishop of Maitland, in the Hunter Valley, who was way outside our listening area but somehow managed to hear enough to write regular letters of complaint to ABC Managing Director Talbot Duckmanton.

The bishop and the Festival of Light's Fred Nile might have been our most prominent external enemies, but there was, in 1976, a more dangerous one right inside the gates. We now know from historian Ken Inglis' authoritative *This Is the ABC* that it was in January that Malcolm Fraser first approached Sir Henry Bland, a retired Public Service mandarin who had closely advised Fraser the previous year, about chairing the ABC. During February, while Bland thought it over, Fraser announced Budget cuts to the ABC: his Expenditure Review Committee, known in the press as the 'Razor Gang', had taken its pound of flesh. There were plenty in Coalition ranks who wanted these cuts applied directly to programs they disliked for political or 'moral' reasons. But there was a clearly established precedent for how the actual distribution of the ABC's Budget money was a matter for its board, and the government had no right to direct, say, a cut in funding to *This Day Tonight* or *Four Corners*. Despite the continuing fury of the deputy general manager, Clement Semmler, Duckmanton decided to resist pressure to close down Double J. We had survived, along with a number of other controversial areas of the organisation.

If the board was the problem, Fraser became more determined to change it. In July he announced the appointment of Bland, whose long record as a Public Service chief covered labour, national service and defence, but had never remotely touched on broadcasting, journalism, music, film or the arts. And there was nothing bland about Bland. Sometimes known as 'Hatchet' because of his often-admirable determination to cut waste in management during his Canberra years, he was forthright and extremely determined. Undoubtedly the ABC suffered from bloat. The journalist Richard Carleton, who'd just left the ABC for 3AW, told a Melbourne audience of political academics in February 1976 that the organisation was grossly overpadded with management. But Carleton also emphasised that, in his view, the program-making itself was generally efficient and professional.

If Sir Henry had stuck to the inefficiencies and sinecures of middle management, things might have been different, but he did not. He tried to make the chairmanship an executive rather than a supervisory role, and in doing so bit off more than he could chew. The most publicised aspect of this was censorship, specifically in that Bland took strong exception to the TV series *Alvin Purple*: a sex comedy based on two bawdy movies whose titular character was, it seemed, irresistible to women. Censorship battles through history have not always centred on classics like James Joyce's *Ulysses*. Indeed, no-one, in retrospect, would describe *Alvin Purple* as a television classic. But equally, the material Bland wanted to censor would seem tame today. Inglis records that during this row, Bland was receiving messages of encouragement and support from the commercial media moguls Kerry Packer and Rupert Murdoch.

But the *Alvin Purple* ruckus was just the visible part of the massive internal battle that Bland sparked at the ABC. Behind the scenes, egged on by Semmler, he was trying to force management to change or control the output of some programs and stations, including Double J. There was a row about the choice of historian Professor Manning Clark to deliver the Boyer Lectures—a yearly series of talks by prominent Australians that was instituted by the ABC—on the grounds that he had been very pro-Whitlam. Bland also took very strong exception to the presence on the board of Marius Webb (one of Double J's founding coordinators) as the ABC's first staff-elected commissioner.

All these factors created turmoil: protests, strikes, bureaucratic battles, and an increasingly unmanageable situation. There was a Sydney Town Hall meeting where 1700 staffers passed a motion of no confidence in Sir Henry, and a 24-hour strike that took the ABC off the air. Sir Henry's overall solution, to dissolve the ABC altogether and reconstitute it under new rules, finally hit a brick wall in parliament, where Coalition backbenchers threatened to cross the floor and forced Malcolm Fraser to back down. Bland was gone before Christmas 1976, his resignation mourned by few.

A postscript to this episode: thirty-eight years later, with the ABC under attack from Tony Abbott, the same Malcolm Fraser tweeted: 'Purpose is to starve, then amalgamate then kill or if value left to sell ABC & SBS. OPPOSE NOW.' Thinking this was a bit rich in the light of history, I replied, 'Dear Malcolm, I'm sure you're sincere now. But I survived Sir Henry Bland. And your Razor Gang. We remember.'

'Touché,' Malcolm returned, 'but different ideology now.'

Chapter 21

Dark Glasses

IN THE YEARS 1975 to 1977, I came of age as a reporter and a broadcaster. Part of it was not just journalism but collaboration and friendship, especially with the late Tony Barrell. I wrote when he died in 2011 of how Tony saw in Double J 'a place where he could do just about anything that there is to do in radio'. What he did then was begin to formulate a radio style of his own, made up of myriad influences.

With the producer and engineer Graeme Bartlett, Tony and I made two programs, one about the American Bicentennial, and the other, called *1984*, about the future. In doing so, I was amazed by Tony's ability to take material which in my hands would have been prosaic, and turn it into a sort of audio poetry—mixing interviews, music, scraps of actuality from here and there, and comedy extracts from groups like The Firesign Theatre. He had a remarkable ability to organise vast masses of material and then juxtapose it in amusing, unexpected, thought-provoking ways in an audio tapestry. The whole concept of large-scale 'sampling' and 'mashup', so dominant in the visual and audio arts today, only became fully technically possible with the coming of digital. But in Tony's brain it was already there, and within our (analogue) capabilities we helped pioneer it.

But there was also 'straight' journalism, from political interviewing and analysis to coverage of the big stories. Few were bigger than when, at 8.10 on the morning of 18 January 1977, a crowded commuter train derailed at Granville, in Sydney's west, hitting a road-bridge stanchion and bringing that bridge down on top of it. I was the only reporter in the newsroom, so I still had to prepare the 8.30 a.m. bulletin and another special report at 9 a.m. before I could leave the building, but as soon as reinforcements arrived I drove out, getting to the scene maybe an hour and a half after the accident. Emergency crews were everywhere but there was little security: you could walk through a fence onto the line a few hundred metres away and then get quite close. Closer than I wanted to, but as a reporter you have to look horror in the face.

The whole bridge—concrete, asphalt, iron girders, the vehicles driving across it—had come down instantly, with full force. The flimsy old Sydney 'Red Rattler' carriages were crushed like balsawood, and it was clear no passenger directly underneath had stood much chance of survival. Of those killed, not all died instantly. Some of those who were still alive were even able to have conversations with their rescuers, and may have thought they'd be all right if they could just get free and into hospital, but they died soon after of internal injuries and something called 'crush syndrome'. They were just ordinary people, mostly from the Blue Mountains, reading their books or newspapers, on their way into the city to do their jobs. The crash killed eighty-three and left over 210 more injured: it was and remains Australia's worst ever rail disaster.

You go numb, trying to cover a story like that for the first time at the age of twenty-five, or at least I did. Some people freeze up entirely: luckily, for me it was not the numbness of paralysis but a sort of emotional shell. You concentrate on your notebook and your tape recorder, try to sort the most relevant points from the least, to do everything you can to stop the emotional blast of what you've seen and heard from interfering with your judgement. You write short, simple, coherent sentences because you know that the facts are stark enough to speak for themselves.

And then, in those days, you faced the most significant challenge: actually filing the story. There were no public phones free in the area. This was of course the era before mobile phones, and while some of the TV journalists had electronic links back to their stations, I was just a guy with a tape machine. You knocked on doors and begged people to let you use their phone, promising to pay for the call. Then they watched aghast as you took their phone apart and connected it with alligator clips to your tape recorder. You filed, you did a Q&A (in this case with the morning presenter, Bob Hudson), then you went back on the track to get more material. It was a dark and terrible day, but I learned from it for the first time that I could, single-handedly, cover a really big and difficult story without falling to pieces.

Much more was to come in 1977. It was the year Don Chipp split from the Liberal Party and founded the Australian Democrats, while Kerry Packer drove a massive wedge through the sclerotic cricket establishment by setting up the breakaway World Series Cricket. It was also one of my favourite years in pop: the year punk started morphing into New Wave, the year of Elvis Costello, Nick Lowe, Blondie, Brian Eno, David Bowie's *Low* and Iggy Pop's *Lust for Life*. In Australian pubs and concert venues there were bands like Dragon and Mental As Anything (who played that year's Double J Christmas party). Punk had exploded into our world, but it was not the dominant force so much as the dam-breaker which allowed a tide of new talent to write concise, sharp, often witty songs of musical and verbal originality. Lyrics, in particular, had evolved: from the in-your-face aggression of 'Oh Bondage! Up Yours' to the delicate, tragic sensibility of Elvis Costello's 'Alison'; from 'God Save the Queen and Her Fascist Regime' to the elliptical irony of Talking Heads' 'Don't Worry about the Government'. In Melbourne I saw The Sports singing 'Who Listens to the Radio?', to which the answer, for our generation, in that city, was: no-one, because you don't have Double J.

Sydney itself was, physically and socially, very different then: a much-lower-slung, less-skyscraper-dotted city with a far busier harbour. Parts of it could feel provincial, with the emphasis on mowing the nature strip and using the incinerator for the weekly backyard burn-off—a social backwater almost unchanged from the 1950s. But because property prices were so low, there was also a Bohemian side to Sydney, a side which is gone now. Before Paul Keating floated the dollar, Sydney was one of the world's cheapest major cities in which to rent or buy. What are now millionaire suburbs like Paddington and Balmain were the haunts of painters, writers and musicians, often paying $30 or $40 a week for a room in a shared house, and using the then-generous social welfare system to prop up their fledgling careers.

My own life revolved around bookshops, cinemas, the beach in summer, and the radio station. It was a time before today's celebrity culture and still, for a journalist, an era where you could often get through to a chief executive or a politician without running the gamut of a whole entourage of PR people. On the other hand, it was also a time when people in general—from public figures to the people you encountered doing vox pops—were far less used to the idea of speaking to a camera or microphone. You had to do much more cajoling just to get people on air, and when you did, they could be monosyllabic. You also had very few research resources: *Who's Who*, encyclopaedias, the phone book (remember them?). When you went anywhere as a journalist, you very definitely took a notebook and pen as well as your recorder, and you very definitely used them to take copious notes: it wasn't possible to wait till you got back to the office to check the spelling of someone's name, or their title, or their CV, on the internet. And your contact book was your most precious possession—direct-line office phones and people's home numbers were just journalistic gold.

* * *

By the Christmas and New Year holidays of 1976–77, my stepfather, Tony Synnot, had been promoted to vice-admiral, and into his new job as head of the Royal Australian Navy (chief of naval staff). He and my mother were living on an old-established property in the NSW countryside, just over the ACT border but only twenty minutes' drive from Defence headquarters in Russell Hill. It was in the kitchen of that house that my mother first admitted to my sister Zoë and me that my father was a spy, and told us a little about how the stresses and strains of intelligence work had contributed to the breakdown of their marriage a decade and a half before.

Mum's account was sketchy, and she emphasised repeatedly that she shouldn't really be telling us anyway: MI6 wives, just like the men they married, were bound to an informal vow of lifelong silence, even though they weren't actually made to sign the Official Secrets Act. Zoë and I were used to a degree of secrecy: Tony's rise through the senior ranks had forced him to be more and more careful about what he said, and us to be more circumspect about what we asked him. But we'd also long joked about Dad maybe being a spy.

Various aspects of his career had always seemed incongruous: he was definitely nothing like other straitlaced, carefully spoken British diplomats I'd met along the way. And things he'd said to both Zoë and me, for instance about the inadvisability of either of us visiting the Soviet Union, for reasons he wasn't fully in a position to explain, had raised more questions than they'd answered. On the other hand, more than one intelligence expert had told me that if Dad had held ambassadorial rank, it was extremely unlikely he was in intelligence, because the mandarins at the Foreign Office were extremely selective about the positions they allowed to be used as 'diplomatic cover', and ambassador rank was definitely out of bounds. (As discussed in previous chapters, it's only recently publicly been revealed that the Mongolia embassy was *the* exception that proved the rule.)

It was liberating in its way to know the truth about Dad, but for me it was also constricting. Paranoia about intelligence agencies was rife among journalists then. Ever since the Dismissal there'd been conspiracy theories involving the US embassy, the CIA and ASIO. They were given new impetus by the arrest in January 1977, and the conviction that May, of Christopher Boyce, a young American who'd been caught selling top-secret material to the Soviet embassy in Mexico. That material, Boyce claimed, included among other things the CIA describing the Australian governor-general as 'our man Kerr'. Boyce's story was soon to become even better known in the form of a book and a film, *The Falcon and the Snowman*. Debate was so intense that in May, Prime Minister Malcolm Fraser told parliament that US President Jimmy Carter had given him a personal assurance that US agencies had not been involved in the events of 11 November 1975.

The arguments over this issue have continued to this day, but what was relevant to me at the time was simply that, as a journalist, the last thing I wanted was to be pigeonholed as 'the son of an MI6 officer'; it was very much in my interest, as well as Dad's, to hold to my promise to my mother and keep the whole thing secret. I can honestly say that I never received or even asked for a story or an inside-track from my father or my stepfather—let alone got 'fed' one—but in those rumour-driven days, there were plenty who might have made assumptions. Especially as my father, whom I hadn't seen since we parted in Ulan Bator, was now living and working in a very senior job in Washington, DC, and I had plans to visit him later in the year.

Apart from Christmas breaks, I hadn't taken a lot of leave since I'd joined the ABC in 1974: I had enough backed up to take eight weeks off. I'd also saved enough to buy a round-the-world ticket, and a two-week Eurail pass, which gave you unlimited train travel anywhere on the Continent west of the Iron Curtain. I would begin with my first visit to the USA, starting on the west coast, moving on to New York, then spending some time with Dad in Washington.

I set off at the beginning of the Sydney winter, headed for San Francisco to visit my friend Roger Allebone. He'd been freelancing for Double J from there for a year or so, covering all kinds of stories the mainstream media largely ignored: the rise of gay politicians like Harvey Milk, the environmental movement and the growth of the porn industry, among others. I walked the trails in Yosemite National Park and explored the Californian seaport, hanging out in City Lights bookshop and buying stacks of volumes to post home. With the Australian book industry then still so locked into British publishing, there was a vast array of books that never normally got to our shores, so along with the latest novels I bought a lot of tomes about American politics, as well as books about the media, such as Jerry Mander's *Four Arguments for the Elimination of Television*, and about cybercrime, like Thomas Whiteside's *Computer Capers*. These were subjects and discussions that had hardly got a toehold in Australia in that pre-globalised world. Books were cheaper in San Francisco than Sydney, but they were too heavy to add to my luggage—I paid so much in postage home that there was little in the way of savings.

Then it was New York, where I stayed a couple of nights in the YMCA before running into an old English friend, Jamie McDonald, now working in finance, who let me stay in his flat for a couple of weeks. You never forget your first time in New York: wherever you were from back then, it turned you into a gawping out-of-towner. A while ago I came across a roll of film I took at the time which mostly consisted of banal shots of the sky, framed by gigantic skyscraper canyons. My memories, though, are all at ground-level: Reuben's delicatessen, with its gigantic heapings of salt beef; jogging round the reservoir in Central Park before walking home on winding paths and under little bridges so bucolic you almost forgot you were in the world's most pulsing city; visiting MoMA and the Met, the Frick Gallery and the JP Morgan Library; more bookshops, of course; having a drink at the Algonquin Hotel, just because Dorothy Parker, Robert Benchley, George Kaufman and Harold Ross used to meet there. I also tried for an interview with one of my great journalistic heroes, John McPhee of *The New Yorker*, only to be knocked back, but I did get in to see Jann Wenner, founder of *Rolling Stone*.

And I had lunch with my dad. We'd arranged for me to stay with him in Washington for a fortnight before I headed across the Atlantic to Britain, France and Italy. But, he told me on the phone ahead of my arrival, we needed to talk. Thanks to the conversation with my mother earlier in the year, I had a fair idea what we'd be talking about.

His venue, characteristically, was an old-fashioned London-style 'gentlemen's club'. I had not known such things existed in New York—my idea of a New York club was CBGB, where I'd seen Jonathan Richman and the Modern Lovers the previous evening—but fortunately I'd packed a suit and tie in my round-the-world travel case, so I was duly admitted to the stately premises of the Knickerbocker Club. There we ascended to a high-ceilinged dining room with tall windows looking directly across 62nd Street to Central Park. The tables, covered in thick white linen and set with heavy silver cutlery, were widely spaced, and the tone hushed. My father liked these places anyway, but you could see why he frequented them professionally, not just socially: discretion was guaranteed and our conversation could not be overheard.

It was a strange reunion. It was the first time I'd seen my father since we'd parted at the Ulan Bator railway station five years before, but the personal pleasure of seeing each other again was a little overshadowed by what we had to talk about. Over lamb cutlets and claret, he told me that I had to be clear that what he was about to say was secret, not to be revealed to anyone, and that if I could not agree to this condition, I wouldn't be able to come and stay with him. There would be colleagues from the London office staying with him at the same time, and people coming for dinner, about whom and around whom I would have to be very discreet. Of course I agreed: there wasn't much of a choice involved. So then he explained to me that his title, councillor (political) at the British embassy in Washington, was just 'cover'. He was in fact the head of station for what I would know as MI6, but what the organisation itself preferred to call the SIS—the Secret Intelligence Service.

Dad outlined the differences between the SIS and the domestic intelligence service MI5. The SIS had an 'intelligence-gathering' remit, with no powers to work inside the UK, while MI5 had the job of 'counter-intelligence', defending the country on its own soil from the depredations of foreign spies, mainly of their mutual enemy, the Soviet KGB. He also explained that British intelligence agencies and their members were known as 'The Friends' and the CIA as 'The Cousins', and that his job in Washington was to liaise between 'Friends' and 'Cousins': between the SIS' home at Century House in London and CIA headquarters at Langley, Virginia. His position was an extremely senior one. Did I know the name Kim Philby? Of course. Well, Philby had been his predecessor in the job during the 1950s, before he was unmasked, and his betrayal had come close to destroying the relationship between the two agencies. My father's was therefore now an extremely senior, delicate and closely watched job. It had taken two decades to rebuild after the damage done to US trust by the defection of the Cambridge spies.

I had read enough John le Carré to have an idea of some of this already, but hearing it from the horse's mouth was the end of a long process of guesswork and confirmation. We parted after lunch with a promise that he'd pick me up at Washington National Airport (since renamed after Ronald Reagan).

My father was a man of great enthusiasms, and in the year or so he'd been there, he'd already fallen in love with a lot about America. His car, he told me with delight on my arrival in the capital, was a Dodge Dart Swinger: a long, low two-door he'd bought second-hand. A friend had told him that its paint job was what American car dealers (accurately enough) called 'babyshit brown'. The thing handled, as many American cars did in those days, like a tugboat, but having driven a series of ancient Minis in Britain, he loved its size and the rumble from under the bonnet. He also took a gleeful pleasure in demonstrating what was then the novelty of a remote control to open your garage door as you approached. And he enthused endlessly about the hamburgers at a bar called Nicky's, where he and my stepmother had become regulars. When we went there a few days later, it was just an American bar, and the burgers, while good, were just burgers, but his fervour was infectious. Another of his favourite places was one just outside the Beltway where they only served crabs. You sat at a table spread with butcher paper, they brought a pile of steamed crabs accompanied by mallets, crackers and long-stemmed forks, you put on a bib and hoed in. I think the place was named Mike's, but there was a notice at the door that said 'The owner of this place is not called Mike. The new owner's name is Bob. DON'T CALL HIM MIKE.'

Two weeks passed quickly in Washington for me. There was so much to see: the National Gallery of Art alone took up two days. I went to see the radical new IM Pei building but stayed to browse through Vermeers and Botticellis, Rembrandts and Goyas, Degas and Matisses. I went to the Freer Gallery, an offshoot of the Smithsonian across the National Mall from the main building, on my father's recommendation, to look at Chinese porcelain. The Freer, like the Frick in New York, is smaller and less well-known than some other great galleries of the world, but they remain two of my favourites anywhere: the Frick because of its presentation of great pictures hung just as they were when their multi-millionaire owner lived there, above and among his furniture; the Freer because as well as Asian art, it houses no fewer than 1300 works by the great James McNeill Whistler.

At the Freer you could see Whistler's extraordinarily prolific originality, and understand how, like late Turner or the French Impressionists, his artistic vision as well as his abrasive nature and sheer arrogance ('I can't tell you if genius is hereditary, because heaven has granted me no offspring') had roiled and defied every tenet of 'respectable' nineteenth-century art. And you could see his Peacock Room, an entire dining room painted and decorated to display the collection of a wealthy London connoisseur of Chinese porcelain, dismantled and reassembled in its entirety: an astonishing thing.

This was also, less than a decade after Neil Armstrong and Buzz Aldrin had landed on the moon, a great time to visit the National Air and Space Museum, not least because it was still such a thrill to touch a mounted piece of moon rock with your own hand. And the huge planes, hanging overhead in that gigantic space, reminded me of the Airfix models I'd painstakingly assembled as a boy and hung above my bed.

As in San Francisco and New York, I spent a lot of time in bookshops, and what sometimes seemed even longer wrestling with the notoriously slow and bureaucratic US Postal Service to send them home. I hadn't then heard the expression 'going postal', meaning 'to fly into a violent rage, especially when provoked by workplace stress', but when I did,

I recognised it from those queues and that attitude. (To be fair, unlike postcards and letters I sent later in the trip from Italy, everything I sent from San Francisco, New York and Washington did eventually arrive in Sydney.)

One night I went to see The Kinks, a band I loved but had managed to miss seeing live at their peak in London in the 1960s. I think they opened with 'Tired of Waiting', I'm sure they played 'Lola', but surprisingly, in retrospect, there was no 'Waterloo Sunset' or 'Days'. The sibling rivalry between the Davies brothers, Ray and Dave, was already notorious, but that night there was no on-stage fistfight between them, despite some fairly obvious tension. Instead, it was Dave and drummer Mick Avory who got into a shouting match during the encore, with Dave kicking down one of Mick's cymbals, and both storming off stage, in opposite directions. All in all, despite the foreshortened encore, the crowd felt they'd had value for money.

Dad took me to lunch a couple of times at one of his clubs. I forget its name, but it was another of those gentlemen-only, buttoned-leather-sofa and obsequious-waiter establishments done up to look like the interior of an English stately home. There I got a glimpse into another aspect of his job: making connections with the media. We were having a drink before lunch when a man called Rowland (Rowley) Evans came over. For decades, Evans and his writing partner Robert Novak put out a hugely influential, widely syndicated column called 'Inside Politics'. They were both fierce Cold Warriors with strong Republican connections, and their usually anonymous sources gave them a lot of scoops. The familiarity and warmth of Rowley Evans' conversation with my father that day left me in little doubt that Dad was one of those sources. It was also clear enough that it was a two-way street: Evans was not just a conduit for planted stories (part of what are known in MI6 as I/Ops), but also, in the opposite direction, a source of gossip and political intelligence for Dad. Clearly, Evans usually knew a lot more gossip and information about Washington political and strategic matters than he could actually print.

From conversations at the time, I know that Dad was also a contact of Jack Anderson, who wrote the 'Washington Merry-Go-Round' column, and who was revealed in a 2010 book to have bribed, blackmailed, extorted, bugged and lied in order to get stories. About this enormously influential newspaperman, *Slate*'s Jack Shafer wrote:

> Anderson's ethical compass pointed wherever he wanted it to, and in this regard he behaved more like a spy than a reporter during his long career. A spy does not mince ethics as he steals secrets, cracks safes, breaks into offices, taps phones and hacks computers, recruits and pays operatives in the field, and blackmails his foes. He lies frequently and brazenly. He swaps information with sources and does favors for them.

Knowing of these relationships left me forever sceptical of all stories involving defence, intelligence and national security that rely on anonymous sources. They're too often tainted, and subsequent events, like *The Spectator* (while I was Europe correspondent during the Balkans war) running two articles by a pseudonymous MI6 agent in Bosnia, have done nothing to change my mind.

Another friend of my father's was Allen Weinstein, then writing his massive and influential book *Perjury*, about the McCarthy-era case of the accused spy Alger Hiss. I'd read a little about the extraordinarily convoluted course of this case, and the way it pitted Hiss against a witness called Whittaker Chambers, but only enough to pigeonhole Hiss in my mind in the same category as others targeted by the House Un-American Activities Committee. Weinstein's investigations of the case were even then causing huge ructions on the Left, because, in exemplary fashion, he had chipped away at the detailed factual foundations of Hiss' defence, finding a host of contradictions which pointed more strongly than ever to the man's probable guilt as a Soviet spy, a KGB 'mole' high in the US State Department.

Staying at the house when Allen came to dinner were two MI6 colleagues of my father's from London. In retrospect, I see myself that night as callow and arrogant. I was foolish enough to regurgitate some half-remembered and thinly understood material I'd read or heard about the Petrov Affair of the early 1950s, and suggested that the evidence that ASIO produced about infiltration of the Labor Party was still regarded by some in Australia as a put-up job by the Prime Minister Robert Menzies. It wasn't just the wrong thing to say, it prompted the 'Friends' from London to furious indiscretion. They told me, without equivocation, that the Petrov defection had been one of the most significant intelligence coups of the century, and that Mr and Mrs Petrov had given them and the CIA essential confirmation of a vast amount of material about KGB infiltration of Western governments. With Weinstein backing them up, I was not just outnumbered but outgunned, and what made it more humiliating was that they so clearly had the facts and I didn't. Nobody mentioned the 'Venona decrypts' of highly secret KGB cables—it would be nearly two decades before their existence even became public—but those documents, and much other evidence that's been released in the last couple of decades, make it clear that I'd made a complete fool of myself that night. Their attack was so ferocious and detailed, however, that my father clearly thought they'd told me too much. The next morning he took me aside to redouble his earlier message about secrecy. There was no real need: I'd been so comprehensively demolished that I had no intention of ever mentioning the incident again.

Perhaps fortunately, I didn't know much at the time about the history of Iran, so I was in no position to repeat my indiscretion when we went to a children's party at the home of a schoolfriend of my young half-brother David. The host was Kermit Roosevelt Jr, a 'friend of my father's in the US Foreign Service', which by now I realised meant 'probably CIA'. A tall, rangy man in horn-rimmed spectacles, grandson of President Theodore Roosevelt, he was the picture of US east-coast establishment benevolence: Anglophile, civilised and charming. In those pre-Google days, I had no way of knowing that he was also the man who'd organised the 1953 coup that toppled Iranian Prime Minister Mossadeq and brought the Shah back.

When I left Washington, there was the usual air of melancholy between Dad and me. We always enjoyed each other's company. For all our political differences we shared a huge amount in terms of artistic and literary interests, among other things, and his enormously wide knowledge of history and foreign affairs was an extraordinary resource to tap for a young man in my trade. But time and distance meant we both knew that the times we had together would always be rare.

As usual, Dad wore his darkest glasses to the airport to say goodbye.

Chapter 22

The Pleasure of Collaboration

I ARRIVED AT THE Sydney Hilton some time between 1.15 and 1.30 on the morning of 13 February 1978. All I knew was that there'd been a massive explosion in George Street, outside the hotel where, earlier that night, I'd spent several hours covering the arrival of Commonwealth heads of government for their regional meeting known as CHOGM. When I'd left, I'd gone back to the Double J offices and filed a fairly lighthearted story for the morning, which focused heavily on the slurred speech and extremely unfriendly words New Zealand Prime Minister Robert 'Piggy' Muldoon had launched at Malcolm Fraser and Australia in general at a hastily convened press conference, after he'd been out on a well-lubricated harbour cruise. I was not to know it when I left the office, but that story would never get to air.

Coming towards the Town Hall, I could see police setting up roadblocks and lights on the corner of George Street directly outside the building. I could see them already turning people, including journalists, away. I went instead through the Pitt Street entrance of the Hilton, thinking security might be less stringent there and I could get to George Street by going down the escalators. I'd guessed right. The security was, at that moment, non-existent: everything had been diverted either down onto George St itself, or to the upper floors where the heads of government were staying. I had no need for the lifts, so whoever was guarding them left me alone. Within about a minute, I was walking down the stopped escalator with my Nagra over my shoulder, looking down at the white marble lobby floor. It was spattered with what looked like shrapnel and other unidentifiable objects, and stained bright scarlet with blood.

Meanwhile, AAP's Peter Logue, who'd arrived from Northern Ireland three years before, was the only reporter allowed to remain on the scene inside the Town Hall cordon. He was on the spot two minutes after the blast. Peter remembers: 'I was on my way to do the overnight shift at AAP. Knew immediately what it was when I heard that crrrruuuummmp! When the cops turned up I got talking to an inspector who found it amusing that I was from Northern Ireland. When they set up barricades and removed the journos he shouted, 'Let him stay, he's a crazy Irishman and he's seen all this before.'

In the Hilton's George Street lobby, with the Florsheim shoe shop on my right, I picked my way through the debris and out onto the pavement, looking left towards the Town Hall. The floodlights were fully up now, and almost blinding. The exploded garbage truck was a silhouette in their beams. Its metal rear had been blown out on each side. It remains as a photographic image burned into my brain, the torn metal of the exploded rear spread out like the wings of a devil in a horror film.

The police worked out fairly quickly that I'd slipped through the net, but I still had my conference accreditation and I persuaded them to let me back into the hotel. And so it was that a small group including Peter and me, along with the legendary tabloid journalist and ex-boxer Jack Darmody and *The Mirror*'s Jim Oram, were there when, at about 2 a.m., Superintendent Reg Douglas briefed us, having to admit that the police had failed in not allowing checks of the rubbish bin which contained the bomb that blew up in the truck's garbage compactor.

I was told that Malcolm Fraser had come down in his dressing gown within minutes of the bomb going off, but my memory is hazy as to whether he also spoke to us. He was certainly holding meetings with police and security chiefs inside the hotel. We did know the damage the bomb had done, though. It had blown two garbage collectors literally to pieces: it was probably the blood of William Favell or Alec Carter I'd seen splashed across the marble. Or it might have been that of policeman Paul Birmistriw, who would die of his injuries nine days later. He and three other policemen were then in critical condition a few blocks away, in Sydney Hospital.

By about 3 a.m., I had enough to head back to the office and put together a new, seven-minute report on everything I'd seen and heard for the morning bulletin. Nearly four decades on, though, despite multiple trials, appeals, retrials, conspiracy theories and reinvestigations, we still do not know definitively who was responsible for that bombing.

* * *

The Hilton atrocity was the last big story I covered for the station. ABC News had decided that I'd been at Double J too long and needed to be brought back into the fold. I'd known it was inevitable, but I'd have liked to make the decision on timing myself. Still, new challenges awaited. I was to be sent to Canberra to be the TV producer for the ABC's federal political coverage, responsible for making sure that the work of the chief correspondent Duncan Fairweather and his deputy Paul Lockyer was properly edited and packaged for distribution down the coaxial cable to Sydney and Melbourne.

After a month of on-the-job training at the ABC's TV studios at Sydney's Gore Hill, I arrived at the Old Parliament House press gallery, which was largely unchanged from my cadetship days of 1974. The lack of technological change in particular was irksome. I'd spend the morning at parliament, but there were no TV editing facilities there, so much of the time after lunch was spent 6 kilometres away at the ABC's Northbourne Avenue office, either supervising the cutting of film with veteran editor Frank Reid, or editing tape upstairs on the huge 2-inch reel-to-reel Ampex machines. Those machines were unwieldy, but so was the system. Shuttling TV material back and forth across Canberra seemed if anything more anachronistic than the run up Cardiac Hill I'd got inured to at Double J. The ABC was trying to introduce smaller, lighter videotape cameras and editing machines, but there was union opposition from film cameramen (they were all men then)—artists—who didn't want to see engineers, who understood the inner workings of the new cameras, allowed to take pictures.

It was frustrating, and with Whitlam gone after the election loss of December 1977, politics that year was fairly featureless. New Labor leader Bill Hayden was only finding his feet, so Malcolm Fraser had the field very much to himself, and the ALP was still only beginning the long process of re-examination and restructuring that would eventually end with Bob Hawke claiming the party leadership in 1983. Hawke was always in and out of Canberra, though, and I was in the pack that interviewed him several times. I thought he always treated my questions with a particular curl of the lip, something that never changed over time. Years later, when he was prime minister and on a trip to Brussels, I asked one of his staffers why he still seemed to single me out as an especially loathsome specimen of a media pack he generally treated with lofty contempt. 'He just hates Poms, mate,' came the reply. Hard, with my accent then, to protest 'But I'm half-Australian by birth.'

Almost every weekend I got a lift to Sydney and back with Duncan Fairweather, so I never truly put down roots in Canberra. I felt I was largely marking time. But I was in luck, because the Canberra political editor that year was John Penlington, a man whose careful and slightly cerebral exterior concealed a history of great and pioneering TV reporting. As part of the team that founded *Four Corners*, he had broken major stories around Australia, covered the Vietnam War, and presented and produced the program: a journalist with a huge reputation inside and outside the ABC. Towards the end of 1978, the organisation decided that *This Day Tonight*, the nightly TV current affairs program which seemed well beyond its swashbuckling peak, should end. It was to be replaced by a new, late-evening program of current affairs and interviews. It was to be called *Nationwide*, it would air at 9.30 every evening, and John Penlington had been chosen as its executive producer. He'd taken a liking to me, understood that I found my current job limiting, and decided to take a gamble by appointing me as one of his small team of national reporters.

So, back in Sydney, I started 1979 working alongside some of the most impressive journalists in TV, notably Paul Murphy, whose talents as a reporter were augmented by a power of vocal imitation that rivalled that of Peter Sellers. The formidable Richard Carleton was back in the ABC's fold as the program's Canberra correspondent and chief interrogator of politicians, and Andrew Olle, battle-hardened by years of on- and off-air skirmishes with the corrupt Queensland Police and the inimitable Joh Bjelke-Petersen, had come down with his family from Brisbane.

I was easily the most inexperienced member of the team, and far down the pecking order, but I set about learning how to work with crews and editors to make film segments of up to ten minutes for the program.

It was hugely enjoyable being on the road with crews like the very clever and experienced John Hagin and Chris Fileman, whose usually blue double-act dialogue could often have you creased up with laughter in the back seat of the ABC station wagon. And I learned how a quick, creative editor like Davey Moore (still, as I write, editing news for the ABC in Sydney) could add to the work you brought in from the road. I'd loved radio all my life, first as a listener, then a practitioner, but at *Nationwide* I began learning one of the great pleasures of television: collaboration. Many of my most rewarding experiences in journalism have come from the ideas of others, either in planning before a shoot or during filming. Working with creative, cooperative crews can be the ultimate demonstration as a reporter of how, with an open mind, you can make a whole that is greater than the sum of its parts.

Towards the end of 1979, I was lent to *Four Corners* for a couple of stories: one on computer learning in schools, another on the economics of the pop music industry. The program at that time was staffed by very senior journalists like Jim Downes and Peter Ross, both of whom were still doing fine work: I remember a vivid piece by Jim about eucalyptus dieback, for instance, and a fine film about racism against Asian immigrants by Peter. But there was also a sense that the program was getting old and tired, not helped by the fact that another reporter, John Temple, a lovely man with an excellent record, had an illness which could make him fall asleep at his desk. Charles Woolley (later to become a *Sixty Minutes* stalwart) and I tended to feel like the token youth reporters.

Looking back, I certainly do not see myself at that age and with that track record as being ready as a film-maker or a journalist to do the kind of really hard-hitting reporting that Paul Lyneham, for instance, was practising at the time at *Four Corners*. But I did just well enough to survive. And when I heard that London correspondent Richard Palfreyman was returning after his three-year stint was up, I applied for the job, though with absolutely no expectation of getting it.

My prior journalism experience seems remarkably limited to me in retrospect, but on paper I had packed quite a lot in, going from cadet to *Four Corners* in six years. And at the interview, I had the great advantage of having no big expectations. I've always found that 'not really caring' is one of the best ways to approach a job interview. Not having your whole future invested in the interviewers' decision gives you the freedom to relax and talk articulately about what the job is and what it could be. I had a broad range of British, African and Middle East stories to suggest: I had some ability with languages, and I was able to talk reasonably knowledgeably about international strategic and other policy areas. At any rate, a week or so later I was told that I'd been appointed.

Chapter 23

The Rule of Revolutions

ON 2 APRIL 1980, cameraman Les Seymour and I drove at high speed down the M4 from London to Bristol in Britain's West Country. Parts of a city which had built much of its prosperity on the trade in slaves and fortified wine were on fire, after a police raid on a café in the district of St Paul's. We arrived to find parts of the area still in flames, others charred and in ruins, and the police still facing off with groups of black and white youths. We filmed the action, talked to young people, found local black community leaders, attended a 3 a.m. police press conference, and I did a piece to camera on the scene. We decided we had enough for a really comprehensive story for that night's 7 p.m. ABC news. We headed back to London, to the headquarters of the international TV newsagency Visnews, later to become known as Reuters TV. At that time, Visnews was the only satellite outlet available: the only way we had to get our footage to air within the time window before it would become 'yesterday's story'.

Driving back up the M4 as the sun came up, we were both so tired that I remember opening all the windows to keep awake, and that we started singing, loudly, songs like 'Yellow Submarine' at each other to keep from dozing off. Exhaustion was quickly replaced by fury when we arrived at the satellite station. Visnews, we were told, was having its 'annual strike' today, apparently a ritual event which both management and staff had just grown accustomed to as part of yearly pay and conditions negotiations. It was bitterly disappointing. We'd shot a really graphic, comprehensive and professional story, which would certainly have run prominently in the bulletin, but there was simply no way to get it back to Australia in time. That was what it was like in those pre-internet days: total dependence on an expensive, monopoly supplier of satellite communication.

But the whole experience, looking back, also functions for me as a parable of what was happening in Britain at that time. Yes, there was growing unemployment, the immigrant community faced disgraceful discrimination by often-racist police forces, and Margaret Thatcher's government, elected under a year before, was just beginning to exert the full force of what would become known as 'Thatcherism'. But here, too, was the reason why Thatcher had been elected in the first place: the accumulated results of two decades of alternating Conservative and Labour governments that had all been too weak to take on the excesses of the unions, preferring instead to do deals with them at what came to be known as 'beer-and-sandwiches' sessions with the prime minister at Number 10 Downing Street.

We drove back to the ABC bureau at 54 Portland Place and I filed the story for ABC Radio News and *PM*, so the night had not been entirely wasted, but the loss of that TV story remains one of the most frustrating experiences of my reporting career. It underlined that old journalistic truism: you can have the world's greatest scoop, but it's not even a story unless you can meet your deadline.

* * *

In 1980, my father was fifty-eight, past the official retirement age for SIS/MI6 officers, and the end of his Washington posting was the end of his official career. While in the US capital he had, however, got to know the chairman and chief executive of Chase Manhattan Bank, David Rockefeller, who appointed him as his personal envoy, based in Hong Kong. Rockefeller had been a founding member of the Office of Strategic Services, the wartime American intelligence organisation that laid the foundations for the CIA. Those connections are never entirely broken, so I've always assumed that Dad's relationship with Rockefeller was intelligence-related in some way. This new position—vice president, international, Asia, Chase Manhattan Bank—gave Dad access to presidents and prime ministers in a wide arc from Delhi to Manila. He rang me one day from Islamabad, where he had been for a week. 'What's it like?' I asked. 'Dry,' was the answer. 'I haven't been sober this long since 1945.'

I have little doubt that my father's reports to Rockefeller revolved around political intelligence and analysis, though probably not of the covert kind. I suspect, too, that much of what he wrote for Chase Manhattan also found its way back to Century House in London. After Dad died, I became aware from various bits of correspondence that the SIS has a system of 'aftercare' whereby what is officially the pensions department keeps in regular contact with ex-officers. No doubt this ensures continuing adherence to the Official Secrets Act, but it can also be useful cover for continuing 'consultancy' work for the service. Later in life, when my father published his memoir, *Twice around the World*, it was heavily vetted by his former employers, and he made little secret to me of the fact that he was in occasional touch with his old workplace. At Chase Manhattan, though he would remain a Cold Warrior at heart, I think his actual war—in terms of spook operations on the ground—was over.

So I think of the 1980s as the time when my father stopped fighting the Cold War and I started covering it. For the next few years, everything else in my professional career, from British politics to the historic Reykjavik, Iceland meeting which led to the first de-escalation of the nuclear arms race in Europe in 1987, would be overshadowed by it.

It's in the nature of history that events often appear inevitable in retrospect. But when you live through an era, not only does the future look unpredictable at the time, you can sometimes see more clearly later where the hinge-points were, and how easily things might have gone a different way. So it was with what we now remember as Thatcherism, or Thatcherism/Reaganism as it came to be seen in terms of global politics. We tend to see it now as progressing ineluctably through the 1980s to an inescapable conclusion: the triumph of Western democracy over international communism, the break-up of the Soviet Bloc and the splintering of the Soviet Union itself. But in practice, the survival of a political philosophy based on the economic ideas of Friedrich Hayek and Milton Friedman was much more precarious at the time.

In the USA, Ronald Reagan had a good chance to win the November 1980 presidential election, but it was the embassy hostage crisis, and particularly the disastrous rescue attempt I witnessed from Tehran, that sealed Jimmy Carter's fate and ensured that Republicans would remain in the White House for the next twelve years. In London, too, Thatcher's future was by no means certain. From reporting on her almost daily, I recall her first years in office as a constant battle for power both inside and outside her government. It was not merely a battle played out in terms of opinion-poll popularity, but a struggle for the soul of her own Tory Party.

Margaret Thatcher was a truly remarkable politician: she had to be, because she rose to head a party that was deeply resistant to her, not only because of her gender but her class as well. She supplanted a leader, Edward Heath, who refused to accept defeat, remaining instead on the backbenches in the long and forlorn hope that the Conservatives would see the error of their ways—though in reality, Heath had few friends and little support. But he was not really at the centre of Thatcher's problem as party leader. What she perceived was a group of 'enemies inside the gate', members of her own Cabinet who she saw as insufficiently tough, insufficiently loyal, and insufficiently prepared to take the hard lines she was certain were essential to reform a country in crisis. She called them 'The Wets', and divided her inner circle up in terms of absolutes. 'Is he one of us?' was the question she constantly asked, so often in fact that her early biographer, Hugo Young, made *One of Us* the title of his book.

Hanging around the periphery of the Westminster political scene as a reporter, you got a flavour of the feeling inside the government from some of the nicknames. Many originated either from the backbencher Julian Critchley or the feline Arts Minister Norman St John Stevas, a Wet himself in social matters, but a loyal Thatcherite in Cabinet and on economic matters. Borrowing from the formal title for the female head of state of Swaziland, they called Thatcher 'The Great She-Elephant'. Lifting directly from John Mortimer's *Rumpole* stories, then hugely popular on TV, they called her 'She Who Must Be Obeyed'—itself a borrowing from the colonial-era adventure writer H Rider Haggard. And perhaps most percipiently, St John Stevas noted that her most frequently used phrase in Cabinet was 'There Is No Alternative', thus the acronym 'TINA'.

The government leaked quite a lot in the early years, with most of the leaks coming from frustrated Wets. Even at the time, it seemed pretty clear—and many subsequent annual releases of Cabinet papers have confirmed it—that Thatcher's reaction to resistance was simply to redouble her determination. The Civil Service, as well as her colleagues, were taken by the scruff of the neck and given a long hard shake. Her handwritten notes and marginalia, to heads of department and ministers alike, were full of absolutes: 'ridiculous', 'too woolly', 'culpable inefficiency'. As St John Stevas wrote in his book *The Two Cities* in 1984, she saw 'everything in black and white [but] the universe I inhabit is made up of many shades of grey'.

Obviously, part of the journalist's job was interviewing ministers when you could, and when the tape recorder was switched off, some of them would give you hints and more of this sort of thing—strictly off the record. But two things became clearer in these encounters. One was that the Wets were also mostly, in British terms, 'toffs'. They included notably Foreign Secretary Lord Carrington, a hereditary peer, and Sir Ian Gilmour, a hereditary baronet. They had made their careers in the tradition of noblesse-oblige Toryism, defined by patronage and continuous negotiation and compromise: 'It is the business of the wealthy man/To give employment to the artisan', as Hilaire Belloc once wrote. It had probably reached its apogee in the prime ministership two decades earlier of Harold Macmillan. The Wets were ill-prepared for the absolutes of monetarist policy, and sometimes shocked and squeamish about the human cost in terms of poverty and unemployment.

In February 1980, just after I arrived in London, Gilmour openly defied Thatcher and her coterie in a speech in Cambridge: 'economic liberalism à la Professor Hayek, because of its starkness and its failure to create a sense of community, is not a safeguard of political freedom but a threat to it'. 'A sense of community': Mrs Thatcher, of course, famously said later, 'There is no such thing as society. There are individual men and women, and there are families.'

And secondly, the Wets were ranged against single-minded people: not just the prime minister herself, but also her closest political friend and adviser, Sir Keith Joseph, an evangelical believer in Friedmanite, small-government, free-market conservatism. Another rising star in the party was the equally uncompromising Norman Tebbit, dubbed the 'Chingford Skinhead', also once labelled by an opponent as a 'semi-house-trained polecat'. Tebbit said later that the insult 'gave my political career a tremendous lift', and literally wore it as a badge of honour by incorporating a polecat in his coat-of-arms when he entered the House of Lords.

Margaret Thatcher was in her way a revolutionary, and a rule of revolutions, even bloodless ones, is that absolutists usually prevail over centrists. It took a few years, but gradually almost all the Wets who dared stand in her way were eliminated.

Out in the real world, thousands of British firms went broke in 1980—more than 3000 in the first six months alone. Their failures had sentimental as well as monetary impacts. Among the hard-hit were the makers of such staples of an English (or Australian) childhood as Meccano construction sets, Dinky Toys, Hornby trains, Scalextric cars, Sindy dolls and Matchbox toys. Everyone who grew up in the 50s and 60s, myself included, had played with at least some of these. Other companies thrived, however, notably the big accounting firms that scooped up bankruptcy business when Thatcher privatised the work of what had been the government-owned Official Receiver.

Apart from bulldozing the opposition within her own party, Margaret Thatcher was also fortunate in whom she faced across the despatch box in the House of Commons. Like Gough Whitlam in Australia in 1975, Jim Callaghan had stayed on as the UK Opposition leader after his election defeat in 1979. Unlike Gough, he had the sense not to fight another election, using the time instead to prepare the party for an orderly succession to his colleague, Denis Healey. That precipitated a leadership election, the result of which was to make Thatcher's job much easier.

Labour was riven by a deep Left/Right split, much of which centred on the question of unilateral nuclear disarmament. It was deeply evident when I travelled to Blackpool, that garish northern seaside town with its mini Eiffel Tower and fairy lights, to cover Labour's annual conference. It was loud, unruly, chaotic. Labour was very slowly beginning to understand that large parts of the party had been taken over by 'entryist' Trotskyites called the Militant Tendency. At their height, the Militants would go on to control (disastrously) local government in the major city of Liverpool, but for now, they were just part of the 'hard Left', which was clearly out to do everything possible to disrupt Callaghan's succession plan. Their hero was Tony Benn, who had made an interesting transition towards their end of the political spectrum since being Harold Wilson's technology minister in the 1960s. They loathed Healey, who had been defence secretary and chancellor of the exchequer, and who was implacably opposed to unilateralism in foreign policy. For me, the complete inability of the party leadership to control events at Blackpool was an extraordinary window into the state of Labour.

Within weeks, deals done behind the scenes at that conference in Blackpool fed into the mess of the leadership contest. Denis Healey was the clear favourite over the Left's Michael Foot in the first round, but it was a four-cornered battle, and most of the votes of the men who came in third and fourth, John Silkin and Peter Shore, transferred to Foot.

A lot is written about journalistic bias, and most of what's said usually focuses on whether we're on the Right or Left. My own experience is that journalists' strongest bias is usually towards drama, character and colour. Denis Healey, whom I interviewed a few times down the years, remains one of my favourite politicians, and I've always regarded him as potentially one of the best prime ministers Britain never had. Healey possessed a near-Keatingesque turn of phrase—famously, for instance, describing an attack by Tory Chancellor Geoffrey Howe as 'like being savaged by a dead sheep'—he was combative and powerful in argument, and, as a convinced ex-communist himself, tough in his determination to keep at bay the forces of the Leninist and Trotskyist Left. It was Healey who defined the difference between politicians with and without what he called a 'hinterland', by which he meant a breadth of interests and activities outside politics. His own hinterland was broad. Widely and deeply read, he was also a talented photographer, easily good enough to have gone professional in another life.

At sixty-seven, blind in one eye and walking with a stick, Michael Foot also had undeniable hinterland. For decades he had been one of the intellectual giants of his party. A distinguished historian and the author in 1940 of *Guilty Men*, a coruscating attack on those who'd appeased Hitler, Foot was personally a well-liked man, with friends and admirers across the political spectrum. His own politics were uncompromisingly of the Left, making him the ideal candidate for those motivated by rage at the growing damage of Thatcherism, but definitely not for those Labour would need to win back the broad centre of British politics. He was also completely unsuited to the needs of a leader in the era of modern broadcast journalism, with his duffel coat and dishevelled appearance making him less than telegenic. I found from painful experience that his rambling delivery, characterised by strange mid-sentence pauses, made him extremely difficult to cut. I've never been a devotee of 'sound-bite journalism', but Michael Foot was almost impossible to use in a Radio Current Affairs piece, let alone a short news bulletin insert.

In Cold War terms, Healey's leadership would have meant Thatcher facing an opponent strongly committed to Britain's defence, including the nuclear deterrent. Instead, the Leader of Her Majesty's Opposition was an elderly, rambling member of the London intelligentsia whom the tabloids labelled 'Worzel Gummidge', after a talking scarecrow in a children's book and TV series. Despite this, the survival of Thatcherism was still not assured. Thatcher's government was determined all right, but that determination was deeply divisive. I saw the results of that resolve never to take a backward step most vividly in the case of the Irish Republican Army hunger-striker Bobby Sands.

* * *

In early May 1981, as Bobby Sands was dying, Les Seymour and I flew to Belfast. We had an arrangement to share footage with NZBC, so we were working alongside their reporter, Peter Newport, a funny, energetic, spirited companion with whom we already had an excellent relationship.

Belfast was exceptionally tense: rioting had already begun and would escalate over the next few days. The leader of the Long Kesh Prison strike, Sands had also been elected, from inside jail, to a sudden vacancy in the House of Commons caused by the heart attack and death of the MP for the border seat of Fermanagh & South Tyrone, a long-time Republican stronghold. It was a seat Sands would never take up. His entire campaign centred on the demand that IRA members like him should be regarded as political prisoners. Margaret Thatcher's view was equally adamant: Sands was a convicted criminal and a senior member of an organisation dedicated to killing others. There was no compromise, and Sands died an awful death, after sixty-six days on hunger strike, on 5 May.

Covering the rioting could be fraught, particularly as a couple of French photographers had been caught paying kids to throw stones at the police. You were in double jeopardy. On one side, Republicans who, attacking first and asking questions later, tended to assume you were the hated British 'Mainland' TV. On the other, the police and the British Army, who now regarded the media with deep suspicion. Rocks and Molotov cocktails on one side, rubber bullets and even live rounds on the other. I remember one nervous half-hour, about a hundred metres from the bottom of Falls Road, keeping watch while one of us changed a punctured tyre on the rented car. Fortunately, we got clear before the conflict got too close.

One thing that was very clear was that the city was absolutely overwhelmed by reporters and news crews. Their usual haunt, the Europa Hotel, had often in the past been a target for riots and bombs, and nobody much liked it anyway, but now it was completely booked out. We ended up at a country hotel about ten minutes out of town.

On the day before the funeral, we'd been among many crews filming on the Twinbrook Housing Estate where Sands' parents lived—there were long queues of supporters lined up outside to pay their respects. We had to plan the next day's coverage of the funeral itself. These were still the days before easy electronic access to shared or agency footage: we had to get all the pictures ourselves. We got up early and arrived outside the Sands' house at sunrise. Ours was the first or second car there, so we parked right across the street and put the tripod on the roof. The plan was that the coffin would be carried up the road mid-morning for a church funeral, then the burial itself would be in the afternoon. It was bright but cold, and Bobby Sands' mother came over to ask us in for a cup of tea. She wouldn't accept our protestations that we wouldn't like to impose, so at about 7 that morning I found myself sitting on a sofa in the Sands' front room, facing the open casket. He was arrayed like a saint in the coffin, his hands clasped on his chest by the embalmer in an attitude of prayer. He was so thin that, as the rising sun shone on to them through the front window, his hands became translucent. It was like looking at a skeleton.

A really big international press pack is not an edifying sight. The scene as the coffin was carried out of the house, placed in the hearse and driven to the church was more like a rolling scrum than a funeral procession. Photographers and camera operators with sharp elbows were jostling for position. Many had stepladders or were standing on boxes, but some were knocked over. Our decision to set up early on the roof of the car proved prescient, as we had good, clear shots of the entire chain of events, but we were worried about what would happen at the burial that afternoon, so the next thing to do was buy our own stepladder. About five hardware stores had sold out, after what the shopkeepers thought was an inexplicable run on the things, but we eventually found one and returned to the hotel to assemble the footage for the first half of our story. Eating a sandwich in the sun, we saw an odd-looking group at the end of the lawn, engaged in some sort of sporting contest. Who were they, we asked? 'The Northern Ireland gumboot-throwing association,' we were told, 'holding their annual championships.' A quarter of an hour away, central Belfast was practically at war. Here, they were chucking rubber boots about for fun.

That afternoon at the burial, the sun was a distant memory as we trudged across Milltown Cemetery in fine soft rain, carrying our newly acquired stepladder. It was almost impossible not to laugh as we arrived at the graveside: the ladder had been rendered completely unnecessary. The IRA had erected scaffolding tiers on either side of the burial place on which we could set up our tripods. Two British Army helicopters hovered noisily overhead throughout, a provocation the Republicans objected to while also taking it almost as a matter of course. The coffin was brought, speeches were made, the rain continued to fall. Slowly, and with several minutes to go, the front of the scaffolding tiers started to sink into the mud. It was clear that if we stayed up there, there was a real danger the scaffolding would sink so far that we would be pitched, face- or lens-first, into the grave. There was a scramble to get off. Balaclavaed gunmen raised their rifles and fired their salute.

It was one of so many scenes I've witnessed as a reporter where the sombre has blended with ridiculous—the kind of scene that means Evelyn Waugh's novel *Scoop*, though written as satire, remains one of the most accurate things ever written about journalism.

* * *

In the autumn of 1981, our longstanding Brussels-based Europe correspondent Malcolm Downing being away, I was sent to Warsaw to cover the growing tension surrounding the Solidarity Trade Union.

I'd grown up on tales of Budapest in 1956, and the promise of freedom before the tanks rolled in. As a sixteen-year-old, I'd watched in frustration in 1968 as the liberation movements in Paris, London and San Francisco were suddenly mirrored by a struggle for freedom against real tyranny in Czechoslovakia, then as all hopes were dashed as Moscow again moved to crush dissent. Now in Warsaw I found myself in the middle of something similar.

Solidarnosc, or Solidarity, had become as much of a social movement as a trade union, heavily buttressed by the strength of Poland's Catholic Church, the force which the communists had never really suppressed and was now resurgent because the Pope, John Paul II, was himself Polish: the former Cardinal Karel Wojtyla. That's not to say it was a religious revolution. Warsaw was in fact a hotbed of secular and moral—as well as Catholic—debate, with a sudden explosion of free discussion in pamphlets, magazines and meetings. But there was also a desperate sense that it was unlikely to last, so there was gallows humour everywhere. The red and white 'Solidarnosc' badges you saw on every second lapel were all rectangular. But people feared (rightly as it turned out) that the crackdown would come soon. Hence the joke I was told: 'You've heard they're making round Solidarnosc badges now? Easier to swallow.'

In much-invaded Poland, there was also historical bitterness about the neighbours—on both sides. 'If the Russians and the East Germans invaded tonight, Sarge, which would you shoot first?' 'The Germans.' 'Why?' 'Duty before pleasure.' Alleged truisms abounded: 'Under capitalism one man exploits another, but under communism, it is the other way around', and 'Capitalism is teetering on a precipice. Soon communism will overtake it.'

I drove to Gdańsk to interview the Solidarity leader Lech Wałęsa. I had a very good interpreter called Agnieska, who was bilingual and smart: she'd talked us through a couple of roadblocks along the way, and I trusted her work implicitly. Wałęsa, though, was mistrustful of the foreign media and somewhat prickly. He insisted on using his own interpreter, whose name I seem to remember was Ewa, pronounced 'Eva'. She wasn't quite as impressive, and bad translation can have consequences.

My experience with Wałęsa was almost an exact mirror of what had happened to the unfortunate US President Jimmy Carter when he visited Poland in 1977. He'd said he was happy to be in Poland. His interpreter turned that into 'I am happy to grasp at Poland's private parts'. In my case, it happened when I asked Wałęsa about General Wojciech Jaruzelski, the prime minister who some then still thought might be capable of reaching deals with Solidarity and the Church, but who others feared (correctly as it turned out) was planning to crush the movement towards freedom.

'You and General Jaruzelski,' I asked Wałęsa, 'may be on opposing sides, but do you respect him?'

He looked startled at the translation, and asked Ewa to say it again. She did.

'Certainly not,' he replied angrily.

I was taken aback. It had seemed a reasonably innocuous query.

'Why not?' I asked.

'Because I am not that sort of man,' he replied.

The interview, which had been proceeding smoothly enough, did not last long after that. Fortunately I had just enough in the can for my TV news package, but I had hoped for much more. Agnieska, who had been chafing in the background, told me as we were leaving what had happened. 'When you asked "Do you respect him",' she said, 'Ewa translated it as "Do you have sexual desire for him?"' Wałęsa, a staunch Catholic and a man's man in a society where homosexuality was in any case heavily suppressed, had been understandably offended.

I left after a couple of weeks with a heavy heart, wondering only when—not if—the inevitable crackdown would come, and then listened with increasing chagrin to my old school roommate, now Warsaw correspondent, Tim Sebastian, reporting for the BBC when, on 13 December, Jaruzelski imposed martial law.

After that, another bleak joke filtered out from an exiled friend. Two Warsaw patrolmen are watching an old man walking down the street a few minutes before the hour of curfew. One of them picks up his gun and shoots the old man dead. The other, aghast, says, 'Why did you do that?' 'Oh, that old guy,' says the first. 'I know where he lives. He'd never have made it home in time.'

Poland's hopes for liberation were dashed, but they had represented another brief flowering of freedom in the Eastern Bloc, another resurgence of the human spirit under communism. Wałęsa was jailed, but he soon received the Nobel Peace Prize in absentia. This time, the world was watching closely, and in Leonid Brezhnev's Moscow they must have been growing increasingly defensive.

The ABC had no Africa correspondent at the time, so I flew in to report stories from Uganda, still recovering from the rule of the madman Idi Amin Dada. I also visited South Africa for the first time. It was the flip side of Poland, a right-wing dictatorship hanging on by crushing the wishes of its own majority, a regime whose survival was only really guaranteed by the refusal of allies such as Reagan and Thatcher to support sanctions, let alone cut the white rulers off from their sources of arms and riot control. The shock of being called 'Master' by a man three times my own age, who insisted on carrying my suitcase at a hotel in Durban, was quickly followed by more stark reminders, such as walking down to the beach to see 'Whites Only' signs delineating the majority of its sand. Later, in Johannesburg, I visited the vast shantytowns of Soweto, and was told the big, well-tarmacked roads that criss-crossed them had been deliberately built to carry armoured vehicles—the rest of the town was alleyways and dirt roads. The tin shacks were sweltering, and the people mostly hungry, though few actually starved. Coming back to the hotel in the evening, though, you could drink dry white wine on the terrace with the rest of the all-white clientele, and eat grilled lobster and salad.

I had a South African friend in London who'd served several months of house arrest because he was the BBC's Namibia stringer. It emerged much later that when he was smuggled out to freedom, it was through the agency of a member of the sinisterly named South African security service BOSS, building his deep cover as a mole within the opposition, while also quietly getting rid of a journalist who had become a PR problem for the government.

Just as I'd found in Poland, and later in the Soviet Union, it was always sensible to assume that you were being followed, bugged or monitored. One of the safety valves by which South Africa survived was to allow 'homelands', dots in the landscape which were technically autonomous. One of those was Sun City, a tiny enclave where people from largely Calvinist Johannesburg and Pretoria could go to drink and gamble. We went there to film, and shot among other things a sequence in which I put a coin in a slot machine. The result was an instant jackpot—coins literally spilling out of the tray underneath, and on the soundtrack, the ching-ching-ching of the machine spitting out cash. I thought it might just have been a lucky strike, until I read years later an article about Sun City which said that every single fruit machine had been closely monitored, and there was a central desk which could dispense or withhold jackpots at the push of a button. It seemed a fitting symbol of the whole phoney set-up. Constant monitoring, constant control. The hallmark of dictatorships, left-wing and right. I never had much time for bands like Queen that took large sums of money to play Sun City, which was just a fig leaf on the appalling system that was called apartheid.

In neighbouring Zimbabwe I attended the anniversary of independence, another long Cold War struggle, in which a liberation fight for majority rule against the rump of minority white settlers had been supplanted by a far-Left dictatorship led by Robert Mugabe. The world was still dewy-eyed about Mugabe then, but the scales fell from my eyes at Harare's national stadium. After leaving the crowd waiting in hot sun for three hours, Mugabe turned up to watch a demonstration of martial arts by his pride and joy, the Fifth Brigade. As they postured, rolled, kicked and punched, the announcer told us with pride that they'd been trained by the army of Kim Il-Sung's North Korea. The Fifth Brigade went on over the next few years to lead the widespread massacres and other brutalities by which Mugabe crushed the heartland of his political opposition, Matabeleland.

* * *

Back in London, Margaret Thatcher was not doing well domestically. Cities like Newcastle-on-Tyne, where I travelled to film the slow death of the shipbuilding industry, were beginning to fall apart, with few plans for regeneration. Yorkshire mines were closing and mining villages were dying, although it would still be a couple of years before the all-out war between Thatcher and the miners' union. The effects of economic belt-tightening were biting hard on the working class in the form of unemployment, and people had not yet begun to see the benefits of major transformational programs like the right to buy, instead of rent, your own council house. Thatcher was trailing in the polls by more than 10 per cent at the beginning of 1981, and even the Labour split which created the Social Democratic Party, or SDP, did not really help her. It was Labour and the SDP which were vying for first place in the polls most of that year and into 1982, and there was even talk, in first-past-the-post Britain, of an SDP-led government, perhaps with Roy Jenkins as PM and Shirley Williams as his deputy.

And the Bristol unrest I'd covered the year before had just been a foretaste. The summer of 1981 was marked by huge riots which racked London's Brixton and destroyed swathes of Liverpool's Toxteth. The press tended to write the Brixton troubles off as race-related, but (to borrow a phrase from the music industry at the time) it was more 2-Tone: disaffected, unemployed black *and* white youth with resentments against the police force in the era of the stop-and-search regime known as the 'sus' laws. Toxteth was an even more serious matter: in parts of depressed Liverpool, youth unemployment was at an astonishing 90 per cent, and Liverpudlians had the very strong sense that the Thatcher government had abandoned them. It was only Thatcher minister Michael Heseltine, given the job of listening to and rebuilding the north-west, who poured oil on the troubled water, but even so, disaffection had burrowed deep and the Conservatives entered 1982 trailing badly.

What saved Mrs Thatcher was the Falklands War, an Argentine invasion which her cost-cutting government had unwittingly triggered in 1981. It had done so by withdrawing one of the Royal Navy's patrol vessels, HMS *Endurance*, from the area. We know now from Cabinet documents released under the thirty-year rule that both Foreign Secretary Lord Carrington and the Navy chief, First Sea Lord Admiral Sir Henry Leach, strongly warned Margaret Thatcher and Defence Secretary John Nott in 1981 that this could 'prejudice our national security', and that 'Unless and until the dispute is settled, it will be important to maintain our normal presence in the area at the current level.' At the time she refused even to see Admiral Leach (a fine man and an old friend of my stepfather's), despite his repeated written pleas, and ignored Carrington. So after the warnings to which she'd turned a deaf ear came true, Margaret Thatcher was extremely fortunate in the magnanimity of these two old-fashioned gentlemen. Lord Carrington 'did the honourable thing' by taking the blame for the invasion and resigning as foreign secretary, while Sir Henry Leach not only did not recriminate, but stood by Thatcher and stiffened her resolve. In response to her doubts, we now know the admiral told her not only that she should, but could, send a naval task force to retake the Falklands. He assembled it, and executed the naval operation which helped her win the war.

So Thatcher and Nott, whose insistence on naval cuts and lack of foresight arguably caused the crisis, survived and thrived. Amid a truly astonishing tide of jingoism and outright racism in the tabloid press, the task force sailed.

These were frustrating days of guesswork and speculation for a reporter. Both my colleague Peter George and I, as dual British passport holders, applied to sail south in the fleet with the other 'embedded' journalists. (Both sons of naval families, we'd earlier discovered that Peter's father had been on board HMS *King George V* when it accidentally ploughed through my stepfather's ship, HMS *Punjabi*, in the Arctic Convoys during World War II.) But the British decision on the task force media contingent was final: only representatives of selected *British* media were to be allowed to go. In practice, of those who did sail, those who were allowed most access were from the most fervently red-white-and-blue of the tabloids. I recall *Sun* reporter Tony Snow reporting on how he was allowed below decks to write a message to Argentina's then president from the paper's readers on the warhead of a deadly ship-to-air missile: 'Up Yours, Galtieri!' Days later, under his by-line, came the sentence, 'I saw *my missile* hit the back of the enemy aircraft. It exploded as advertised. His plane was in flames.' (My italics.)

After that, it hardly came as a surprise when *The Sun* reacted to the sinking of the Argentine warship *General Belgrano* with the infamous headline 'GOTCHA'. There'd been 1095 human beings on that ship, and 323 of them were now dead. But what else was *Sun* editor Kelvin McKenzie going to go with? After all, he'd already used 'STICK IT UP YOUR JUNTA'.

In the London bureau, we pieced together a daily news jigsaw, not helped by the daily obfuscations given at dictation speed, as if to a very slow secretary, by government spokesman Ian MacDonald. The task force reporters were heavily censored, often counterproductively to the point of not being able to give details such as how many aircraft had returned to a carrier unharmed—Argentina was falsely claiming to have shot down dozens, if not scores, of British planes. The BBC's Brian Hanrahan got round the restriction on his ship with the famous phrase 'I counted them all out, and I counted them all back'.

As well as radio and TV reports, you could build a partial picture through a careful reading of all the broadsheet reporters' stories, and listening to the 'white noise' coming out of Whitehall. My only notable victory in terms of analysis (and it was a tiny one) was an *AM* piece in which I said the barrage of denials of an early landing by ground forces was now so intense that it was extremely likely that such an attack would take place within the next twenty-four hours. This extrapolation proved correct: I filed it that evening, London time, and woke up the next morning, 22 May, to hear that British forces had indeed landed at San Carlos.

Like all wars, the Falklands conflict was nasty: both at sea, where the British as well as the Argentines lost a lot of men, and on land, where the battles took a mental and physical toll in death and injury on many. Years later, freed from censorship, *The Guardian*'s Gareth Parry wrote:

> In the task force, if not in the saloon bars of England, there was little taste for glory achieved at such a cost. Even seasoned officers said they never wanted to return to Goose Green, the insignificant hamlet where 300 men died in a few hours. The scene after the battle was ghastly. There were rows upon rows of corpses badly charred by the phosphorus of artillery shells. In several places there were rifles stuck in the mud with helmets on them, marking where men died.

To anyone familiar with the reality of armed conflict, whether or not they had been among the war's backers, the triumphalist words of Margaret Thatcher, 'Just rejoice at the news and congratulate our Forces and the Marines', were hard to swallow. But the opinion polls, the street parties and the bunting-strewn homecomings showed that most people not only agreed with her, but had also come round to the iron-willed determination of the Iron Lady more generally. By the time I finished my London posting at the end of 1982, I was fairly convinced that she would be elected to another term and that Thatcherism was there to stay.

Chapter 24

Obviously KGB

IN THE NORTHERN autumn of 1984, having become the ABC's Europe correspondent, based in Brussels, I found myself reluctantly heading for Moscow. The reluctance arose from repeated warnings by my father that, because of him, I would be a KGB target, and unpleasant things might happen. Because of the continuing barriers to revealing anything about Dad's real job, however, this was not something I could tell anyone else.

I'd spent just over a year back in Sydney, at the beginning of which my career had hit a small speed bump. Although it was generally agreed I'd done a good job in London, no department had a vacancy for me. So I spent some time in ABC limbo, increasingly worried, on something called the 'unattached list'. Eventually, Managing Director Keith Jennings heard of my plight, called me in, and told me he'd try to get something organised. Simultaneously, my friend Paul Murphy, now the presenter of *PM*, lobbied the head of Radio Current Affairs, Russell Warner, to hire me. Warner asked me to come in for an interview.

I arrived wearing a rather expensive Italian red knitted-silk tie. Beetling his brow, Warner, a manager of the old school, asked me, 'Does that tie represent your politics, boy?' Throwing caution to the winds, I decided to be cheeky, rather than defensive, in response: 'In the sense that it's red, or that I bought it on the Ponte Vecchio in Florence?' He had the grace to laugh, and ten minutes later offered me the job.

I started as senior reporter just in time for the dramatic events of February 1983, when Malcolm Fraser tried to steal a march on Labor by calling a surprise federal election. Unknown to him, the ALP had chosen the same day to axe their own leader, Bill Hayden, and replace him with Bob Hawke. I put together a quick and dirty special on Hawke, and helped with coverage of the election over the following month. Hayden, who said he felt 'flensed' after the coup (a term whalers used for stripping all the skin off the beasts they killed), has always said a 'drover's dog' could have won that election. We'll never know, but I think it's fair to say that Hawke won a bigger majority than his predecessor, a decent and intelligent but uncharismatic man, ever could have.

There were certain frustrations in the job as Senior Reporter, Radio Current Affairs, notably the fact that some of my new bosses regarded me as a News interloper—an indication that the old enmity between News and Current Affairs was still alive. The place was also teeming with internal backbiting and resentment, caused partly by an outdated system of promotion by length of service, which engendered a massive and widely divisive conflict between two senior reporters. But I thought some of the factionalism and gossip was caused by a degree of overstaffing: too many people seeing their stories go unused because the two programs, *AM* and *PM*, were oversubscribed with content. Partly to soak up the overspill, I started agitating for an hour-long lunchtime current affairs program, which seemed rather obvious to me after three years in London: the BBC, after all, had had *The World at One* since the mid-1960s. After a certain amount of departmental infighting, it happened, and I became the first presenter of the brand-new *The World Today*. A year or so on, however, my good friend Malcolm Downing was finishing the last of many terms as Brussels correspondent, and he suggested I apply as his replacement.

The Moscow assignment was my first field experience after arriving in Brussels. I believe the director of ABC TV News, Jack Gulley, had been given indications that visas might be available for an ABC TV crew for what was then a fairly rare chance to travel in the Soviet Union—albeit under controlled conditions—and I was the one to go. Gulley, at any rate, knew an Australian woman called Daphne who was bilingual in English and Russian, and who, he very strongly suggested, should travel with us as our interpreter.

On paper, this was the year Konstantin Chernenko was the leader of the Soviet Union; his predecessor, Yuri Andropov, had died after just over a year in office, having achieved very little of any visibility. In reality, to all intents and purposes, we were there—had we known it—to chronicle the end of the Leonid Brezhnev years. Chernenko himself was wheelchair-bound and not long for this world, and the Soviet Union itself was still in the long slow decline it had been suffering at least since Brezhnev had ousted Nikita Khrushchev in 1964.

The Moscow where we landed would be almost unrecognisable to those who know it now by its oligarchs, limousines, expensive hotels, restaurants and nightclubs. Back then, at the National Hotel on Red Square, where we stayed, there was an elderly female 'concierge' on every floor—not to look after the guests' every need but to note all their comings and goings, and (reputedly) search their belongings when they were out. In the restaurant at breakfast, it usually took up to a quarter of an hour to get the attention of a waiter, even for something as simple as a coffee and the little food available. At dinner, there were thick, leather-bound menus listing many delicacies, such as sturgeon and bear steak, which were somehow never actually available.

At a table next to us one night, an American went through the options with the surly waiter, eventually establishing that only two out of the dozens listed could be ordered: chicken or fish. 'Which is better?' he asked. 'Chicken, fish, both good,' came the reply. He persisted with the question but kept getting the same answer, until, suddenly inspired, he drew a Havana cigar in a silvery tube from his coat. 'The chicken. Or the fish?' he insisted. 'Take the chicken,' said the waiter, palming the cigar swiftly into his trouser pocket. Foreign goods and foreign money were the key to almost everything among ordinary people. Scarcity was the norm, and dollars or pounds, Western records, jeans and other consumer goods could open many doors.

Our first port of call was the media authorities, whose word would be crucial in allowing us to film. There it became clear that the Soviet Government was as greedy as its people for foreign currency. Even though we had a highly competent interpreter of our own, we would have to pay for Irina, a starched, judgemental young woman who would accompany us everywhere. She never did any actual interpreting for us, but her presence was necessary when filming because she carried the permits and the ministry credentials that would keep police and militia members at bay. The rates were exorbitant, as they were for the minivan with driver the authorities insisted we hire from them to get around.

That morning we also had to negotiate a filming schedule, including not only the subjects we'd be covering but the people we'd be talking to. With round-the-clock surveillance, and this being my first visit to the Soviet Union, there was no chance whatsoever of interviewing dissidents or doing any serious investigative journalism. On the other hand, Sydney had also given me to understand that this was on some level a reconnaissance mission, a chance to work in a country where we might ultimately try for what were then extremely rare permissions to set up a bureau. So we worked out a schedule whereby we would make a colour story on Moscow's underground rail system, a piece about the Soviet nuclear power industry, a story on the trans-Siberian pipeline which was just about to bring Russian gas to Europe, a short film about Russian conservation and environmental measures, and a piece about the Baltic states, for which we would travel to Estonia.

It all started out auspiciously enough in the Moscow Metro, where we were making a ten-minute story for the Sunday night ABC News program *Weekend Magazine*. Built in the 1930s, the heart of the metro was a series of stations of unparalleled magnificence, a relic of a time when the Soviet Union was trying to persuade the West of the superiority of its system—an era when Lenin, then Stalin, wooed intellectuals like George Bernard Shaw, Sidney and Beatrice Webb, and Andre Gide with visits from which they would return with glowing reports of how nothing was too good for workers in the Soviet Union. The stations are of varying design, some almost baroque with chandeliers, others with marble walls and gilded neoclassical columns holding up their vaulted ceilings. There are mosaics and stained-glass panels and statues. Though millions of people used it every day, it could have more of the feeling of a museum than a public transport network.

We then went by railway to Voronezh, about eight hours south of Moscow, where we were taken out to film the nearly completed gas pipeline and interview the gas-exporting authorities. First, though, there was a dinner hosted by the local mayor, who insisted on toasting us with vodka shots which had to be downed in one. We were expected to toast in return—'To the friendship between our peoples', etc.—in a ritual which looked as though it could only end in mutual oblivion. Protestations that we had to work in the morning, weren't used to drinking so much, and so forth, were brushed away. I lost count after about twelve shots. We staggered back up the street to our guesthouse, arm-in-arm with the mayor, singing drunkenly. Before we could sleep, our freelance sound-recordist, who I won't name to spare his blushes, was violently sick over himself, cameraman Les Seymour, and me: we had to strip him and spend about half an hour hosing him down in the shower.

My piece to camera the next morning, which involved climbing a high ladder and standing on a gantry above the pipeline itself, was one of the most difficult I've ever done. I was on the verge of retching throughout, and my head felt as if a steam hammer was repeatedly striking a big brass bell somewhere between my ears. I saw it years later, and was surprised to find that you couldn't tell.

The next day involved a visit to the Novovoronezh nuclear power station, with interviews about the superiority of the Soviet scientific and technical system. They would have been more persuasive had the power station itself not had such a retro look: unwieldy dials and levers, with very little in the way of the sophisticated electronics that were already going into Western power technology, let alone any sign of computerisation. It was fascinating to find that so much of what the Soviet Union offered for filming as 'modern' at the time looked old and clunky to our eyes.

Our minder Irina had been difficult, moody and unhelpful from the start, but problems started to escalate with the next story, planned for convenience in the same region. The idea was to film a piece about Soviet attempts at conservation, centred on scientists working in the field to ensure the survival of beavers in the area's forests, streams and lakes. I assumed that 'in the field' meant just that: we would have a day or two tramping around, David Attenborough-style, watching the creatures build their dams. Instead, on arrival at the 'field station', we were shown a sort of large, roughly built wooden dolls' house, complete with little wooden ladders, intended to replicate the inside of a beaver dam. The Soviets would bring in semi-domesticated beavers and we could film to our hearts' content. I told them we couldn't possibly go along with this: we were trying to film reality, not a stage set. They told us that it was always good enough for Russian TV. We relented enough to film a couple of minutes for show, but it was equally clear that they knew we felt let down. There was no alternative offer, but much shrugging and resentment.

One of the people we were to interview for this story was an entomologist, a pleasant and helpful man with good English. At one point, while Irina was out of the room, we talked off-camera about his work, which, being about insects, meant crunching huge amounts of data. 'Where's your computer?' I asked. 'I don't have one,' he said. 'I send all the data to Kiev and get the computer results a couple of months later.' I knew that no similar science department in Britain or Australia lacked at least some basic computing power: the Soviet Union was lagging far behind. I pointed to his very large desk calculator and he grinned. 'In the Soviet Union,' he said, 'we have a joke: our scientists are racing to build the world's biggest computer chip.'

Back in Moscow, we filmed another equally unpleasant Soviet science story, about brain research, in which we were invited to film in a laboratory full of monkeys attached to the wall by electrodes in their skulls and given periodic stimulation and electric shocks. The terror in those animals' eyes was palpable to me, but seemed so normal to the white-coated scientists and laboratory assistants.

In the Soviet capital, I felt ever more under surveillance. A correspondent from the Soviet newsagency TASS, formerly based in London and Washington, with perfect English and excellent manners (therefore obviously KGB), invited me to lunch and tried to quiz me gently. He got nothing because there was nothing to get. Things came to a head when we were called into the media ministry, and under Irina's stern eye were told that we had been 'breaching the terms of our agreement'. I had absolutely no idea what they were talking about, especially when they claimed we'd been going out at night interviewing dissidents. I protested absolute and unfeigned ignorance of this, but they were adamant: this was our final warning, and the trip would be over if this behaviour continued.

It was only that evening that Daphne, the translator imposed on us by Jack Gulley, admitted to me that she'd been leaving our hotel every night and visiting her many academic and intellectual friends, mostly in Moscow's Arbat district. She'd been doing so for entirely personal reasons—she had no intention of writing about them or feeding information to us—but she had put the whole trip in jeopardy, and once again (because of the secrecy still surrounding my father's role) I was left unable to explain why what she had done was so particularly dangerous for me.

The last leg of the trip involved another train ride, to Estonia, just across the water from Finland. The historic capital, Tallinn, was an eye-opener, far more northern European than Russian. The language spoken there is closely related to Finnish, and the town was full of Finns who mostly came over on big ferries to take advantage of more liberal drinking laws—having a beer in a bar one night, Les and I saw a tall Finn, stupefied with vodka, stand up and fall straight forward like a tree in a forest, smashing a glass table in the process. We filmed bucolic farm scenes, tickled trout in an aquaculture facility, spoke to local government officials who predictably extolled their semi-autonomous status within the Soviet Union. But there was an undercurrent of discontent everywhere: the differences of language and culture were far too great, and it felt like a Russian colony, not a province.

I was relieved when we arrived at Moscow's Sheremetyevo airport to leave for London and Brussels: the trip had become increasingly oppressive as it had gone on. But it wasn't over. We went through passport and Customs control and waited in the departure lounge to board our British Airways flight. Almost there. But as the plane boarded, two plain-clothes officials took me aside and into a small room. They demanded to search my hand baggage. I objected quite strenuously, more on principle than because I had anything to hide. I said my colleagues were already on the plane and would be worrying about me. They were menacingly insistent, saying that they would actually ground the plane if necessary should I refuse. I demanded a call to the Australian embassy. They refused. Eventually, against my better judgement, I let them look inside my briefcase. They rummaged through it, finding nothing of interest except my Filofax—a leather ringbinder that served as a calendar, diary, notebook and contact book. They told me they were taking it away, and when they brought it back I could get on the plane. Forty minutes passed in silence. Long enough, I supposed, to photocopy the whole thing.

It was the 1984 equivalent of someone taking and copying everything on your smartphone: a gross invasion of privacy. I still don't know what they were looking for. If it was my dad's address and phone number, they could have got that from the London telephone directory. There was nothing else in my Filofax to interest them.

They returned and told me I was free to go. Shaken, angry and humiliated, I boarded the plane. I was leaving the Soviet Union and I never wanted to go back.

Chapter 25

The Edge for the Scoop

In May 1985, forty years after the end of World War II in Europe, I found myself driving at insane speeds between Bitburg, a German war cemetery where Ronald Reagan had elected to lay a wreath, and the concentration camp at Belsen. It seemed obscene to many then—it still seems to me now—that Reagan should have so chosen to pair a visit to the graves of Wehrmacht soldiers with another to one of the worst sites of the Holocaust, the place where the BBC's Richard Dimbleby gave one of his most famous broadcasts, just after liberation: 'I passed through the barrier and found myself in the world of nightmare.' He tells the story of a woman who begged a British soldier 'to give her some milk for the tiny baby she held in her arms. When the soldier opened the bundle of rags to look at the child he found it had been dead for days.' Dimbleby, in a masterpiece of broadcast writing that can still bring me to tears, leaves the worst till last: 'In the frenzy of their starvation, the people of Belsen had taken the wasted bodies of their fellow prisoners and removed from them the only remaining flesh—the liver and kidney—to eat.'

There's little to see at Belsen, because the extent of disease was so great that the liberating forces had to bulldoze and burn most of the buildings: there are none of the sights that give employment to tour guides at Dachau and Auschwitz. But something about its very emptiness, and the photographs and films that are on display of what the British forces saw at the time, may, for those with a sense of history and human suffering, even increase the starkness of what happened.

Reagan had to be lobbied hard to go there, because, he initially said, 'since the German people have very few alive that remember even the war, and certainly none of them who were adults and participating in any way ... they have a feeling and a guilt feeling that's been imposed upon them'. This caused a justified furore, especially from American Jews. Being himself an adult during the war (he did not serve overseas but did make a number of army propaganda training films), Reagan must have known that this was simply factually incorrect, even if he couldn't grasp its insensitivity.

At Belsen, he redeemed himself somewhat with a well-tuned speech:

> Here lie people—Jews—whose death was inflicted for no reason other than their very existence. Their pain was borne only because of who they were and because of the God in their prayers. Alongside them lie many Christians—Catholics and Protestants. For year after year, until that man and his evil were destroyed, hell yawned forth its awful contents. People were brought here for no other purpose but to suffer and die. To go unfed when hungry, uncared for when sick, tortured when the whim struck, and left to have misery consume them when all there was around them was misery.

But for me the memory remains: screaming to a halt at the Bitburg German war cemetery as Reagan's helicopter rattled overhead, trying but failing to get film as he and Chancellor Helmut Kohl laid wreaths in the deliberately far distance—wreaths to soldiers whose colleagues had committed the atrocities of the Belsen plague-pits.

I remembered Belsen, and Dachau, which I'd visited previously, the next May as I sat on a high-speed train heading south from Paris for the trial of the SS Hauptsturmführer and member of the Gestapo, Klaus Barbie, the 'Butcher of Lyons'. In the seat opposite me sat a balding, grey-haired man who, like me, was reading through a large file of recent newspaper articles about Barbie. Thinking he might be another journalist, I asked if he was going to be attending the trial, and we got talking. He told me he made documentaries, though he did so in such a modest way that it didn't at first register. It was only after about half an hour, when I asked his name and he said 'Marcel Ophüls', that I realised that I was travelling with the director of *The Sorrow and the Pity*. This classic, Oscar-nominated film had rocked France to its foundations in 1969 by forcing the country to look hard for the first time at the reality of wartime collaboration with the Germans, and in particular of French complicity in the forced transportation of the Jews.

Barbie had not only tortured French men and women in the Lyons Gestapo headquarters, he had sent many Jews and Resistance fighters to their certain deaths in concentration camps. He escaped to South America after the war but was finally extradited back to France in 1983. Now Klaus Barbie was to stand trial for crimes against humanity, central among which was the rounding up of forty-four children at a refuge in Izieu, and an order he personally signed for them to be transported, ultimately to the gas chambers. Not one of them survived.

It was Barbie's lawyer, Jacques Verges, who turned the trial into a grotesque piece of theatre, with Barbie seeming to exert an almost hypnotic hold over the French media. A Maoist and lifelong friend of the genocidal Cambodian dictator Pol Pot, Verges was determined to frame proceedings not around Klaus Barbie, but around the entire history of French imperialism. 'French society is sick,' he said. 'It does not want to recognise the lies on which it constructed its existence.' This appeared to chime with something in French intellectual life at the time. Verges' entire strategy, it gradually emerged, consisted not of defending Barbie's innocence as such, but of proving a parallel between the Nazis' Final Solution and France's actions in Indochina, Algeria and Central Africa. Whatever your views about those issues, for anyone brought up in the British, American or Australian court systems, this seemed like a derailing of the natural order of justice. It was Barbie himself who was accused of committing appalling crimes: even if Verges thought he could prove a moral equivalence between two political systems, how could that be a reason for letting this one war criminal go free?

Inside the courtroom, the first day of proceedings consisted entirely of a recitation of the many crimes alleged against Barbie—despite often monotonous reading by the lawyers, an accumulation of true horrors which couldn't fail to have their impact as I scribbled away in my notebook. Barbie himself, white-haired, jut-jawed, stared impassively out at the public and the press. At one point, for some reason, he fixed his eyes on me for what seemed about five minutes. They were piercing and hard, and his expression was not merely stony but contemptuous. That stare is forever printed on my brain.

Fortunately, it was not Verges' posturing but the testimony of victims that swayed the jury in the end. The ones who had suffered most, of course, could not be there: they had died in the gas chambers and their remains were burned to ash in the ovens. But even the survivors' testimony was heart-rending, like the woman who remembered how, as a thirteen-year-old, she had suffered water torture at Barbie's own hands: '"You'll talk", said Barbie. In the bath, when he pulled up my head, I was thinking, What would happen if I didn't speak? … It was said that you must swallow right away in order to drown yourself. I couldn't. I never recovered from the torture.'

On 3 July 1986, Barbie was sentenced to life in prison. He died there four years later. But the trial did more than bring one man to justice. For my train companion Marcel Ophüls, for instance, it provided vindication at last. *The Sorrow and the Pity* had been banned from French television until 1981. Now France could no longer look away from the consequences of its own people's wartime collaboration with officers like Barbie and the genocidal ideology they represented.

* * *

In early 1985, just months after my visit to Moscow, rumours had begun circulating that the Soviet leader Konstantin Chernenko was not just severely ill, but dying. In mid-March, the Kremlin made it official: there was to be another state funeral, the third in two and a half years.

The Soviet system was genuinely sclerotic, partly because it had tested the theories of centralised economic control in a socialised economy far beyond their limits, but also partly because it had been led for two decades by sclerotic old men. Finally, after decades of promotion by pure seniority, the Central Committee of the Soviet Communist Party saw the sense in appointing a younger, more energetic, more outward-looking leader. The man they chose was almost unknown outside his own country at the time but was soon to become world-famous, better known as a person and a politician than any Kremlin leader since the startlingly colourful Nikita Khrushchev twenty years before. The new man's name, of course, was Mikhail Gorbachev, and Kremlinologists both inside and outside the Soviet Union immediately began the guessing game: who was he, and what would he do next?

News travelled more slowly in that era. It was about three weeks later that I got a call from a current affairs producer in Sydney: 'I've been reading about this fellow Gorbachev. He sounds interesting. Could you get us an interview with him in the next couple of days?' It wasn't the only time I had to explain such things as the distance between Brussels and Moscow, the difficulty and delay in getting visas, or the fact that every resident Moscow correspondent was already begging vainly for even a few words with Gorbachev. After all, around the same time, ABC News briefly had a foreign editor whose proud boast before taking the position was that he had never left NSW, let alone Australia.

The BBC's Moscow correspondent, my old schoolfriend Tim Sebastian, said on Gorbachev's appointment that despite his lively and flexible manner, the new leader was 'still a strict, orthodox Marxist: in no sense has he shown himself to be a liberal'. Even Soviet Foreign Minister Andrei Gromyko, nominating him for the leadership, said that behind Gorbachev's disarming smile there were 'teeth of steel'—a particularly Soviet metaphor, since many victims of Russian dentistry did actually have steel teeth. But Margaret Thatcher made a point of attending Chernenko's funeral, and, having met the successor on a recent visit to London, Thatcher said, 'I like Mr Gorbachev. We can do business together.' It was one of the most influential statements she ever made, because it began the process of persuading her friend and ally, US President Ronald Reagan, to take seriously the new man at the top in Moscow.

I'd already been reporting regularly on the increasing crisis over the nuclear arms build-up in Europe. That year I went to West Germany to film US Abrams tanks on exercises, interview arms experts and nuclear-free-zone proponents, and film a length of the sinister border with East Germany, where long lines of barbed wire interspersed with Warsaw Pact army watchtowers still marched through the dense forests that had haunted my dreams since reading the Brothers Grimm as a child. On another occasion, without a crew, I walked through Checkpoint Charlie, in the guise of a tourist, and spent the day exploring East Berlin, a city almost as grey, lacking in vim and plagued by scarcity as I'd found Moscow the year before. In strategic terms, both sides were deploying or threatening to deploy more intermediate-range nuclear missiles on European soil. There was even increasing talk of 'battlefield nuclear weapons'. American officers appeared on TV telling of how they were trained to use 'flash-to-bang time' to calculate how far away a nuclear explosion had hit—the old thunder and lightning trick: see the flash, then the number of seconds till you hear the bang is the number of miles away it is. The nuclear annihilation of large swathes of Europe didn't seem probable, but it certainly didn't seem impossible. Now, we journalists quickly had to learn the meaning of words like 'glasnost' ('openness') and 'perestroika' ('restructuring'), and, almost as quickly, to start analysing deeds as well as words.

A month after he became leader, Gorbachev announced that the Soviet Union would not, after all, deploy intermediate-range nuclear SS-20 missiles into Eastern Europe. On the one hand, this was a major gesture of appeasement in the best sense. On the other hand, it could be viewed as a clever tactical move: it ratcheted up the pressure on Western leaders like Thatcher and Reagan to make their own gestures towards disarming Europe. In Britain and Germany, particularly, there were big and vocal unilateralist disarmament movements. Some—a tiny minority but a dangerous one—were bent not on pacifism but extreme violence.

The annual summit of the G7, the world's richest industrialised nations, was held in May 1985 in Bonn, then the West German capital. Filming anti-nuclear demonstrations, Les Seymour and I suddenly found ourselves in the midst of mayhem: black-clad anarchists in masks and balaclavas rampaging though the streets smashing windows and using catapults to fire ball bearings. Sheltering in a doorway, we looked at each other. We'd both been in dangerous situations in Africa and the Middle East, he more often than I, but there was something completely visceral and unpredictable about this. These people might have seen governments as their enemy, but they were quite indiscriminate about the damage to anyone or anything that got in their way. And that included news crews. Flying glass from shop windows was the biggest danger, but I escaped with no more than a scratched hand. Bonn—Beethoven's birthplace, immortalised by John le Carré as *A Small Town in Germany*—seemed the most unlikely venue for such mayhem.

That sort of encounter was unusual in the Brussels job, though. When I think of those years, I think of the title of Mark Lawson's amusing travel book *The Battle for Room Service: Journeys to All the Safe Places*. At that same G7 summit, the press room was on a high floor of a tower block beside the Rhine. The German hosts had laid on unlimited supplies of food and Henkell Trocken sparkling wine. My old Double J friend and colleague Jim Middleton was now Washington correspondent, travelling with the US president's press pack. He and I drank a glass or two while looking out of a window down to the street below, laughing as we watched a hilarious stand-off between the motorcades of the US and French presidents Ronald Reagan and François Mitterand. Our bird's-eye view gave us the perfect vantage point from which to see secret service officers threatening to duke it out in the building's driveway. It took about half an hour before they reached some sort of compromise.

It made you wonder: if allies found it that hard to give any ground on such a tiny matter, what about enemies, when the issue at hand was nuclear war?

Not all of the 'battle for room service' was played out in the theatre of Cold War summits. In Vienna, for example, there was also the hotel where the oil cartel OPEC held its meetings: meetings on whose results, announced by the camera-hungry Sheikh Yamani, the world's markets regularly swung. I was discreetly shown around the basement garage, where Rolls-Royces, Cadillacs, Bentleys and various high-end sports cars sat, permanently garaged under dust cloths. Some of them were owned by oil barons and sheikhs who drove, or were driven in them, once or twice a year. Others were thick with dust: clearly left there indefinitely, just in case, by people who probably had dozens of similar vehicles in similar garages all over the world.

As a reporter at OPEC, instead of hanging around waiting all day, you could often find out when the announcement was coming, giving you time to spend in the Kunsthistoriches Museum, looking at Raphaels or the world's largest collection of Brueghels. There were also, at the Belvedere Museum, more modern works. One day a British colleague thought he was absolutely hilarious when he replied 'Typical Aussie' on hearing that I was 'going to the Belvedere to look at the Schieles'.

I also spent a lot of time in hotel rooms in Paris, sometimes getting there at extremely high speed down the road from Brussels after another in the wave of terrorist bomb attacks, now almost forgotten, which hit the French capital and other cities like Frankfurt in the 1980s. Many were blamed on Libya, others on Syria, others on various Palestinian liberation organisations. In a pattern that's become all too familiar more recently, there was little discrimination when it came to the victims. Among the wounded at the Tati department store in Montparnasse, particularly, I remember women in hijabs and small children among the mainly Muslim immigrants killed or wounded.

There were also days in Paris, in mid-1985, spent trying to uncover the truth of the sinking of the Greenpeace ship *Rainbow Warrior* in New Zealand. It was difficult. President Mitterand's defence minister, Charles Hernu, and the minister for overseas territories, Georges Lemoine, ran what was essentially a brick wall defence. As it turned out, Hernu himself had ordered the mission, but nobody at that time would say so. I made contacts, especially through the assistance of *Le Monde* investigative journalist Edwy Plenel, and passed them to my colleague Chris Masters, who made better use of them than I could, with my daily deadlines fairly soon dragging me back to Brussels to cover the rest of Europe. Chris dug deep, and found intelligence sources to give him the real evidence, which he and producer Bruce Belsham put to air in what remains one of the great *Four Corners* investigations.

It was also in Paris, in October 1985, that I saw Gorbachev for the first time in person. He had just sacked Andrei Gromyko as foreign minister, an extraordinary moment as 'Old Grom' ('grom' is the Russian word for 'thunder') had held the post for an astonishing twenty-eight years. It was the clearest indication yet that Gorbachev had ambitions beyond domestic glasnost and perestroika. He wanted to take command—with the Foreign Ministry's Eduard Shevardnadze at his side—of international policy. Security in Paris was so tight that at one point we sat in a traffic jam for two hours on the Left Bank as the military blocked off streets and roads for the Gorbachev motorcade. But once indoors with the press pack, security was almost non-existent. As Mikhail and Raisa Gorbachev walked through the rococo drawing room of the prime ministerial headquarters known as Le Matignon, I was in the front row among scores of journalists, with nothing but a velvet rope and less than a metre of space between me and the leader of one of the world's two superpowers.

It was a stark contrast to a news conference in Bonn in May, where our tripods had been corralled at least 20 metres away from President Reagan, as we tried to peer over the shoulders of a line of tall Secret Servicemen with dark glasses and earpieces. A French photographer tried to nudge one of them into moving. 'Don't touch my body,' he said though gritted teeth. She tried again, and he turned round, leaned down right into her face and said, 'Read. My. Lips. Don't Touch. My. Body.' Mind you, to be fair, in 1981 Reagan had taken a bullet to the chest from the mentally disturbed John Hinckley Jr in Washington, so his protective detail had plenty of reasons to be careful.

Also on the list of 'the safe places' to and from which I commuted often during that time was Geneva, site of many UN agencies, including the Disarmament Commission. Gorbachev's Paris visit turned out to be a curtain-raiser for his Geneva Summit with Reagan a month later, where he started to build a real relationship with the US president. This meeting was frustrating for anyone who hoped to be able to report on concrete results, real advances towards peace. But we know now, and even at the time there were indications, that it laid the foundations for what would eventually become the first de-escalation of the postwar nuclear arms race. It was there behind the scenes that Reagan and Gorbachev forged a personal relationship which would ultimately lead to the Intermediate-Range Nuclear Forces Treaty.

Geneva also led me, unwillingly I must emphasise, to mislead the ABC audience as to my own linguistic abilities, basically because the press centre where the summit was being held was wired in a very peculiar Swiss system. The time zone was perfect for the ABC's new TV news and current affairs program *The National* to carry live coverage of the summit's close, when Reagan and Gorbachev would emerge from their private talks to give formal speeches. There was no problem feeding out the video and audio of Reagan, but with Gorbachev there was a snag: the simultaneous translation was being distributed around the building by a curious low-voltage electronic system which had one massive limitation. If you plugged your transmitting equipment into it, even putting alligator clips on and feeding it through a Nagra as an amplifier, you would drain it in some mysterious way, to such an extent that the whole system would blow. It wasn't a myth: other broadcasters had done it earlier in the day, with disastrous results. The only way to get sound was to listen through the system's wired-in headphones. My job was to talk *The National's* presenter, Geraldine Doogue, through the preamble to Reagan, throw to him, then come back to her for the transition to Gorbachev. The only way for the audience to hear what the Soviet leader was saying in English, therefore, was for me to listen to the translation and simultaneously parrot every word I heard into a microphone back down to Sydney. One result is that I still, very occasionally, meet people who were watching that night and who are under the entirely erroneous impression that I speak fluent Russian.

In my view, the first real test of Gorbachev's grip on power, and his genuine intention to bring about transparency, or glasnost, came about five months after the Geneva Summit, with the Chernobyl disaster. It happened on 26 April 1986, but the first reaction was the traditional Soviet one: cover it up. The Moscow authorities said absolutely nothing about it for two days, and even then their reaction was only triggered by the Swedes, who had detected unusual levels of radioactivity at one of their power plants more than a thousand kilometres away. Nuclear scientists around Europe started seeing similar results, and the Soviets were forced into a brief admission: 'There has been an accident at the Chernobyl Nuclear Power Plant. One of the nuclear reactors was damaged. The effects of the accident are being remedied. Assistance has been provided for any affected people. An investigative commission has been set up.' Moscow correspondents reported that even this terse press release was the result of a debate inside the Central Committee—a debate which Gorbachev had had to fight hard to win.

The fact that he did win, though, was extremely significant. Only through decades of persistent scientific detective work did we know back then that there'd been a huge radioactive leak after an accident at a Soviet reactor in the eastern Urals in 1957. Nearly three decades later, in the teeth of all the evidence, Moscow was still denying that one. The Chernobyl admission had taken less than three days.

As prevailing winds drifted the plume of radioactivity across Eastern and Western Europe, the Soviet Union became more and more cooperative, and it became possible to report considerable detail of what was happening. My partner Michele and two-year-old son Nicolas and I were advised to shift to London for a few days as the radioactive cloud blew over Belgium. There we met up with my sister Zoë and her husband,

Mark Higgie, then posted at the Australian embassy in Belgrade—the meandering path of the plume had hit what was then Yugoslavia quite hard, and they too had a toddler, Anna. For some odd meteorological reason, the plume was forecast to bypass the British capital, though it did rain radioactive particles on parts of Wales.

I was in the London office briefly, trying to assess the significance and detail of the disaster in reports for ABC News, *AM* and *PM*. The footage we'd filmed in the Novovoronezh power station in 1984 came in useful—not many people had film from inside a Soviet reactor plant. Then I travelled to Finland and filmed inside the world's only exported Soviet-built nuclear reactor. The Finns pointedly showed us the myriad ways they'd modified the system they'd bought: modern dials and especially electronics, extra layers of reactor shielding, a system whereby the pressure inside the building was lower than that outside so any breach would mean air rushing inwards rather than exploding outward. If anything it simply reinforced my sense in 1984 that, unmodified, the Soviet plants were ramshackle and dangerous.

Returning to Brussels a week after the news broke, I filmed in fruit and vegetable markets where people were suddenly avoiding produce like apples from Austria, and leafy greens, like spinach, in general. As it turned out, Belgium, one of Europe's dampest countries, caught a lucky break that week: there was hardly a drop of rain to precipitate the radioactivity to the ground. But the suspicion about what you could and couldn't eat persisted in much of Western Europe for months, if not years.

* * *

My time in Brussels was due to be over at the end of 1987. I'd had an extraordinary three years, marked by many new friendships in the international press corps, most closely with Éamonn Lawlor of the Irish broadcaster RTE, with whom I shared an office and who remains a lifelong friend. He and other members of the Brussels press corps, like Martin Sixsmith of the BBC, Quentin Peel and Will Dawkins of *The Financial Times*, and Derek Brown of *The Guardian*, were competitive with each other on the big Euro-stories, but had nothing to lose by giving me advice or a helping hand. I'd also got used to sharing crews, footage and notes with massively experienced BBC broadcasters like John Simpson, with whom I worked covering many major events. What I hadn't had was much competition. I was Australia's only full-time broadcast correspondent in Europe, and although I was busy, I occasionally wondered whether I had the edge for the scoop.

In May 1987, I got the chance to find out. I was in Paris to interview Foreign Minister Bill Hayden on his visit to the Organisation for Economic Co-operation and Development when ABC News Foreign Editor John Tulloh rang to say that NSW mafia boss Robert Trimbole, Australia's most wanted fugitive at the time, was reported to have died in southern Spain. The trouble was that the story of Trimbole's life as a fugitive had been one of false sightings, an arrest and failed extradition in Ireland, and erroneous reports of his death. Now the chase was on to prove whether, this time, it was really him and he was really dead. But, this being the ABC, they didn't want me to leave Paris without the Hayden interview, which meant that I would arrive in Alicante half a day behind the commercial stations.

At the airport of the Spanish port city, I met a veteran Visnews stringer cameraman, Mike Gore, who was bilingual in Spanish and so was also able to interpret. Our first port of call was a *tanatorio* (undertaker) called Siempre Viva—Eternal Life. As we arrived, however, my heart sank. The commercial TV crews, led by Paul Lyneham for Channel Seven, Robert Penfold for Nine and Mike Tancred for Ten, were just leaving. It looked like we were way behind. They made a lot of jokes about the lateness of the ABC, particularly when I mentioned the reason for the delay: an interview on the very dry subject of Australia's position at the OECD. I gritted my teeth, grinned, and hoped that we'd be able to catch up. It was early afternoon and we and the commercials had a joint, four-way, one-hour satellite booking at 8 p.m. up the coast in Murcia. I had to get something together fast.

We went in to see the undertaker, a surprisingly cheerful, bearded man in his thirties named Jose-Luis Vacca, who asked if we'd like a cup of coffee. I'd worked enough in southern Europe to know that you take the time for such courtesies, so we sat down for a chat and a small cup of black, thickly brewed espresso. I knew he'd done an interview with the other TV crews, and he quickly agreed to one with me. As we drank our coffee, I asked if, apart from receiving the body and meeting a man who said he was Trimbole's son Craig, he'd seen any documentary evidence of the dead man's identity. Oh yes, he said, the passport.

'Do you have a copy?' I asked.

'Yes, of course.'

'Could I see it?'

'No problem.'

Not only did he fetch several copied pages of the passport, including one with Robert Trimbole's photo, but he also brought a death certificate signed 'Craig Trimbole'.

'Could we film these?' I asked.

'Of course.'

'Did you give them to those other guys?'

'No.'

'Why not?'

'Oh, they were in a big hurry. They didn't want to sit down for a coffee. So they didn't ask. You did. You asked.'

For the rest of the day, we kept arriving just as the others were leaving: at the cemetery where the embalmed body had been moved, at the supermarket where Trimbole was reported to have shopped, in the hills above Benidorm where we searched for his elusive home address. On each occasion, their teasing of us for being in the rearguard got more raucous. Knowing I had in my briefcase the proof of death they lacked, I just smiled and soaked it up.

By the time I'd done my piece to camera in Benidorm, we had to leave fast for the coastal drive to Murcia. We arrived just after the satellite feed had started, to another chorus of 'Late again, ABC'. I must say, this is an anecdote I would never even tell if the others hadn't been so triumphalist. But they'd grabbed the first three-quarters of the hour-long feed, so I had to sit there pretending to look glum as I saw their stories go out. Their voice-overs were all still speculative—Trimbole was 'probably' really dead this time—but as I'd thought, none of them had the crucial proof.

They were cracking open some cold beers at the back of the control room when my story started to feed out, leading off with the passport pages.

Shot of passport, including photo.
It's the documents that have turned this report of Robert Trimbole's death from a rumour into a near-certainty. His Australian passport, issued in 1979, may have expired but this photograph has now been matched with the dead man's features.

Shot of death certificate.
The death certificate says Trimbole died of a heart attack at 8 p.m. on the 13th of May. He checked into the La Villa Joyosa hospital under the alias of Robert Witt, a Swiss citizen.

Shots of cemetery.
He died there, and his embalmed remains were removed to this cemetery. The body is still there under guard.

Shot of Craig Trimbole's signature.
This document, signed Craig Trimbole, authorises the undertakers to make the necessary arrangements.

I kept my eyes fixed on the screens, but Mike Gore told me he could practically see the other reporters' jaws dropping. What was worse, the feed being a shared one, their news editors back in Sydney were seeing my story come in, so the others had little choice but to get back in the saddle to try to match it before airtime.

In the ABC, of course, no good deed goes unpunished. Instead of a herogram, I got told off by Foreign Editor John Tulloh. My crime? I'd done what I was supposed to do and filed the story for Radio News and *AM*, who put it to air at breakfast time, thus spoiling what he thought should have been a 7 p.m. TV News exclusive. But by then, one thing I'd learned was that 'foreign correspondent's paranoia' was a feature of the job: you were never going to please everyone, so you might as well just do the best job you could.

Chapter 26

Human Stories

ON SOME LEVEL, I think of my career before the return to Sydney from Brussels at the end of 1987—all thirteen years of it since my first day as a cadet—as little more than an apprenticeship in journalism. Yes, I had done a lot, seen a lot, been to dozens of countries. But most of what I had done was daily reporting, reacting to events rather than trying to anticipate them. What I lacked was the experience of investigative journalism, or even of long-form explanatory work. I had no idea whether I was capable of it. So when the executive producer of *Four Corners*, Peter Manning, said he wanted to appoint me as one of the program's reporters, I was initially reluctant.

Like many so-called 'high achievers', I've always suffered to some extent from Impostor Syndrome—that sneaking feeling that much of what you've achieved has been the result of luck as much as talent. I feared that *Four Corners*, which had emerged from the doldrums in the mid-1980s to become one of the most influential journalism platforms in the country, would tear aside the curtain and reveal my hidden weaknesses. I was in awe of the investigative and film-making skills of colleagues like Chris Masters, Tony Jones, Marian Wilkinson and Paul Barry, and very much aware that although I had real skills in writing and interviewing, the creation of coherent film sequences to tell stories within an integrated structure over forty-five minutes involved a whole new set of skills, which I would have to learn extremely quickly or fall by the wayside.

I was fortunate to join *Four Corners* when I did: although Jonathan Holmes, who had led the program's renaissance, had moved on, his deputy Peter Manning had taken over, and done so with inspiration and guts. The 'culture' of the unit was very strong: constant fact-checking, right up to transmission time; endless arguments—usually constructive and creative—about how to tell the story; an obsession with picture and sound quality; and a collaborative sense in which every member of the team on a given story was encouraged to contribute. Peter used to address the troops with a rousing speech at the beginning of every year, and I remember how we started 1988 with his clarion call about doing serious journalism for people who otherwise might never see it: 'Yes, we need to do *National Times* stories, but they need to be understandable to a tabloid audience.'

It was a high bar. *The National Times* was famous for breaking massive, complex stories about everything from organised crime to espionage and national security. Our job was to do that, but also to be storytellers, capable of drawing an audience in and holding it.

It was at least a year before I even began to feel equal to the task. I made films about what even then seemed the growing discontent with big-party politics, about multiculturalism (in the midst of a controversy stirred up by then Leader of the Opposition John Howard), and about the future of the Melbourne *Age*, then in grave danger of being taken over by the British media magnate and (as it turned out) swindler Robert Maxwell. None of these stories was completely without merit, but they weren't going to set the world on fire. Above all, in retrospect, I hadn't started working as a *film-maker*. I was instead a journalist who happened to be working in the medium of film. But I was unquestionably learning, and over the next few years, I came to internalise the process: to think simultaneously about how to 'do a story' *and* 'make a film'.

In 1989, for instance, my second year at *Four Corners*, I travelled to Namibia to follow a refugee, Ndeutala Hishongwa, back to her homeland. It was an early foretaste in miniature of the end of apartheid. South Africa was being forced to withdraw from its nearest colony, formerly known as South-West Africa. Its troops and armour were still in the country, but a UN Transitional force, UNTAG, was going in to supervise their withdrawal and maintain stability: Australia was contributing a force of engineers. Ndeutala had left Namibia in terrifying circumstances in 1974, the South African Police banging down her door while she escaped through a rear bathroom window, leaving her tiny baby son behind. She'd spent the first part of her exile at university in Sweden, then moved to Melbourne to complete a PhD at La Trobe University. She'd had two children in exile, a girl, Hippulengwa, and a boy, Nyoma, with Australian accents and Australian expectations, who were now going to see Africa for the first time, and if all went well, meet the half-brother they'd never known—the baby Ndeutala had been forced to abandon.

Potentially an indigestible foreign affairs and politics *essay*, it was instead a human *story*, with the journey of the Hishongwa family, among the first group of refugees to return to Namibia, as its through-line. Its most climactic moment came by sheer coincidence. We'd been to Ndeutala's home village, in the country's north-west near the Angolan border, but been unable to find her son. He'd gone to the seaside, we were told, to collect salt. No-one knew when he'd be back. We'd almost given up, and were driving to another location, when we saw something potentially photogenic in the distance. The cameraman, Dave Maguire, stopped the car and set the camera on its tripod. Out of the shimmering heat haze we could see emerging the outline of a vehicle of some sort ... a cart ... a donkey cart ... driven by a teenage boy ... Suddenly, behind me, Ndeutala started ululating, in that eerie way you hear so often in Africa. Had she recognised the boy? Could she really do so, at this distance, after all these years? In a minute or two he was beside us, and they fell into each other's arms. It remains one of the most moving and dramatic scenes I've ever witnessed, let alone filmed.

I think it was only with that film that I began to feel comfortable with long-form journalism, but the lessons I'd learned in the first eighteen months at *Four Corners* stood me in good stead for the rest of my time there, and onwards into my years making films for *Foreign Correspondent*, *7.30* and *Lateline* in Europe and Africa.

* * *

For my sixtieth birthday in 2012, my brother- and sister-in-law took me to the Sydney Opera House to see the singer-songwriter Nick Lowe, whose work I've admired since the mid-1970s, when he produced the early Elvis Costello albums, was house producer for Stiff records, and put out what remains one of my favourite solo albums, *The Jesus of Cool*. He'd followed them over the years with a series of beautifully crafted songs that ranged from rock to country, but always, whether funny or plangent, contained a recognisable intelligence and wit. A man less celebrated than his own songs, and a backroom muse to many, Lowe ran the concert gamut from '(What's So Funny 'bout) Peace, Love and Understanding', which he wrote for Brinsley Schwarz all the way back in 1974, to 'Stoplight Roses' from his latest album. As he was coming towards the end of the set, I yelled out from the balcony for 'The Beast in Me', the song he wrote but which was first recorded by his father-in-law, Johnny Cash—Cash's self-lacerating rendition of the piece had haunted me since 1994, and Lowe's own recorded version was scarcely less affecting. Nick Lowe looked up towards where I sat and said slowly, 'Yes. Well. [Long pause] There are a lot of good songs.' Then he dashed my hopes by playing something else entirely.

Yes. Well. There are a lot of good stories. By the time you get to my stage in life, the playlist is always too long for one concert.

Between 1988 and 1998, in fact, there was a whole decade of long-form stories, from the one that helped end the move of the RAN base at Sydney's Garden Island to pristine Jervis Bay, to the Kimberley cattle station where thirty-two of a total of fifty-six Chinese asylum seekers suddenly appeared out of the bush in early 1992, with a police rescue operation eventually finding the entire group alive. From a corrupt Ferdinand Marcos–era oligarch with massive landholdings in Australia who briefly looked set to become president of the Philippines, to the Cambodians desperately struggling to live normally again during the United Nations transition that theoretically returned their country to democracy. From Serbia as it pursued its territorial ambitions over what remained of Yugoslavia, to the mountains of Calabria and evidence of close connections between the 'Ndrangheta organised crime group and Australia. There are so many stories, in fact, that perhaps one day they could fill another volume.

There's also the personal story which has dominated my last two decades: the story of the freakish medical accident—a virus triggering an autoimmune reaction—which turned an assignment in Rwanda, covering the unspeakable atrocities of that country's 1994 genocide, into an encounter with a disease that came close to killing me, the rare ANCA-positive polyangiitis. It's a story I've tried hard not to allow to define me, or if it does, to define me not as a victim but a survivor. It's the story of the months in which that disease went undiagnosed, and the cortisone-induced near-psychosis as I haemorrhaged internally and doctors pumped me full of chemicals which undoubtedly saved my life; my mother flying to London from Australia and my sister from Budapest, after the specialist told them it might be their last chance to see me; my father trying hard to conceal his fear that I would die, as he sat beside my bed for many, many days; the three months in Charing Cross Hospital before a brief remission was replaced by a new affliction which put me back 'inside' (yes, if you spend enough time in hospitals, your mind subconsciously starts confusing them with prisons); the recovery and return to the road, first on 'light duties', then back to making stories for *Foreign Correspondent*. And the twist in the tail when, in the freezing northern December of 1995, I was making a film, about the fragile future of the beauties of Venice, that turned into another nightmare. As a side-effect of all that cortisone a year before, my hips had turned to chalk overnight—something called avascular necrosis—and in Venice, which is all alleys and bridges, you need to be able to walk. I returned to London to have the hips replaced, and a few months later, still on crutches, went to Bosnia to do a piece on the divided city of Mostar.

There's the story of my return to Australia in 1997, and the gradual deterioration of my kidneys to the point in 2010 when I had to accept that my only alternative was to go on dialysis; and the story of how Mary-Ellen Field, whom I first came to know as a journalist interviewing her about how Rupert Murdoch's *News of the World* hacked her voicemails (when she was model Elle Macpherson's business adviser), decided to give me a kidney, and how well that kidney has worked ever since.

But this has essentially been a book about what now looks like the postwar interregnum: the period in which the locked-in struggle of two nuclear superpowers kept us in a mutually assured state of fear, while at the same time giving us the illusion that this was the way it would always be. A mirror of Orwell's *Nineteen Eighty-Four* dystopia: 'Oceania was at war with Eastasia. Oceania had always been at war with Eastasia.' Apart from occasional diplomatic skirmishes and quite a few proxy wars, the world we lived in *was* the world drawn up by Joseph Stalin, Franklin Roosevelt and Winston Churchill at the Yalta Conference in 1945. Now, thanks to the collapse of the Soviet Union, we could suddenly see that binary opposition as more impermanent than perhaps we ever dared expect.

But I began this book with the Iranian Revolution of 1979, and I think with hindsight we can see that, too, as a hinge-point, presaging a new era even before the new one was over. An era in which other forces would arise to challenge the old strategic assumptions. A new 'asymmetric' world in which forces other than capitalism and Marxism would enter the field, and warfare itself would become increasingly asymmetrical.

It was from afar that I had to watch the collapse of the Soviet Union's Eastern European Empire: I was in Sydney at *Four Corners*, and the Berlin Wall fell at the end of the year, when all the program's slots were already filled. Besides, since we were still working entirely on film (beautiful but unwieldy), it would have been extremely difficult to get the story to air fast enough. We had to leave it to the nightly news and current affairs programs.

It was frustrating, but in the back of my mind the thought was already forming: what happens next? What does a post-bipolar international landscape look like? I was to find out soon enough, in early 1990, when we began planning a trip to Ethiopia.

* * *

One of the first consequences of Moscow's weaker hand was a dwindling of the massive aid it had given to many of its allies in Africa. High among them was the Marxist government of Colonel Mengistu Haile Mariam in Addis Ababa. In Ethiopia's north, Eritreans had long been fighting for independence, and their neighbours in Tigray, in recent years, had been doing the same. But as my *Four Corners* colleague Chris Masters had reported in a searing piece a few years before, Mengistu was ruthless—so ruthless that he was prepared to use famine as a weapon of war. That was the time of Live Aid, and the notion was widespread that, somehow, large injections of Western money would provide answers, when the root of the starvation was as old as humanity itself—at least as old as the Four Horsemen of the Apocalypse: Death, Famine, War and Conquest.

The Forgotten Famine, the film we made about the unheralded return of that humanitarian disaster in Tigray, involved by far the hardest trip I ever made. We travelled with Community Aid Abroad, which has since merged with Oxfam, in a train of ancient, badly maintained trucks, on terrible roads which often turned to quagmire and bogged the entire convoy. There was no strictly legal way into Tigray: you had to go via Khartoum, and get the Sudanese authorities to give you a month's visa while turning a blind eye to the fact that you were going to slip across the border into neighbouring Ethiopia. Once inside, all travel was at night: a couple of weeks beforehand, Mengistu's air force had bombed an aid convoy, and Britain's ITV News had filmed the carnage. We parked under trees or in sheds in villages during the daytime—reading or sleeping in the shade, or under whatever cover we could find—and never set off till the hour before sunset. On many days, we saw Soviet-built MiG fighter-bombers flying overhead, but we were lucky. Even so, on many nights, the roads were so bad and the trucks so dilapidated that we could only cover 60 kilometres before dawn.

My wife Michele was expecting a baby in late April. When we set out, Community Aid Abroad seemed sure the trip would take no more than a month. I should be back in mid-March. Plenty of time to be there at the birth. As it was, it took ten gruelling days just to get to Aksum, still well outside the worst famine zone. There we all, one by one, contracted dysentery. I was hit last, only to discover that the ABC had provided us with only enough Flagyl and antibiotics to cover three people, when there were four of us. Fortunately, we found a pharmacy of sorts, where I learned from experience a hard truth about life in the developing world: antibiotics are diluted by black marketeers, so that to be sure of any effect you are wise to take at least triple the stated dose.

After a few days of near-delirium, combined with disgusting sanitary facilities, we were able to continue. Aksum was just far enough from Addis Ababa to have escaped the worst of the bombing. Its ancient cathedral, claimed to contain the Biblical Ark of the Covenant, was still practising a form of Christian service that dated back 1600 years.

The town was dotted with dusty cafés containing beautifully decorated chrome Gaggia espresso machines, left over from Mussolini's occupation of what was then called Abyssinia. They, like the bakelite telephones and art-deco lamps, were all useless because there was no electricity and all phone lines were cut.

Now it was onward through Adwa and Adigrat, and into some of the most remote and difficult territory I've ever seen. It was all stones and rocks and dust on steep harsh slopes, completely impassable to trucks. We filmed thousands of people making day-long marches to get grain handouts, up and down mountain ranges and across deserts. They'd been encouraged to stay in their towns and villages, to avoid the mass starvation in refugee camps and along the roads of the 1984–85 Live Aid exodus. They'd obeyed in the belief that the world would help. But the aid was too little, too late. They walked with staffs, in robes and sandals or barefoot. It was a picture from a Biblical famine, not a twentieth-century one—a panorama almost unchanged for centuries. The bishop of Adigrat, Kidane Mariam, told me, 'Now nobody is helping and no food is coming. They have to stay at home and die there.'

In one village, Dera, we filmed a family trying to survive. Their grain crops had failed months before because of drought. The head of the family, Germay Seneslet, told me of how he'd had to sell his cow and calf, then finally, a few months later, his ox. Finally, desperate, he'd had to hire his twelve-year-old son out to a local merchant as a shepherd. The boy's wage: a mere 5 kilograms of barley for a full month's work. When we went back to see the Seneslet family the next day, Germay's wife, who we'd filmed talking and heating tiny handfuls of grain for her children, was lying exhausted. She was clearly dying. We stopped filming and withdrew, to leave her at least some dignity in the death that followed soon after.

We pushed on south. In a clinic in Mekele we saw babies dying of TB. The elderly Irish nurse looking after them told me how there'd been medicine to treat them, but now it had run out. It is appalling at any time to watch children dying: when you want to be with your pregnant wife thousands of kilometres away, and know that whatever happens your baby will be well cared for, it seems even harder.

But this turned out to be a historic moment in what eventually became the fall of Mengistu and his Derg government in Addis Ababa.

The further south we went, the more we could see the signs that the Ethiopian Army, deprived of Moscow's strong backing, was in retreat. Wrecked tanks, armoured cars and jeeps littered the roadsides. From a hilltop, we could see in the distance an Ethiopian air base put out of commission by Tigrayan shelling. We could hear artillery to the south, and were advised this was as far as we could go. We were close to the front line, and it was clear that the line was moving steadily towards the capital, Addis Ababa.

In now-empty trucks, getting out was faster than getting in, but still not fast enough. After six weeks completely out of touch with my family, I needed to get to Khartoum as quickly as possible, and then on a plane back to Sydney. I was reckoning without the fundamentalist Muslim government of Omar al-Bashir.

We arrived back in Khartoum on 29 March. We'd overstayed our visas, a formality in normal circumstances, requiring only a stamp to allow us to depart. But Ramadan had just begun, and all government offices were closed. The prospect loomed of weeks of waiting. As it was, the stamping happened within days, but it was already too late. On 3 April, my sister-in-law Marilyn rang to tell me that there'd been an emergency—placenta previa—which entailed Michele being rushed to hospital and my son William being born prematurely. I remember lying on my bed beating the pillow and crying tears of frustration and rage. It wasn't till nearly three days later that I first looked into the piercing blue gaze of the son whose birth I'd managed to miss.

The fall of Ethiopia was one of the first harbingers of what both US President George Bush Snr and Mikhail Gorbachev had been calling the New World Order. The nature of that 'Order' began to crystallise four months later, when the Iraqi dictator Saddam Hussein invaded Kuwait. *Four Corners*' Executive Producer Marian Wilkinson sent me to Baghdad to watch as Saddam prepared his nation for war. In a hotel reputedly purpose-built with two-way mirrors and microphones for the bugging of every room, accompanied everywhere else we went by minders, we had just one advantage over other television crews. *Four Corners* was still made on film, rather than videotape—in the days before digital, not only were the pictures better, but you could do much more in editing and post-production. For once, we found, this was not a hindrance but an advantage. Iraq no longer had processing facilities for TV film, and therefore, unlike video, no means to censor what we filmed. A long meeting at the Information Ministry ended with officials reluctantly giving us the go-ahead, but intensifying the minder oversight.

They could not, however, do much about it when they took us to a 'model village' in Kurdistan, to show how well the people were treated, and we discreetly filmed a menacing truck with a heavy machine-gunner on the back patrolling up and down to keep the populace quiet. Nor did they know that we had filmed from our hotel rooms the large numbers of anti-aircraft gun emplacements on the roofs of every building nearby. The only images to be seen in public places in Baghdad were huge, flattering paintings of Saddam himself, but you weren't supposed to film them. We did.

There was a great deal more: the massive parade of reserve troops that turned out to be a showcase of the very young, the very old and the infirm, but was supposed to persuade the world that Iraq was ready to take on all-comers. The propaganda play we were allowed to film, full of ludicrous anti-Western caricatures. The multimillion-dollar memorial to the dead of the Iran–Iraq war, which had been turned into a hagiographic museum of the life of Saddam Hussein.

Yet there were many all over the Middle East who believed in Saddam. We opened our film with a mass rally in Jordan of Shi'ites, offering heartfelt support to Iraq despite its long, primitive and utterly deadly war with Shi'ite Iran. In a sign of the global changes of the last year, I reported, the Soviet Union, Egypt and Syria had joined the Gulf states threatened by Iraq's military might in an 'unprecedented coalition'. But when I interviewed Jordan's Crown Prince Hassan, he told me of 'the sense of disillusion and despair' in a region with 300 million people, '70 per cent of whom are under the age of fifteen, many of whom are unemployed, embittered, see no hope in terms of Western promises and political solutions ... if the Gulf had been producing bananas we wouldn't have seen this rapid response'. And in Saudi Arabia, I interviewed obdurate sheikhs who said that the oil kingdoms didn't need democracy because—a circular argument in the absence of elections—they already had the wholehearted support of the people.

The resulting *Four Corners* film, broadcast on 12 November 1990, seemed prophetic in many ways, not only about the first Gulf War which started two months later, but about the second in 2003. I narrated the following:

> From here in Baghdad, Saddam Hussein will try to control the rage of Islam to his own ends. But the chances are that he will fail. Saddam's military, if it comes to war, will almost certainly be outgunned and outclassed. But the West hardly seems to have thought about the dangers of total victory. If Saddam Hussein were removed, Iraq would become a massive power vacuum. The opposition has been systematically eliminated. This is all there is. The consequences outside Iraq may be just as dire. Israel will find itself more threatened than ever before. Saudi Arabia and the Sheikhdoms will find for all their riches that rule of the many by the few is harder to justify in victory or defeat. Saddam Hussein opened the bottle and the genies of war have escaped. We will all have to face the consequences.

* * *

In early January 1991, I flew to London to pull together a fast-turnaround follow-up piece on the war that was clearly just about to begin. The 747 was almost empty. Tough-guy movie stars Clint Eastwood and Sylvester Stallone had cancelled trans-Atlantic trips to Europe because of the perceived threats to aviation: certainly very few Australians wanted to overfly the Middle East on their way to London, and Britain's tourism, along with Qantas' business, was hurting.

I stayed with my father, who saw the complexities of what was about to happen with equal clarity. He was particularly concerned, based on long connections with contemporaries in the CIA, at the way American intelligence had systematically shed Middle East expertise, even down to the number of people who spoke Arabic or Persian. He had little faith in American military and strategic thinking.

We talked a lot that night, and inevitably the conversation turned to the last forty-five years—the Cold War which he had fought secretly from the inside, which I had observed as a child and been trying to make sense of ever since. Just as I'd been worried about the Iraqi power vacuum, I could see trouble coming in the former Soviet Union. He, too, could see that the blight of Soviet totalitarianism wouldn't necessarily be replaced by a new utopia. But of one thing he was very sure: anything was better than Stalinism and its heirs.

I remembered another conversation, years earlier, when he'd asked me why I kept on being a reporter, rather than a commentator. It obviously puzzled him, as someone who'd spent his whole career having opinions and making predictions. I'd said something about never being sure enough about anything to write editorials telling people what to think. In the years between, I'd moved subtly from that position to another: now I *was* prepared to prognosticate, up to a point, but only after I'd had the chance to examine all the facts, preferably on the ground. But what remained consistent was my addiction to reporting first, concluding later. In fact, my real interest was, had always been, in the opinions and perspectives of others: in walking around a subject, as one walks around a building or a sculpture in a museum, trying to see it from every possible angle.

He was a grandfather now. I was a father. It seemed we were somehow on a new level, more equal than before. We could argue without falling out, we could understand each other's point of view. It was easy and comfortable, sitting on the sofa, working our way through a bottle of red while a gangster film played in the background. We were not so very different, except in this one respect: he had always been firmly on one side, a purist for the Cold War.

What I really remember about that night is the moment I asked my father what he thought about the mirror-world of moral grey areas, dilemmas, paradoxes and complexities explored in the novels of John le Carré. 'What about you?' I said. 'Was it always absolutely clear-cut? Did you ever find any ambivalence or ambiguity about what you were doing?'

'Never. Not once. Not for a single minute,' he replied.

I had—in a way that was arguably equally purist—devoted myself to not taking sides, to trying at all times to see the other person's point of view. Each was a tenable position, each was understandable in the context of the lives we had led and the trades we had followed. We each understood that, but there it was, the fault line across which we viewed each other.

Postscript

THE LAST STORY I actually reported from the field was in New York, on the first anniversary of 9/11. Michael Carey, Virginia Trioli and I had done a three-and-a-half-hour live broadcast on the city's commemorations, but afterwards I was on a promise to supply a piece to *The World Today*. I went for a walk with a tape recorder, but I think it was the spirit of Alistair Cooke, my favourite broadcast journalist, that impelled me to write a purely spoken piece. This is part of it, about the 'message wall' set up right across Union Square:

> Here were stories, all right. So many that by the time you'd read from one end of the wall to another, new sheets were papering over the place where you'd started. So this is a record of the Union Square wall during just one hour of September the 11th, 2002. An hour later, the stories would have been different.
>
> There were memories of the lost: 'You are in our hearts forever. We all miss you, Aunish. I know you're here with me. You never left. Your sister, Nidhi Arya.'
>
> And this: 'It was my third day of teaching. The principal told us we could not tell the children yet. We needed to just teach. I looked at my lesson plan for the day, shaking. I began to read. The class was silent. They listened. I stopped. James Baldwin wrote years before, for me?

for this moment?, that without love we cannot survive. I asked the students to write and write all they could on this one sentence. Then they were taken away and told. Without love we cannot survive.'

There was much patriotism on the Union Square wall, many God Bless Americas, some paeans of hate for Osama bin Laden, and these three short lines: 'I will not forget. I will not forgive. I shall not understand.'

There were at least as many calls for peace, and protests against American foreign policy.

But the dominant tone was of love for the city of New York itself, almost as if it were an independent state and not part of America. And not just from people who have lived there all their lives.

This for instance: 'I am Australian and always will be, but New York is my home. I always loved this city and its people. September 11th changed us all and I fell more in love with this city and its people all over again. Thank you.'

But for some, finally, words were just redundant: 'I've talked about it. I've listened to others. I have nothing left to say. I have too much to say. There is too much loss.'

I turned away from the Union Square wall to a commotion by one of the tables. A young man was writing the word 'Love' on a piece of paper. An older man was shouting at him. 'I'm sick of this left-wing political agenda. It's all political.'

A middle-aged man with a voice disconcertingly like Woody Allen's yelled back, 'Bush wants to start a war. What's that if not political?'

Suddenly everyone was shouting, in a rapid escalation of political assertion and personal abuse.

I looked at one of the organisers of the wall project who was standing beside me.

'What did you expect?' she said. 'New York is New York.'

I thought it was as good a piece of radio reporting as I'd ever done. It encapsulated what I believe about the value of being a reporter. Christopher Isherwood's line 'I am a camera' springs to mind—the single pair of eyes recording the precise moment, the words recorded painstakingly in my notebook, the single perspective on what's known as 'the first draft of history'. Something about that wall made me think of history, too, with its steady accretion of new messages slowly covering, without destroying, the ones that had gone before: like the many layers of ancient Troy, one displacing another for hundreds of years until archaeologists come and cut through them in cross-section to try and guess what the past really looked like.

It can be frustrating to know that you're still able to tell first-hand stories as a journalist in the field, yet return to being desk-bound. I could still walk long distances in 2002, and therefore function as a reporter, but very soon those days were gone. As a side effect of the long treatment of my illness, I lost the cartilage in my right ankle, which made walking extremely painful, and the cortisone-induced brittleness of my bones meant that parts of my spine were starting to collapse. I began living more and more in the virtual world, playing video games for a while, but also leaping in imagination from continent to continent in search of news sites and blogs, reading more and more online to supplement my long-term book addiction.

Then, in February 2009, I had a minor fall and broke my upper thigh, the fracture uncomfortably close to the hip replacements I'd had in 1996, and, during a fortnight's stay in hospital, discovered Twitter. Once I'd realised that the 140-character rule was not as limiting as I'd thought, because of the ability to include links, the appeal was immediate. I'd long been sharing articles and pictures among friends but had never wanted to start a full-time blog. Nonetheless, I'd learned a lot from some of the blogs I'd read: enough to realise that you could use Twitter as a microblog, a place where you could share and exchange without having to write an essay every time you did so. I followed a wide variety of interesting people, and gradually got more and more of the information I'd been used to scouring the web for, directly from Twitter.

And so in June 2009, without leaving my desk, I found myself—in a virtual sense—back on the campus of Tehran University, nearly thirty years on from the events with which this book began. In the weeks of turmoil after Iran's most recent elections, it had become increasingly clear not only that there was a revolt going on over the rigged result, but that the state was doing everything it could to prevent news of that revolt getting to the outside world. It wasn't for lack of trying by Western reporters. The ABC's own Ben Knight was pumping out as much information as he could, for as long as he was allowed to stay. My old BBC friend John Simpson, bringing the perspective of thirty years in and out of Iran, plunged into crowds to interview and report, despite knowing that foreign journalists—and eventually anyone with a camera—was a target for Basij militia thugs or Revolutionary Guards. But it was a losing battle. The BBC's resident correspondent, John Leyne, had already been expelled. John Lyons of *The Australian* remained as long as possible, filing copy until he too was thrown out. Soon, almost all of them were gone.

What was worse was that the US networks, once so powerful, chose at first almost to ignore the situation. CNN in particular, still then highly influential in the news business, gave it so little coverage that a hashtag sprang up and went viral: #CNNFAIL.

For me, among others, this was the first moment when, in the absence of traditional media source material, Twitter started to become a genuinely useful primary source for journalism. It was by no means easy or reliable: there was a vast amount of miscellaneous material coming out of Iran, with no way of verifying it absolutely. But if you had a sharp eye for detail, you could pick up indications of whether someone was truthful or not.

If they referred to protest action in a particular square, were other people saying the same thing? Quite often I would find three Twitter sources, all apparently in different parts of the crowd, reporting on the same event, though from a different perspective. Time came into the judgement as well. Was this someone whose tweets yesterday and the day before had been proved to be true by other reports later? One Twitter user, 'Change_for_Iran', reported, in a series of messages, being under siege in a university dormitory. Another, from another part of the campus, reported seeing the same thing from another angle. A day later, pictures started coming through confirming the damage done in the attack. It starts to add up to something like credibility.

I found I was developing a method of triangulation, applying the old journalistic methods of verification to a new medium. When one reliable tweeter, a student I'd been following since the unrest began, sent out a stream of 140-character messages, I'd developed enough faith in his reliability to link his tweets up and have them voiced over and put to air:

> It was a nightmare, I can barely breathe & my face is burning, Masood got shot in the arm & Shayan's brother is missing. I don't know where

> to start with, first they attack our peaceful memorial gathering in front of the university with water gun. The university's doors were closed, we couldn't run everywhere! & then they start shooting tear gas at us. They were so many! riot police, normal police, intel, IRG [Revolutionary Guard], Basij! ... We didn't realize for a moment they started shooting at people, the gun's sound was like a toy gun, not loud & the soldiers were smiling. I was going to tell Masood they are using fake guns for scaring people! until people started screaming in agony ... We ran as fast as we could in the opposite direction, at the same time Basiji bastards started to hit fleeing people. I think I saw 2 or 3 people lying on the ground in blood & IRG started to move them, probably hide them.

He disappeared off Twitter soon after, never to be heard of again. At around the same time the Iranian Government started to muddy the waters with fake accounts and black propaganda. Still, we'd had a glimpse into a scene the government didn't want us to see, and I'd learned lessons that we could apply in subsequent stories.

When a talented young woman called Jess Hill started researching for us at the beginning of the Arab Spring, she built on those lessons, using Twitter, Facebook, YouTube and Skype to make contacts all over the Middle East. She was tireless, and highly effective in breaking down dissidents' natural suspicions: state secret police were posing as journalists in sting operations, so that in itself required persistence and talent. The result was that I was able to talk to people in places and situations which would have been completely inaccessible in previous contacts: a photographer speaking to me live as Bahraini troops attacked a peaceful demonstration; a young woman in Misrata on the Libyan coast describing, live, the experience of being under siege by Colonel Gaddafi's artillery; a young man in the remote mountainous south of Libya, describing the advance of Gaddafi's tanks across the plains below; a dissident in Der'aa, Syria explaining the revolt against the Assad government in the days before the opposition was taken over by crazed fundamentalists like ISIS and Jabhat al-Nusra.

So the new media technologies have given me a virtual telescope through which to bring the world closer, now that I am so much more limited in going to view it in person. But they've also brought me closer to the audience. Because of my Twitter feed, no-one any longer thinks of me as 'just a newsreader'. They get a daily feel, whether they listen to the program or not, for the breadth of my reading and the depth of my experience. And they can judge for themselves whether I am, as I am occasionally accused of being, a 'right-wing stooge' or a 'lefty nutjob'.

I don't link to a lot of articles about Australian politics, but when I do, it's because they're well written, amusing, or contain unusual insights, not because I endorse everything in them. Of course, I have to accept that people who follow me over time will make assumptions about what I do and don't agree with. Sometimes they'll be right, sometimes wrong. I have striven throughout my career not only to appear, but to be, fair to all sides in politics, something I don't find hard because I've never belonged to a political party, or been tempted to.

I'm not a political eunuch, though, and in international affairs, even within the bounds of my ABC role, it's possible to express some opinions. I don't like dictatorships. I don't like regimes that imprison writers and dissidents. I don't like torture. I read *Nineteen Eighty-Four* and *Darkness at Noon* at an impressionable age, and I got the message.

As I've recorded, I reported from the Soviet Union and its satellites, and from apartheid South Africa; I travelled through China in the throes of the Cultural Revolution; and I experienced life under the Iranian theocracy. I know what dictators look like, and I've seen at first hand what happens to their victims.

My heroes include Andrei Sakharov, Nelson Mandela, Desmond Tutu and Václav Havel. I have always done my best to spread news about the oppressed, the tortured and the gagged in countries like Iran, Burma (Myanmar) and North Korea.

A few months before I was stricken with chronic illness in 1994, I'd done a short internet course at the BBC in London, enough to convince me of its revolutionary potential both in my life and my work. In the six months or so I spent in hospital in late 1994 and early 1995, one of my chief frustrations was the inability to use a modem to hook my laptop up to the web in my hospital room: the ability to span the globe from a keyboard had already become that important to me.

A fear of boredom runs in my family. For me, the questing for action in the field, the travel (when I could still travel frequently), the voracious consumption of books and newspapers, the round-the-clock trawling of the internet, are all probably symptoms of that fear of the empty moment. As illness and disability have encroached over the last two decades, the virtual world has only become more important to me.

And my good fortune has been that the deterioration of my health and mobility has coincided with an enormous improvement in the availability of virtual experience. Encyclopedic knowledge at the touch of a key, music and vision flowing as from a tap, books downloaded to an e-reader the moment they're released in London or New York, groceries or clothes ordered online and delivered to your door, and free calls to friends and relatives anywhere in the world via Skype or FaceTime—it's all come at the right time for me.

So I'm thankful to be able to end this narrative with two words: Never Bored.

Acknowledgements

THE FIRST PERSON to thank is my mother, Anne Synnot, for giving me the peace and quiet at her farm that I needed to write most of this book. She celebrated her ninetieth birthday part way through the process, but proved (if proof were needed) that age had not even slightly affected her memory or mental acuity. Many of the details in the account of my early years emerged from conversations with her: she read the manuscript and provided corrections, clarifications and constructive criticism.

My sister Zoë also contributed hugely, both by adding her own perspective on shared experiences and because, as a former Hansard reporter, her grammar and punctuation are far better than mine.

If I owe my mother thanks for bringing me into the world, there are a number of people I must also thank for keeping me alive for the last two decades and more. They include Dr Andrew Keat, then of Charing Cross Hospital, London; Professors John Charlesworth, Bruce Pussell and Zoltan Endre, and Dr Grant Luxton, all of the Prince of Wales Hospital in Randwick, Sydney; Dr Andrew Lennox, whose surgical skills allowed me to have a new kidney; and above all, Mary-Ellen Field, whose absolute conviction that her kidney would be a match for mine and that I should accept it was beyond generous, liberated me from the difficulties of dialysis, and has so far given me an extra three years and more of productive life.

It was a good time to write this book, because the wall of secrecy around the SIS in the relevant years is slightly more porous than it used to be.

By a stroke of fortune, Paddy Hayes' book *Queen of Spies*, about my father's colleague and contemporary Daphne Park, came out just when I was beginning my research. Not only is the book a cracking read, but it also supplied new clues and revelations about two of my father's most significant postings—Hanoi and Ulan Bator. Paddy was also personally very helpful in pointing me in the right direction for further research.

The intelligence historian Professor Richard J Aldrich, Director of Research Degrees in Politics and International Studies at the University of Warwick, knew my father and hosted him and other former SIS colleagues at seminars. Professor Aldrich gave me new information and pointed me in the direction of more.

The BBC Security Correspondent Gordon Corera contacted me some time ago to tell me of a CIA officer he'd interviewed who had sung my father's praises. Gordon's book *The Art of Betrayal: Life and Death in the British Secret Service* is an important contribution to espionage history. It was invaluable in writing this book, shedding particular light on the chapters which cover the 1950s.

Professor Scott Lucas, of the University of Birmingham, helped me to understand the UK/US manoeuvrings behind the Suez affair.

Thanks to the espionage writer Nigel West for confirming to me that his 'outing' of my father in *The Faber Book of Spies* was done with official sanction.

I'm grateful to Matthew Parris, whose published collections of diplomatic despatches have both amused and enlightened many readers in recent years about the work of the foreign service. Matthew referred me to Joe Lloyd, who spent a week researching for me at the Public Records Office in Kew, and unearthed large numbers of declassified cables from my father's Vietnam and Mongolia postings.

In another accident of fortunate timing, Adam Sisman's biography of John le Carré was published just before I wrote this book. Le Carré (real name: David Cornwell) was employed at different times by both major branches of British intelligence. Sisman's account describes le Carré's time in Austria, working for MI5, shortly before our time there, and gives details of his SIS training in 1950s London not long after my father joined the service. Sisman's work helped me understand considerably more about the world in which my father worked.

On events in Malaysia and Indonesia in the late 1950s and early 1960s, Leon Comber's *Malaya's Secret Police 1945–60: The Role of the Special Branch in the Malayan Emergency* shone a light on one aspect of my father's activities, and David Easter's paper *British Intelligence and Propaganda During the 'Confrontation', 1963–1966*, in *Intelligence and National Security*, 2001, was helpful in providing clues to his role during the Indonesian Konfrontasi.

Simon Kear's paper *The British Consulate-General in Hanoi, 1954–73*, in *Diplomacy & Statecraft*, 1999, was also useful.

Sarah Ferguson, Andrew Sholl, James Jeffrey, Jim Middleton, Peter Logue and Peter Newport were among those kind enough to give me feedback on chapters of this book while it was in the making. Thanks also to Tim Curnow, and a warm thanks to John Spence in the ABC Archive.

Finally, to the team at MUP. This book would not have been written without the frequent encouragement of Louise Adler, who first asked me to write it some years ago and was patient enough to wait until I was ready. Sally Heath has been an enormously encouraging and constructive midwife to the work, and I thank her for her patience when a medical crisis interrupted work for some time, about two-thirds of the way through. And many thanks to Paul Smitz, whose copyediting has been meticulous and who has corrected and guided my copy with friendly courtesy and admirable attention to detail.

Mark Colvin
Sydney, July 2016

Index